Chocolate Surrealism

ANTON L. ALLAHAR AND NATASHA BARNES
Series Editors

Chocolate Surrealism

Music, Movement, Memory, and History in the Circum-Caribbean

Njoroge Njoroge

UNIVERSITY PRESS OF MISSISSIPPI • JACKSON

www.upress.state.ms.us

The University Press of Mississippi is a member of the Association of American University Presses.

Copyright © 2016 by University Press of Mississippi
All rights reserved

First printing 2016

∞

Library of Congress Cataloging-in-Publication Data

Names: Njoroge, Njoroge, author.
Title: Chocolate surrealism : music, movement, memory, and history in the
    circum-Caribbean / Njoroge Njoroge.
Description: Jackson : University Press of Mississippi, [2016] | Series:
    Caribbean studies series | Includes bibliographical references and index.
    | Discography: pages
Identifiers: LCCN 2015043008 | ISBN 9781496806895 (hardback : alk. paper)
Subjects: LCSH: Folk music—Caribbean Area—History and criticism. |
    Blacks—Caribbean Area—Music—History and criticism. | African diaspora.
Classification: LCC ML3565.N56 2016 | DDC 780.89/960729—dc23 LC record
available at http://lccn.loc.gov/2015043008

British Library Cataloging-in-Publication Data available

To my sister, for teaching me how to read

Contents

Acknowledgments - ix -

Introduction - 3 -

1. "Headless Heroes of the Apocalypse"
   The Trinidadian Calypso to 1940 - 15 -

2. "Cuba Libre"
   Clave Consciousness and Montuno Aesthetics 1945–1955 - 49 -

3. Dedicated to the Struggle
   The Aural Making and Unmaking of the Third World 1955–1965 - 73 -

4. "Cosa Nuestra"
   Salsa "Folklórico y Experimental" 1965–1975 - 107 -

Conclusion - 134 -

Notes - 138 -

Bibliography - 164 -

Select Discography - 178 -

Index - 181 -

Acknowledgments

This work is dedicated first and foremost to my family: my parents, Mbugua and Josephine Njoroge, without whose loving support none of this would have been possible, and my sister, Wanjiku Njoroge, my closest friend and confidante who—both literally and figuratively—taught me how to read.

There have been many, many people who have contributed to my personal growth and intellectual development; here I can list only a few. George Yúdice was a steady source of encouragement and critical feedback, as well as a good friend and colleague. Michael Gomez's pioneering work on the African diaspora has not only helped reconfigure the field but has also been a model for my scholarship. Adam Green consistently challenged me to deepen my analyses, and his exacting critiques helped bring this writing to fruition. The insights, knowledge, and enthusiasm of Jairo Moreno played a vital role in the project's completion, and it was a pleasure to have his formidable academic and musical arsenal (generously) at my disposal. Christopher Winks has been a wonderful friend whose encyclopedic erudition I have had the great privilege of benefiting from through countless and ongoing conversations. Finally, Steven Feld has been a true inspiration (intellectually and musically); it is difficult to express my gratitude for the many ways in which his brilliance, guidance, kindness, and support have been crucial to this endeavor.

The ideas and themes in and around this work actually began to develop through writings and discussions with David Anthony, Angela Davis, Herman Gray, and Nathaniel Mackey. Each in their own way has contributed much to the project, and the seeds sown have been cultivating for many years. Manthia Diawara, Robin D. G. Kelley, Tricia Rose, Brent Hayes Edwards, Fred Moten, and Steven Gregory were all and always supportive. In addition, (the late) Juan Flores and Miriam Jiménez Román have been good friends and key interlocutors throughout. I must also give special thanks to

Timothy Reiss and Patricia Hilden for their support, assistance, encouragement, and feedback. Inspiration and encouragement also came from Ngũgĩ wa Thiong'o and Kamau Brathwaite.

The Black Marxist Study Group in New York helped my thought immensely and the book project was refined and strengthened through hours of conversation, argument, and hilarity with Peter Hudson, Ifeona Harrison, Ted Sammons, Forrest Hylton, Seth Markle, Sobukwe Odinga, Daniel Rood, Hillina Seife, Khary Polk, Natasha Lightfoot, Rich Blint, Tanya Huelett, Chris Winks (again), Adam Waterman, Fanon Howell, Erik McDuffie, and Michaela Harrison. I also had the privilege of learning at the feet of the "master," C. Daniel Dawson, who was generous to a fault in sharing his unrivalled expertise.

Here at the University of Hawai'i, Mānoa, I must thank a number of colleagues: Paul Lyons, Monica Ghosh, Cindy Franklin, Laura Lyons, Charles Lawrence, Mari Matsuda, Mike Shapiro, David Hanlon, David Chappell, Marcus Daniel, Vina Lazona, Matthew Romaniello, Ned Bertz, Noelani Arista, Shana Brown, Karen Jolly, Herb Ziegler, Margot Hendrickson, John Zuern, Craig Howes, Stan Schab, John Rosa, Ned Davis, Leonard, Andaya, Hokulani Aiku, Matthew Lauzon, Wengsheng Wang, Yuma Totani, Paul Holtrop, Lori Yancura, Gary Pak, (the late) Jerry Bentley, and, of course, my dear friend Giovanni Vitello. I would also like to give special thanks to Craig Gill, editor-in-chief of the University Press of Mississippi, for his patience and unflagging support in making this book possible. And thanks to the anonymous readers for their exacting and insightful commentary.

I must make mention of my extended family in New Jersey. Steve and Dequandra Fradkin, and their beautiful children Asha, Nadia, Ivan, Amanda, and Steve Jr., have always freely given much love and support (and, often, an open home and a hot meal). Jamie Wilson has been a friend, a brother, and a model of pedagogy, fortitude, and general "right on-ness." Victor Viesca and Melany De la Cruz have been compañero/as, collaborators, and indispensable allies from beginning to end ("en el espíritu de la resistencia"). Kristy Ringor, Greg Chun, and Alice have been true forces for good in the world and our lives. The genius, wit, and friendship of my comrade, colleague, and co-conspirator Kobi Abayomi have been indispensable to my sanity and insanity. Stan Pyrzanowski has been a true friend and soul brother and I am grateful for his music and companionship. Lastly and most importantly, I must thank my partner in life and love, Suzanna Reiss.

"What do I have that I have not received?"

Chocolate Surrealism

Introduction[1]

In those days it was either live with music or die with noise,
and we chose rather desperately to live.
—Ralph Ellison

Black music has always been a tremendous source of information and inspiration for musicians, dancers, and music lovers. Listening to the music opens new worlds and windows onto the rich history of black music, society, and struggle in the circum-Caribbean, and provides a rich archive of the creative musical genius of the African diaspora. Music always expresses the interrelationships of movement, memory, and history, but this is preeminently true of the music of the African diaspora. This book uses music as both optic and focus, to examine and rethink both the modes of black cultural production and social formations in the African diaspora. The music has always been both an expression of "black" life and part of the philosophy that developed and emerged with that life, "as history and as art" (Baraka 2009, 9).

This book attempts to uncover the ways in which these "black" identities (ethnic, racial, religious, sociocultural) were constructed, transmitted, fashioned, and refashioned in and through music and music-making in order to create habitable spaces within the tumult of New World experiences. What is this "black" in black music, and what can the music relate about the maintenance and creation of Afro-diasporic cultural identities, memories, histories? As Marx has written, "it is not the consciousness of men . . . that determines their existence, but instead their social existence that determines their consciousness." What can the musical forms and rhythms of the African diaspora tell us about consciousness and existence? Music offers both historiographic and musicological spaces of inquiry; but at the same time, as an aesthetic experience music is not entirely accessible through either methodology. The analysis of the development of New World black music reveals the complexity of stylistic evolution, historical change, and the interrelations between consciousness, culture, and material history.

The music of the African diaspora demonstrates coherent tendencies, a decidedly "black" style, and reveals dynamic, creative consciousness and meaningful responses to particular historical situations; here we can speak of "traditions of mobilization" and the "mobilization of tradition." The music represents ways of being in and through time, and it is precisely in the polyrhythmic fabric (the weave of the "flows" and the "breaks") of the musical traditions of the African diaspora that we can echo-locate black sensibilities in time and space: "Lived history . . . is produced out of the clash of contending temporalities" (A. Johnson 1999, 10). Using polyrhythm as structure and process, we can analyze the way the music of the African diaspora, heterogeneity and stylistic hybridity, keeps time.[2] The music "makes an abstract world concrete" (Friedmann).

The power of black music lies in its ability to re-present the significant structures toward which the thought, feelings, behavior, and values of the cultural community are oriented; the social context and performative dimensions of the groove give maximum possible coherence to the real and potential consciousness of the African diaspora. The music remembers Africa, the Middle Passage, and the history of the black Atlantic. There is a rigorous homology between cultural forms and social structures, and the depth of integration of black musical traditions in patterns of social and political life make the music a critical site of memory and imagination that opens onto a sea of meanings and experiences. Music means and makes sense at the intersection of the most abstract level of collective consciousness and the most concrete level of social practice and aesthetic sensibilities: "Its [styles] and instrumentation change to reflect the level of people's productive forces and the social, political, and economic structure of those people's lives" (Baraka 2009, 20). Through uncovering the multiple layers of clashing temporalities and crossing rhythms, the epistemological force of black music reveals a different and dialogical understanding of time, history, and the practice of diaspora.

In conjunction with the polyrhythm, the concept of rootwork is used here both as an historical methodology to re-present subaltern strategies and as an expression of cultural practice. Refracted through the lenses of the African diaspora, this notion alludes to conjurational practices (e.g. Hoodoo, Vodûn, Obeah, Palo Mayombe, Candomble), as well as the material operations, philosophical transformations, historical meditations, aesthetic mediations, and spiritual invocations that shape and embody the tradition: "a complete and conscious return to which assimilates all the wealth of previous development" (Marx 1970, 87). Highlighting what Gilroy has called "the antiphony of roots and routes," thinking of black musicking[3] and musical traditions as rootwork enables a move from the general ontological categories to epistemology and specific socio-historical context, a move from "folk hermeneutics" to historical praxis, to uncover the continual reciprocity between culture, ideology, and consciousness developing under definite conditions. Rootwork expresses the dialectics of production and reproduction, transit and transition, in the invention of tradition. We can think of rootwork as a theory of practice, a "black unconscious" and system of dispositions reflecting an internal coherence of dynamic structures whose efficacy and vitality, "as with all symbolic reduplication lies in the extent to which it brings *to* consciousness all that is implicitly assumed in the unconscious mode of the [Afro-diasporic] *habitus*" (Bourdieu 1977, 216).

Here we can think about the *work* of art. Examining the music of the African diaspora helps reframe the interrelation of popular cultural expressions and social formations, and allows us to rethink the relationship of Afro-diasporic culture to the making of the modern world. By centering music as method and subject, its explanatory and elocutionary force provides a view into the critical work of cultural creation, the politics of time and temporality, and a different and perhaps deeper way of rendering New World black experiences. Placing music at the center, as both the subject of historical analysis and mode of examination, and using rootwork and polyrhythm as theoretical and structural anchors, we can develop and elaborate a methodology for Afro-diasporic historiography and the study of expressive culture more generally.

The more we attend to the uniqueness of music as a social and cultural phenomenon, the more the concepts we have inherited from the social sciences are challenged. As a medium, method, and expression of social organization of sound in motion, music transcends such "classical" antinomies as form and content, emotion and meaning, signifier and signified; form and content are expressions of each other (Baraka 1968). Listening to music can tell us not only about political, ideological, and cultural logics but also about the "practice of everyday life." Looked upon from different vantage points, music can be conceived as at once an activity and an artifact, as process and product. Taking the music seriously demands that we attend not only to its production and reception, but also, critically, to how music continually makes meanings and feelings available to its creators and participants—audiences, musicians, dancers, and singers.

John Shepherd has written: "Music seems to most faithfully reflect the intangible, fluid, and dynamic characteristics of social relationships" (1991, 81). We can push this further. Music not only "reflects" social relations but, in many ways, is constitutive of social relations and socialization. Humanly organized sound expresses humanly organized behavior.[4] The interrelationship of music and sociality illuminates historically and culturally specific politics of time and temporality—in a word, style. The power of music lies in its ability to at once communicate the incommunicable and to "keep time," to narrate and describe the experiences of collectivity. Movement, affect, memory, and history are all united in the "innate mythopoeia of music" (Soyinka 1976). The dialectics of music and history shape the production, reception, and interpretation of symbolic forms, "affecting presences."[5] The music can shed much light upon the history of historical consciousness.

The peculiar phenomenology of music as sound, sign, and symbol lies in its ability to simultaneously present and represent, to historicize and poeticize existence. Music expresses cultural patterns ("structures of feeling") and at the same time, articulates a relationship between communication and social structure.[6] Music is both media and mediation: society is "as much 'in' music as music is 'in' society" (J. Shepherd 1991, 190). Modes of musical and cultural expression exhibit an extreme sensitivity to their historical contexts and conditions. Music means and is made meaningful in the context of social interaction, of its communal creation and reception in time and space. Thus music gives us unique insight into the nature of cultural production in general.[7] Ellison has said, "one of the chief values of living with music lies in its power to give us an orientation in time. In doing so, it gives significance to all those indefinable aspects of experience, which nevertheless make us what we are. *In the swift whirl of time music is a constant, reminding us of what we were and of that to which we aspire*" (1964, 197; emphasis added).

Black Marxism and the Philosophy of Music

The history of the expressive cultures of the African diaspora provides a locus for exploration of many of the issues of music, memory, movement and history. Interrogating the "black aesthetic" provides both a multiperspectival historiography and sonic holography. In black music, black culture is politicized and poeticized in such a way as to make it a rich analytic.[8] As Marx and Engels have said: "History is nothing but the succession of separate generations each of which exploits the materials, capital funds, the productive forces handed down to it by all preceding generations, and thus, on the one hand, continues traditional activity in completely changed circumstances and, on the other, modifies the old circumstances with completely changed activity" (1972, 57).

The histories of Africans in the Americas are histories of enslavement, resistance, "downpression," displacement, encounter, and survival. From the middle passage to the slave cabin, from plantation to ghetto, the music of the African diaspora has nourished, sustained, and preserved Africans and their descendants in the so-called New World. The histories of the musics of the black Atlantic reveal the dialectic between the succession of modes of cultural production and the revitalization of traditional activity: the expression of "discontinuous continuity" (Bastide 1978), "coherent deformation" (Mackey 1993), and "consistent modes, attitudes and approaches within changing contexts" (Baraka 1963, 153).[9] Further, these cultural practices and processes eloquently express the Caribbean counterpoint that underpins the shaping of the modern world system. The Caribbean region as locus, Africans in the Americas as actors were central to the construction of modernity, and these expressive cultures provide an "alternate archive" in which the histories of these countercultures of modernity are inscribed (Gilroy 1993).

The semantics and semiotics of musical communication reveal the dense interrelations of experience and expression. The complex interplay of music and sociality and its affecting presence in Afro-diaspora also enables us to glimpse some of the modalities of insurrection, accommodation, and resistance embedded in black cultural practices and politics played out on a lower register ("bass culture"). Historically, we can think of the popular musics of the African diaspora as a form of low-intensity peasant and proletarian warfare (Wolf 1969; James 1995). Not only do the musical conversations of the African diaspora enable and embody ways of retheorizing and remapping the geographical, cultural, and imaginative bounds of the Caribbean region; examining these expressive cultures and their production as popular styles (grooves) also enables us to "read" social history of the region "from below" and explore a different level of productive activity and cultural creation, beneath the ground of political economy.[10] Through tracing some of these musical styles from slavery to freedom and through the first half of the twentieth century, we get a sense of a different level of productive activity and cultural creation; we can begin to echo-locate an "Atlantic Sound." In addition, we can examine some of the sociological, philosophical, and feelingful dimensions and functions of the music: the politics of music and the pleasure of meaning.[11]

The complexities of transculturation, ethnic differentiation, gendered identification, class, status, and state formation in the Caribbean over time are such that we can speak of Creole identities (Brathwaite), plural societies (Smith), proto-proletarians (Craton), reconstituted peasantries (Mintz), and lumpen and comprador bourgeoisies (Rodney; Frank). New social and cultural forms emerged in the Caribbean that were neither determined by the African past nor reducible to the idealized structures of political economy.

The massive demographic displacement of the African slave trade, and the socio-political derangement and dis-integration that ensued on the African continent ensured that a wide spectrum of diverse peoples with varying cultural competencies and social statuses were recruited into the New World labor regime. This had profound effects on the making of black culture in diaspora. Differences in age and sex as well as regions of provenance and time of arrival are also important variables that further complicate theories of cultural transmission and contact. Processes of transculturation among African groups in the circum-Caribbean region reveal that these intricate sociocultural interchanges had more to do with the historical patterns of interaction on various local levels than simply ethnic origins, class formations, or demographics.[12] Shared experiences, cultural sensibilities, economic conditions, and New World labor discipline enabled and fostered the formation of coherent, if contradictory, pan-ethnic African-based worldviews and cultural networks. But this process was by no means automatic; the question is how these "black" identities were constructed, refashioned, and expressed in and through music and music-making. As James Snead observed: "Black culture highlights the observance of [. . .] repetition, often in homage to an original generative instance or act. Cosmogony, the origins and stability of things, hence prevails because it recurs. . . . Periodic ceremonies are ways in which black culture comes to terms with its perception of repetition, precisely by highlighting that perception" (1981, 149).

The central role of music and dance in black cultural life survived the middle passage. Music has always been a crucial part of a wider African and Afro-diasporic cosmology and worldview, inseparable from a variety of related media and relations. There is a deep structural integration between music and virtually all other aspects Afro-diasporic performance. "Music and dance are so closely bound together in the thinking of many West Africans that it is difficult to separate song from movement or playing the drum from speech. The various media blend into one another as when the drummer might say of a dancer, 'The dance she spoke'. It is in fact, difficult to find a word in any of the West African languages that is equivalent to the Western idea of 'music'" (Stone, 15). The continued implication and imbrication of music and performance in the social lives, cultural productions and political articulations of the African diaspora are testimonies to the profound resourcefulness of the enslaved, the deep necessity of innovation and adaptation, and the critical role of song and dance in cultural and communal preservation. "Culture is not a fixed condition but a process: the product of interaction between past and present . . . it is not one of survivals but of transformations" (Levine 1978, 5). In West and West Central Africa, the main areas of catchment and embarkation for enslaved Africans can (roughly) be divided into six overlapping cultural zones ("clusters") that shared numerous underlying cultural similarities (as well as marked differences).[13] Similarly, the New World context of the Caribbean provided common conditions and experiences as well as a host of new differentiations and stratifications. The power of black music lies in its feelingful representation of these transformations of African peoples into black folks.

Black Science

The concept of rootwork is more than just metaphorically suggestive, but also is historically and empirically verifiable when we turn to the diaspora as a whole and maintain a focus on cultural production as process. Polyrhythm provides an analytical and methodological tool to examine the multiplicities of time and space, musically and historically in the Caribbean region as a whole. There is an unmistakable family resemblance between the musics of the African diaspora, a kinship based upon lineage and history and shaped in and by the "Caribbean crucible," while still enabling these various local traditions to maintain their subtle individuality. This work uses four musical genres to outline a general historiography of the African diaspora and its musical and aesthetic expression. Since black labor was critical to the creation of white capital, and given the centrality and ubiquity of music in the cultures of the African diaspora, these musical traditions have much to tell us about the lives and histories of people of

African descent. By placing music and cultural production at the center of historical analysis, we can create a more (w)holistic historiography of the circum-Caribbean region, theorizing the area as integrated culturally and conceptually while paying close attention to the fractures, fragmentations, and historical particularities of development and, at the same time, holding the region as both crucially constitutive of wider Atlantic history. Black music provides the "back beat" to the making of the modern world.

Utilizing archival sources and research, oral interviews, secondary historical works, musicology, ethnographic and linguistic literature, and drawing from a broad framework of cultural studies and critical theory, I investigate the musical cultures of the African diaspora, both in their relations to the African origins of the enslaved, the New World context, and their ongoing transformations in relation to political economic change and social flux. The techniques, content, and structure of these musical modes reflect and engender shared conceptual frameworks, cultural strategies, and creative approaches that give meaning and coherence to the idea of a "black aesthetic," understanding "blackness" as processual and contingent, imagined but no less real. Afro-diasporic musical traditions reveal deep structural forms and aesthetic grammars of the historical imagination,[14] at the same time they encode and embody an alternative archive of the processes of historical development, transculturation, ethnic identification, and the significance of African origins: the changing same.[15]

The point is not to reduce the complexities of the histories of the African diaspora and the lived experience of black peoples in the Western hemisphere to some static, cultural common denominator stemming from the shared experience of enslavement and continued oppression (although this is crucial), but instead to theorize the profound impact of the African slave trade, racism, colonialism, and black creativity and cultural genius manifested in resilience and resistance as critical to and constitutive of the making of the modern world. The history of black music in diaspora chronicles the "great transformation" of modernity, and registers the development of capitalism as a world system. The different modes and moods of this work combine to explicate the transformations of Africans in the Americas as slaves and freed people, and the subsequent role of black music in registering the development and underdevelopment of Caribbean societies in late capitalism. There have been many pioneering historical studies of slave culture, plantation societies, "peasantology," and wonderful ethnographic and musicological analysis of African "syncretisms," "retentions," and transculturation in the New World, but fewer attempts at connecting the issues of historical materialism directly to culture, ideology, and the practices of everyday social life. As Eric Wolf has said, "we need a more theoretically informed history and a more historically informed theory" (Wolf 1997, 21).

The "elective affinities," iconicities, and deep grooves densely woven into the polyrhythmic nature of Afro-diasporic musical idioms—syncopation, offbeat phrasing, and melodic accentuation—combine to embody a radically democratic ethos of rhythmic inclusion. At the same time, the antiphonal and improvisational praxis of musicians, dancers, and audiences structure forms and figures of individual expressiveness within a context of collective participation and affirmation. Black musicking taken as a whole expresses and articulates the ontological totality.[16] Through the dynamism and feelingfulness of its very nature—as communally organized, produced, and experienced—the music *re*-presents and remembers the unity in difference of the Afro-diasporic cultural continuum. In short, the music is the message (as Marx put it, "the concrete is concrete" [1959]).[17]

The four chapters that make up the book are conceptually distinct and aesthetically intertwined; the musics tell many stories. The first two chapters work together to give a picture of the spectrum and continuum of "plural societies" in the Caribbean and the processes of transculturation from bondage to freedom through the first half of the twentieth century. Trinidad, a former Spanish colony, partially occupied by the French and finally under direct British rule, was never dominated by the machinery of the plantation; however, that system necessarily shaped the sociocultural and political economic contours of the island. Trinidad's unique position makes it a critical site for the examination of issues of nationalism, race, class, and cultural creation in a colonial state. Cuba, in contrast, was a late, great sugar-producing society, almost entirely dominated by the plantation complex; a Spanish colony afloat on British and later American capital, whose commercial importance and slave imports soared in the late nineteenth century. In Cuba issues of American empire and national consciousness intertwine with Afro-Cuban cultural creation and modes of industrial production. The chapters continue through the interwar period to trace the development and transformation of ex-slaves into proletarian subjects, still in the "shadow of the plantation." These first two chapters seek to explore practices of identity formation and their musical articulations in response to late capitalism as well as the roots of underdevelopment in the Caribbean (it is important to recall that the two islands contributed to the first foreign popular dance "crazes" in the United States). The calypso of Trinidad is often considered the most "logocentric" of African diaspora, while the son/

rumba complex of Cuba is widely acknowledged (on both sides of the black Atlantic) as dance music par excellence. As such the juxtaposition provides insight into the interrelationships between rhythm and the voice in circum-Caribbean music.

The second part operates in the post–World War II context, to chart two distinct yet interrelated visions of diaspora and decolonization. Chapter 3 uses "third world creative music" (jazz or so-called hard bop) and the sonic imagination to explore the lineages and developments of the so-called Second Reconstruction, from the Bandung Conference and the *Brown v. Board of Education* decision, and the politics of liberation and neocolonial domination. The politics of nonalignment, third world unity, and afro-diasporic consciousness found eloquent expression in the sonic imaginary of the late fifties and early sixties. The fourth chapter shifts to New York City, urban renewal, black rebellion, and the beginnings of deindustrialization to examine the birth of salsa, concurrent with the rise of the civil rights movement, and its stylistic consolidation concurrent with the rise of Black Power. Countercultural rebellion, "montuno aesthetics," barrio iconography, and urban realism found a unique and exciting vehicle for expression in the controlled chaos of salsa and Latin soul. These two chapters interrogate diaspora as a "post-national" space in which potential consciousness is circumscribed by objective possibility (the idea of the third world is juxtaposed with the reality of Puerto Rican migration), and in which music becomes a means to realizing unity in the flux of constantly changing social and political relationships.

The thesis is that a critical account of the historical development of the Afro-diasporic musical tradition must be re-presented as one of resistance, accommodation, creolization, and transculturation, as reflected in these four cases of stylistic evolution. It is the role of music in society and society in music that holds these four "case studies" together. At the same time, I examine some of the recurrent features ("repeating islands") and strategic differences (counterpoint) that distinguish these musics while binding them in a collective groove. Given the strictures of slave society and the structures of continuing domination after emancipation, music became the primary mode of black expression and cultural creation. As such, the "black aesthetic" is always already a musical one (and necessarily so). Each of the four overlapping movements represents unique yet vitally interrelated musical, historical, and epistemological moments. The first two chapters are bound by the period between the two world wars, characterized by a heightened sense of "new nationalism" in Africa and the Caribbean and reflected in various political and artistic movements ranging from Garveyism and Afro-Cubanismo to Negritude and the Harlem Renaissance. Chapters 2 and 3 are linked through contexts of intensified anticolonial struggle, third world consciousness, and the Cuban revolution. Finally, chapters 3 and 4 examine the transition from civil rights to human rights, and the increased militancy and radical self-awareness of the Black Power movement. Throughout, the "nation" as a unit of analysis is problematized. The first chapter on Trinidad presents us with a "national" case, an island that has been subject to all the major imperial powers and whose music reflects the complex stylistic amalgam of the "neo-African" cultures of the Francophone, Hispanophone, and Anglophone Caribbean. The Cuban case reveals the dynamics of intra-imperial expansion and bilateral relations, national consciousness, and the dialectics of underdevelopment between insurgent Cuba and a consolidating US empire. The third chapter takes on a truly international vision of the African diaspora; the "Black revolution in music" (Kofsky 1970) reflected a transatlantic consciousness and sonically realized an international awareness of the necessity of black liberation. Lastly, the Puerto Rican/Nuyorican example is instructive in that the island is at once a neocolony, semi-sovereign protectorate, and (in New York) a "nation within a nation." "Borinquen" is quite literally and figuratively an "imagined nation."

In many ways, the project is a symbolic and sonic dialogue with the "specter of Haiti." After the black victory in Haiti, I argue, many (if not most) of the Afro-diasporic "revolutions" were social, cultural, and above all, musical, registering and grounding subaltern politics and survival strategies on a lower frequency. These musics are "rituals of intensification": "In a situation in which the system is continually able to absorb revolt, to incorporate it into its growing totality . . . critical activity is, in fact, often [elevated] to the level of ritual" (Mayrl, qtd. in Goldmann 1976, 21). After all, it was the French planters and their slaves from Haiti who brought the Carnival traditions to Trinidad that would prove so important in the development of kaiso; and it was the Black Revolution in Ayti and its aftermath that sent slaves and planters to Cuba and colonial Louisiana. After the revolution, rhythms of the slave trade and the circum-Caribbean cross-fertilizations of the late nineteenth and early twentieth centuries coalesced (around roughly the same time) into Cuban rumba/son complex, Trinidadian calypso, and the early blues and jazz in the Mississippi Delta region. In the post–World War II period these musics were remembered and reinvented in the harmonic improvisations of bebop; later, the African and Afro-Caribbean roots of jazz were forcefully reasserted in the new creative music of the Bandung period. By the late sixties and early seventies, Puerto Rican musicians were drawing heavily on Afro-Cuban son and the black roots of the rumba, and combining Afro-Boricua traditional musics with "soul power" to create salsa.

By exploring these "national" musics as communal ritual, danced religion, and regional history as well as modalities of ethnic assertion and identification, we can see not only the continuous revolution, renovation, and reinvention (rootworking) of significant structures of feeling of African origin and New World elaboration; we can also examine the deep polyrhythmic interrelationship and iconicity of styles in the expressive cultures of the African diaspora. The musics' performance and performativity invites theorizing of the polyrhythmic nature of historicity and Afro-diasporic consciousness as well as the intermeshed complexities of popular expression and commodification.

We can say that one of the functions of black musicking is to "*awaken our historical self-consciousness and keep it awake*" (Lukács). The music moves through myth and memory, and the groove keeps it all together, carrying the feeling of black people making music, making a living, making history. I have worked toward rendering a complex history of both the stylistic and cultural transformations of some of the musical traditions in the African diaspora (a rich, if unstable mosaic) using the examination of local musical responses to global movements in the circum-Caribbean, to echo-locate "an analytically effective picture of the past and present of the region as a totality" (Mintz 1974, 52). The different yet intermeshed movements, musics, memories, and histories in the following chapters provide the "phonographic" plates that record the interference patterns of black musical traditions—reflecting, refracting, crossing, splitting—to create a "four-dimensional" soundscape of black experiences in the circum-Caribbean: a holographic imaging and imagining of *Chocolate Surrealism*.

1. "Headless Heroes of the Apocalypse"
The Trinidadian Calypso to 1940

> Everything that happened in Trinidad with the real calypsonians, they recorded it. So the history of Trinidad can be found in the calypsos.
> —Roaring Lion

Kaiso and Kalinda

By the mid-1930s what had begun as the "folk" music of the Afro-Trinidadian working and under-classes had achieved international recognition and acceptance. The music known as calypso began crossing transatlantic circuits with the first recording of the music in New York in 1912. With the growth and development of the recording industry in the 1920s, and the expanding international market for recorded music, US recording companies began searching for "new" sounds as well as catering to new tastes (outside the Euro-American classical and popular music audiences). In the United States, this was reflected in the rise of the "race" records and the first recordings of "hillbilly" music; internationally, this meant forays into the Caribbean and Latin America, as the search for new sounds followed the penetration of US financial capital and foreign investment.

Brisk sales of calypso recordings in the West Indies, the United States, and Britain led to fierce competition among recording companies. In the calypso market of the 1930s the main players were Decca and RCA Victor's Bluebird label. The battle for the local market share of music sales in Trinidad erupted in a small "war" between the Decca distributor, a businessman of Portuguese descent named Edward Sa Gomes, and the distributor for Bluebird, a Chinese man named Akow. Perceiving Bluebird as a potential threat to his monopoly, Sa Gomes falsely reported to the colonial administrators that a recent shipment from the United States of Bluebird records contained obscene material. The British authorities, ever vigilant to protect the morals of their colonial subjects, listened to a few of the songs and ordered the entire shipment dumped into the ocean(!). Furious, Akow retaliated by reporting that the Decca shipment also contained indecencies, and, sure enough, Sa Gomes's shipment was seized and buried at sea (Shapiro 1979).

This episode highlights the "audible entanglements" that inhere in listening to the kaiso:[1] poetics and politics; censorship and creativity; capitalism and colonial control; marginal practices and metropolitan values. Here race, class, and gender imploded in a conflict that resulted in tens of thousands of records being buried at sea. Following Guilbault (2007) we can use the analytic of "audible entanglements" to "*foresound* sites, moments, and modes of enunciation articulated [*in* and] *through* musical practices. . . . [F]ar from being 'merely' musical, audible entanglements . . . also assemble social relations, cultural expressions, and political formations" (41–42). As the epigraph that begins this chapter states, the history of Trinidad is in the calypso. Thus the story of the kaiso is also about a "history of the voice," subterranean convergences, creolization, masking, and power. The history of calypso sounds the musical and social development of the Afro-Trinidadian community, the transition "from shared experience to conscious expression." "[M]usic is, in fact, the surest threshold to the language that comes out of it" (Brathwaite 1993, 270).

Further, Trinidad provides a unique location from which to explore and interrogate the socio-historical dynamics of the circum-Caribbean as a cultural area writ large. As Peter Wilson has said: "the island's singular status gives it the peculiar distinction of being an amalgamation of much that is typical in the Caribbean" (1973, 188). Having been subject/prey at various points to all three major Caribbean imperial powers (Spain, France, and England), Trinidad offers us a microcosm of the region as a whole and a site to theorize the complexities of creolization and the "fragmented whole" that is the circum-Caribbean. Kaiso emerged out of this transcultural complex of music-dance-language and religious beliefs, in the context of social conflict, repression, and resistance that characterized black colonial life in Trinidad. The music developed in the late nineteenth century, through the intermingling of the once largely rural proletariat: unemployed and underemployed ex-slaves, formerly indentured Africans, and other creoles (and some Asians), mainly (though not exclusively) in the urban context of

Port-of-Spain. The calypso tells the history of migration and immigration, urbanization, proletarianization, underdevelopment, and black reconstruction in the post-Emancipation period. The kaiso emerged in and developed from the barrack yards, stick-fights, road marches, carnival tents, rum-shops, and city streets and became a national popular music and symbol.

Using humor, hyperbole, narrative detail, deft allusion, satire, wit, suggestive imagery, and verbal violence, the kaiso narrates the story of the Trinidadian social system, black life beneath colonial rule, the nature of male/female conflict and gender roles, the interpenetrations and clashes of classes and ethnicities; it tells of immigration, censorship, industrialization, and Carnival. It is about language and power, pun and proverb, survivalism and surrealism, and the endurance and aspirations of the dispossessed. The calypso is related to all Afro-diasporic musics and shares traditional African traits—songs of praise, blame, derision, protest, satire, celebration, affirmation, and contestation; dense rhythmic structures, dramatic syncopation, and improvisation; the interweaving and intereffectivity of speech and song, dramaturgy, drive, and eloquence. The calypso is oral history as well as "auriture," a repository of living folklore and political commentary chronicling historical transformations, collective aspirations, and social tensions; it has faced similar strictures, censorship, and repression as have all black musics in this hemisphere.

The Cedula of Population of 1783 encouraged and attracted labor and capital to Trinidad from other West Indian islands, like Martinique, Guadeloupe, St. Vincent, St. Kitts, and Grenada. Before the cedula, two-and-a-half centuries of Spanish colonial neglect had left the island largely uncultivated and underpopulated. The cedula changed the composition and complexion of the colony as the influx of planters and slaves from the French colonies overtook the Indian and Spanish settlements. After 1789, in response to the fluctuations of French Revolution, French planters and free people of color (of diverse political leanings) and their slaves left the French islands for Trinidad. The cultural dominant of this new society was essentially "Afro-French." The arrival of French planters and enslaved Africans began the complex creolization process that would stamp the island with its uniquely Caribbean and cosmopolitan character.

Prior to the cedula, slavery was inconsequential to Trinidad's development; however, by linking land grants with slave ownership, the cedula ensured the massive influx of slaves and the creation of a slave-based economy. Particularly after 1795, there was a dramatic increase in migration and population, as French planters fled with their slaves Saint Domingue and the advancing armies of Toussaint L'Ouverture, Andre Rigaud, and Jean-Jacques Dessalines. The arrival of the Haitians, enslaved peoples from other French colonies and Africa, along with their (fearful) masters was to place a lasting and distinctive imprint on the emerging national culture of Trinidad. With the arrival of the French, the plantation-complex that syncopates the Caribbean meta-archipelago was introduced to the island. Between 1783 and 1797, French immigrants established 468 plantations, with 159 sugar mills and hundreds of smaller holdings processing coffee, cotton, and tobacco (Pearse 1956, 176).

As early as 1784, the British had begun their economic penetration into Trinidad. While the French planters concentrated on agriculture, the British established a strong hold on the island's trade, disproportionate to their actual numbers. Thus, despite Spanish capitulation to the British in 1797, the "open door" policy would continue to provide a steady influx of French speakers and slaves, and the French/Afro-Creole cultural matrix would remain at the center of black cultural life throughout the nineteenth century (Wood 1986, 32).[2] The British takeover of the island added new layers of cultural complexity and contradictory pressures to an already diverse colonial scene. The underdeveloped state of the island and abundant land proved attractive to a number of English planters, who came with their patois-speaking slaves. The coming of the British also meant the ascendancy of "King Sugar," and the rationalization of the plantation regime that was to rule imperiously throughout the nineteenth and early twentieth centuries. British capital made the rapid rise of the sugar industry possible; large amounts of arable land and fertile soil (in comparison with the older colonies) made the island attractive to merchants and planters alike.

With the coming of the British also came the beginnings of the crown colony system and a more rigid racial stratification. The installation of crown colony status was used principally to deny the right to vote to the free people of color who numbered more than double the whites at the beginning of the nineteenth century. Under Spanish law the free coloreds enjoyed almost equal status to that of the whites; however, the succession of British governors sharply and systematically curtailed those rights. "The taint of republicanism associated with many of the Colored immigrants from the French islands, and the *shades of* Haiti which they evoked, were enough to compel competing groups in the white upper class to momentarily sink their differences in their universal apprehension for the security of the stratified social order, the maintenance of which they regarded as fundamental" (Singh 1994, 3; emphasis added). With the coming of the "age of revolutions" to the Caribbean, the specter of Haiti, the independent black republic, loomed large in the planter imaginary, and the colonial elite—formerly divided by nationality, religion, and language—forged an uneasy peace in order to maintain social control. As carnival developed, it would play an important role in consolidating the ruling classes.

Trinidad's development as a slave society began late. In 1813 the majority of the slaves were African born, and slaves were still concentrated in relatively small holdings. Bridget Brereton writes: "As late as 1834, the average owner had only seven slaves; 80% owned less than 10, while only 1% held over 100 slaves. An unusually high proportion of Trinidad slaves were urban: about 25% lived in Port of Spain in 1813, and this pronounced urban orientation was to be important for the development of post-emancipation society" (1981, 55). The late development, erratic growth and the competition from larger sugar-producing islands ensured that the Trinidadian economy would never be wholly dominated by the plantation. In 1810 "only" two-thirds of the population was enslaved, a much smaller proportion than the territories boasting "monster" plantations: Jamaica, Barbados, Brazil, and later Cuba. Slave mortality generally exceeded fertility and the population had to be regularly replenished.

Oral and recorded evidence reveals that diverse groups of Africans were brought to Trinidad. Higman (1984) has shown that the majority of the Africans imported were Mandika, Fulbe, KwaKwa, Yoruba, Hausa, Igbo, and Kongo.[3] A complex pan-African cultural base was forged from the diverse ethnic groupings of slaves, and while many maintained their "national" affiliations, internal and external forces in the context of plantation production necessitated the creation of a common community. This transformation from "ethnicity" to "race" was paralleled in the development of the creole language or "nation language" (Brathwaite 1993).

African slaves, like those born in the Americas, tended to marry endogamously, thus facilitating the transmission and retention of core cultural and linguistic codes, values, and practices beneath the oppressive weight of the slave system. Since few of the African-born slaves could speak French or English, or had mastered the Afro-French creole, they had no other recourse but to their mother tongues, which in turn continually transformed and "Africanized" the already multi-inflected creole. The linguistic history of Trinidad reveals the significance of social context, the period and provenance of African migration, and the varying levels of accommodation, adaptation, and transculturation between ethnic and racial groups. Rex Nettleford explains: "For not only does Africa ride the sense and sensibility—and bodies—of her offspring in the diaspora, she fertilizes the [Caribbean's] Creole languages in dynamic interaction with the masters' tongues as part of the all-pervasive process of cross-fertilization. Syntax and structure, idiom and lexicon are transformed to create 'third tongues'" (1978, 31).

In addition to and inseparable from language, slave song, dance, and religious ritual were vital nodes of resistance to the brutal dehumanization of enslaved life and served as crucial sites of opposition and affirmation, creating the "living room" necessary for the slaves to preserve and express a sense of humanity not constructed by the plantation, a humanness that resisted reduction to their legal status as property and their economic status as units of production. Music, dance and aesthetic production and celebration were critical to the survival and maintenance of slave culture. Slave dances had been tolerated and accepted in varying degrees at varying historical points throughout the circum-Caribbean. They were generally allowed in the French and Spanish colonies as a safety valve and a means of control; however, in the British colonies slave activities tended to be more circumscribed.

Like the carnival traditions (as we will see below), black musicking and celebrations in the early colonial period provided not only a means of social control for the planters, but more importantly, these practices also provided a means of social cohesion for the diverse population of enslaved Africans. And while the dances served to reinforce the common stereotypes that underwrote many of the moral justifications for slavery and reassured the planters of their (tenuous) hegemony, lurking behind the wavering tolerance and racist stereotypes lay the genuine and well-justified fear of the numerically superior slave caste. The planter class realized early on that black music and performance often masked potential subversion.[4] This dialectic of repression and tolerance by the elite dependent upon social conditions would continue to characterize ruling-class attitudes and actions regarding the expressive cultures of the slaves and their descendants.

Kalinda[5] emerged as a general term for an entire complex of slave song/dance and ritual activity, and was observed and documented throughout the circum-Caribbean, from Louisiana to British Guiana. According to J. D. Elder: "The term ... seems to be well known in other islands of the Caribbean, e.g. Haiti, Carriacou, and in Bequia, the form the institution takes in Trinidad is unique in respect to the music and dance and the 'stick-fight' which is its most important feature" (1966, 192). The ubiquity of the term in various accounts of slave culture can be explained by several factors: in the ongoing internal and inter-island creolization processes, song and dance complexes were simplifying and merging throughout the nineteenth century, while others died out altogether. Songs/dances like the Jhouba (juba), Bel-Air (bele), and bomba were transforming, adding and subtracting elements and developing through pan-Caribbean exchanges. Another factor that may explain the term's wide usage is that most white traveler-reporters had neither the inclination nor the ability to distinguish one dancing style from another. Pierre Labat, one of the most perceptive early commentators, wrote of kalinda in 1724: "The dance which pleases them [the slaves] greatly, and which is their most customary is the kalinda. It comes from the coast of Guinea, and according to all appearances from the Kingdom of Arada [the present-day Benin Republic, formerly Dahomey]. The Spanish learned it from the Negroes and dance it all over America in the same way as the Negroes" (quoted in Emery 1988, 25). The kalinda in Trinidad was an articulation of diverse modes of African-rooted ritual, which included song, dance, and stickfighting—a body of practices brought from the shores of Africa and syncopated to and transformed across the region by the rhythms of the plantation. From the eighteenth century on, kalinda (the dance), stickfighting, and their musical accompaniments were to play a decisive role in slave culture celebrations and the development of the kaiso.

There are conflicting legends as to the origins of the kaiso; Mitto Sampson gives two versions. In the first tale, a French planter known as "Lawa" ("King") Begorrat, who came to Trinidad from Martinique in the late eighteenth century,

> used to hold court in his cave to which he would adjourn with his favorite slaves and guests on occasions to indulge in a variety of entertainments. The court was attended by African slave singers of "Cariso" or "Caiso," which were usually sung extempore and were of a flattering nature, or satirical and directed against unpopular neighbors or members of the plantation community, or else they were "Mépris," a term given to a war of insults between two or more expert singers ... Gros Jean [a slave] was said to have been the first of these bards of "chantwells"[6] to be appointed Master of Caiso, or Mâit Caiso. (Sampson in Pearse 1956, 253)

Many of these early "chantwells" were reputedly obeahmen, and, assumedly equally respected and feared for their musical and magical prowess. They were larger than life figures with names like Papa Cochon and Hannibal the Mulatto.

The second myth of origin recounted by Sampson comes from legends passed on by Surisima the Carib, one of the few Amerindian kaisonians that has come down through history. According to Surisima, the word *cariso* is descended from the Carib word *carieto* (see fn. 3), which were traditional indigenous songs used to "heal the sick, embolden the warrior, and seduce the fair" (Sampson in Pearse, 296). Atilla[7] traces the roots of the modern kaiso back to the *gayap*,[8] or communal work effort and the musical accompaniment that both rhythmatized the labor and eased the strain of the work load, as slaves would prepare (their) ground for planting and divide themselves into gangs, each vying to outwork the other. As Atilla relates:

> Each gang had a leader whose main duty it was to set a rhythm by improvising and chanting a song, the refrain of which was taken up and maintained in unison by the whole gang as they worked their implements in time with the rhythm. The leader always chose a sonorous and important sounding name like Elephant, Thunderer, Trumpeter.... At the end of the day as they gathered around the cooking pot and made preparations for the evening meal, the gang that had done the most work would extol their prowess in the field and the leader would improvise ribald ditties making fun of the other gangs and their inability to do as much work as the victors. Thus, no doubt originated the "picong" which distinguishes the earliest forms of kaiso. (Quevedo 1983, 5–6)

Finally, Liverpool (2001) traces the origins of kaiso to praise-singing traditions and griottage of West African derivation. What these diverse explanations have in common is the affecting power (natural and supernatural) of word and sound, the presence of the musical form, and its functional and symbolic efficacy.

Carnival and Canboulay

After the abolition of the slave trade by the British in 1807, an inter-colonial trade developed in the region. Slaves from less profitable and productive islands were transported to the more fertile soils of places like Trinidad and British Guiana. The higher value of slaves and the newer, virgin soils inaugurated and sustained the inter-colonial trade. Between 1813 and 1821 Trinidad received over 3,800 slaves from neighboring islands, of whom nearly 1,100 came from Dominica and nearly 1,200 came from Grenada (E. Williams 1964, 76). The inter-island trade would complicate the already diverse pan-African/French/Spanish core culture of the island, and leave a significant mark on Trinidad's emerging Creole culture. With the rise of revolutions in Latin America after 1810, the island witnessed the migration of Spanish and (twice dislocated) French planters and their slaves, as well as mestizo *peones* from Venezuela and other parts of the Spanish Main. Trinidad in the first half of the nineteenth century was a French Creole society built on an Amerindian and African foundation laid by the Spanish, with a British superstructure and institutions. We can only understand these multifaceted histories of creolization once we grasp the layers of cultural, social, and demographic complexity.

By 1820 slavery in British possessions was coming to an end, although it would persist for another fourteen years, due in no small part to the profits being reaped from the sugar industry and the inter-colonial slave trade. In 1834 the slaves were "indentured" for a six-year contract, with emancipation arriving "early" in August 1838. At emancipation there were 20,656 "apprentices" and approximately 12,000 free people of color, the majority of who spoke French or patois. The newly apprenticed former slaves protested their status and demanded "full free." The former slaves blamed the local colonial elite, saying "their masters were 'dam tief,' the Governor an 'old rogue,' and the King not such a fool as to buy them half free when he was rich enough to pay for them altogether" (Cowley 1996, 28). After emancipation the demography of the island (and the region) was drastically altered (again); many slaves "voted with their feet," responding to the newly found mobility that freedom offered. Immediately after abolition the sugar industry in Trinidad lost some 20 percent of its labor force. Some freed people sought to buy the land that they worked, others simply squatted and farmed, still others moved into the urban areas of Port of Spain and San Fernando.

There was an intensification of the political impositions of the English after emancipation, in response to internal needs and external market pressures. English law and language supplanted French and Spanish institutions. Although there was still a clash of culture and custom between the French Roman Catholic and British Protestant elites, a détente emerged around issues of economics and labor control. The older French and Spanish upper class increasingly accommodated to the strictures of the crown colony system, in part due to the growing homogenization of interests among the planters and the ruling classes as British capital and imperial policy moved toward "free trade" and the self-regulating market over the course of the nineteenth century. More importantly, the evolution of a "community of interests" of the ruling classes was also a response to the growing political agitation of Trinidad's large free black and colored middle- and working-class peoples, particularly in the latter half of the century. The nature of the economy and mode of production militated against any radical structural transformation of the body politic, while the racialized relations of production ensured class and caste hierarchy would necessarily be sustained. As far as the ruling classes were concerned, the fundamental problems of post-emancipation Trinidad revolved around the procurement and disciplining of labor.

The problem of labor would continue to plague the planter class throughout the nineteenth century and into the twentieth, and the ruling class would traverse vast circuits of empire to fulfill its laboring needs. To meet the demands of production after emancipation, extensive immigration and importation of ex-slaves from Barbados, St. Vincent, Grenada, and other West Indian islands was undertaken. Trinidad became a mecca for "small islanders" (as they were derogatorily called). From around 1840 the island absorbed a continuous influx of inter-island migrants, cresting around the last quarter of the nineteenth century, when between 1871 and 1911 some 65,000 immigrants entered Trinidad, most of whom settled permanently. After abolition the island also received approximately 36,120 post-emancipation Africans, contributing to a re-Africanization of Trinidad's Afro-Creole culture. These "liberated" Africans had been either captured by British naval patrols or condemned by the mixed commission in Rio and Havana enforcing British law against the slave trade. The prospect of employment opportunities and better wages also encouraged emigration and many Africans arrived from Sierra Leone and St. Helena. In addition to the Africans, a small number of free blacks arrived from the United States. However, the attraction of Trinidad's sugar economy was short-lived for the Africans and others of the diaspora, and the sources of labor and immigration were too irregular for the planters and sugar estate owners. They had to look elsewhere in the far-flung British empire for a reliable labor supply. Thus between 1845 and 1917, some 143,000 East Indian indentured laborers were imported into Trinidad to resuscitate the sugar industry. The internationalization and Afro-diasporization of the Trinidadian labor force was to have profound effects on the development of this creole society and the kaiso.

The new Africans in Trinidad tended to live amongst their own countrymen, and continued to marry endogamously. For example, in Port of Spain, the "Radas" tended to settle in Belmont, Yoruba in St. Mary's and other areas. The Yoruba in particular (who made a large proportion of the liberated Africans and were to leave a pronounced mark on Trinidadian culture), like the East Indians, settled into insular communities and maintained and reproduced, to a large degree, their indigenous cultures; language, music, and the Shango religion are all testaments to the tenacious preservation of Yoruba heritage. The arrival of these Africans, as Maureen Warner-Lewis has said: "could not but serve to reinforce African customs existing since slavery. The cultural unity of Africa was real enough to ensure that an African rooted culture would survive the slave experience. This coalescence and synthesis of overlapping cultures took place again among the indentured laborers, further ensuring the maintenance of pre-emancipation traditions" (Warner-Lewis 1991, 54).[9]

The various patois and creoles of the small islanders combined with European, African, East Indian, and Chinese languages to add to the linguistic and cultural complexity of the island. The contiguity and simultaneity of all these dialogues, dialects, and cultures reflects and refracts the larger polyphony of social and discursive forces that were shaping the cultural systems of the entire region. This was also a period when folk-song melodies and rhythms from all over the West Indies and Latin America were being introduced into the colony, carried on the tongues of the migrating islanders, sailors, and dockworkers. The song/dance/language complexes traveled with the formerly enslaved and "liberated" Africans, and would contribute to the development of a multilayered, multi-ethnic cultural matrix.

After emancipation, when the planters and the English ruling class made it extremely difficult for the former slaves to acquire land, a period of "urban drift" (paralleling the inter-Antillean movements) set in. Poverty, unemployment, and unequal opportunity intensified conflicts between races, classes, and men and women. Seeking to reduce their dependence on the plantation, black laborers headed for the towns. The influx of freed people and new immigrants caused constant urban unrest. In their powerless position the working people of Trinidad formed bands, generally along territorial lines, fighting amongst themselves since they were unable to attack the true sources of oppression.

The French elite brought their carnival celebrations and customs to the island. Prior to emancipation slave participation in the festivities varied from plantation to plantation, town to town, and master to master. During carnival season the white elite masqueraded as *negres jardins* (field slaves), and would travel from estate to estate, feting one another, and participating in the *Cannes Brulees*, or "burning of the cane." After emancipation the formerly enslaved began to take on carnival as their own festival and an interesting inversion of this masking took place as ex-slaves themselves appropriated "canboulay," singing, stick-fighting, and dancing the kalinda. As Andrew Pearse notes, they "began to represent this scene as a kind of commemoration of the change in their condition, and the procession of 'cannes brulées' used to take place on the night of 1st August, the date of their emancipation ..." (1956, 182).[10] This play of inversions, this masking of politics and social relations and layering of cultural codes, reveals the "kaiso epistemology" that critically (in)forms the development of calypso in Trinidadian society. The canboulay masquerade of the ex-slaves was a (re)presentation of the creolization, masking, and rootwork at the heart of Afro-diasporic cultural practices: ways of being and doing which "re-veil" and reveal the iconicity between musical forms, linguistic structures, and traditions of performativity in the flux of historical change.

As early as 1838, blacks began to make their presence felt in the carnival celebrations, and canboulay, with its torchlit procession and stickfighting, came to mark the inauguration of carnival season. Adding a sense of racial solidarity and class consciousness to the proceedings, the canboulay was a multimedia, symbolic ceremony pitting African traditions and expressions of freedom against European moral codes (Elder, 1998). The ethnic intricacies of the island and ongoing political and economic inequality forced the ruling classes to remain constantly alert to the threat of the formation of volatile coalitions of urban "roughs" (ex-slaves and migrant workers) and the equally "exploited and explosive" East Indian and Chinese populations. This threat was felt acutely as the ex-slaves began to take over carnival in earnest in the 1860s. The formerly elite carnival became a truly "popular" celebration. The pronounced effect of slave culture on carnival turned the event into a ritual of "annual confrontation," a world turned upside down in which all sectors of Trinidadian society "faced" themselves (albeit masked). Trinidadian carnival simultaneously highlighted and heightened the conflicting interests and positions between the European ruling classes and the urban proletariat.

In the latter half of the nineteenth century, with massive immigration and overall population increase as a result of continued augmentation by East Indian indenture, the urban population of Port of Spain continued to grow. The sharp decrease in employment due to economic depression and collapsing infrastructure of the sugar industry (particularly after 1884) led to the flight of agricultural workers and the swelling of the ranks of lower-class blacks, concentrated in the heart of the city. Large numbers of Afro-Trinidadians (male and female) were habitually unemployed or underemployed, forming a "lumpen" population existing at the edges of the economy and society. The vast majority of these city dwellers were concentrated in the notorious barrack yards. The yards were the centers of sociocultural life, used for subsistence farming, informal gatherings, recreation, and so on. To quote Donald Hill, they were the "hub of the everyday world for rural Creole families and the center of local activity for denizens of the barrack houses in urban Port of Spain.... Yards were for chores, socializing, and other diversions, and for ritual ... washing, shelling corn, cooking, gossiping, playing cards and dominoes and holding prayer meetings, and other funerary or proprietary rituals..." (1993, 24). At the same time, the barrack yards were also overcrowded and dilapidated, without suitable ventilation or sanitation. The yard-dwellers were the victims of endemic disease (malaria, dysentery, yellow fever, etc.), high infant mortality, grinding poverty, and "mass human suffering" (as one nineteenth-century observer put it). The yards also supported the "gray" economy of the lumpen population composed of working poor, unemployed, petty criminals, prostitutes, vagabonds, gamblers, and, of course, musicians: the *jamette*, from the French *diâmetere*, meaning "underworld."

The *jamette* environment bred gang warfare and turf battles, trouble, misery, resilience, and musical creativity.[11] From the eighteenth century onward, sugar plantations and estates had rivaled one another in stick-fighting competitions (*bois bataille*), which, like the music and religious assemblies, were alternately permitted and censored. After emancipation, the freed people carried these notions of territoriality, masculinity, and violent conflict resolution to the urban barrack yards. As Atilla has testified: "The kaisonian was inseparably bound up with the institution of stick-playing known as kalenda, by his connection with that class of society" (Quevedo 1983, 23). The tensions between the lumpen unemployed and underemployed were ritualized in the stick-fight. Gordon Rohlehr gives an eloquent assessment: "The kalinda stick-fighting bands were the results of displacement and urbanization with their attendant conflicts and cultural processes of syncretism and assimilation. The landless were defining their territorial boundaries, making ritual claim to the land into which they had been so harshly indigenized, but to which they had no legal title" (1990, 52). Issues of status and identity in such a fragmented and plural society; defining gendered roles and "masculinity" in a patriarchal capitalist system; the politics of survivalism; "claiming turf" in a situation where land ownership was prohibited: amidst a wide and turbulent array of languages and cultures, all contributed to the shaping of the kalinda/stickfight complex.

The stick fight became highly formalized, with distinctive costumes and uniforms, behaviors, rules, codes, language, and musical style. The fighting bands themselves emerged from the confluence of a variety of cultural institutions. Slave networks and secret societies (replete with "kings" and "queens," traditions that had roots in African soil), were incorporated into the carnival celebration and provided early organizational structures for the bands. The mutual aid and self-help societies that proliferated after emancipation also contributed organizational components to the stick fight/calinda matrix. Most importantly, the barrack yards in which the freed people lived, congregated, and communed were central to the formation and affiliations not only of the fighting bands but also the larger Afro-Trinidadian creole community. The yards established the territorial perimeters and cultural parameters of the kaiso epistemology and the kalinda complex.

The jamette subculture of Port of Spain was based in the barrack yards, populated by the working poor, the destitute, the kaiso singers, drummers, stickmen, prostitutes, hustlers, and badjohns. The stick bands, competing for limited urban space, divided up the city, each major band having its own territory and boundaries that were often violently defended.[12] These rivalries were both means of empowerment and identification, and modes of aggression and sublimation. The violence of the stick fight ritualized and refocused the tensions of immigration, multiracial/multi-ethnic society, class conflict, cultural collision, and erosion among the urban and rural "underclass." The physical violence of the stick fight was iconically coupled with a violence of the tongue.

Each stick-fighting band consisted of a fighting leader (king or *pierrot*)—leading on holidays or festive occasions, a lead singer or chantwell, a corps of fighters, and a group of women backers usually led by an older female called a matador. The task of the chantwell was to steel the fighters' courage, sing the praises of the champions, empower the leader, and "to harangue the stickfighters into action and pour scorn on their rivals." The chantwell was supported by chorus made up of the women, hangers-on, and members of the band who sang in response to the singer's call.[13] In African antiphonal fashion a lead line would be given by the chantwell, who would alternate the verse with the refrain from the chorus. As the fighting bands moved through the streets, open and intense hostilities occurred when they met other bands. The kaiso epistemology and the kalinda complex were communal creations and re-creations, the joint product of inspired folk artists, skilled fighters, and the men and women who traveled with the bands, spontaneously producing songs for the occasions: popular music.

Upon encountering a rival band, the pierrot would deliver a spirited and fiery oration, dealing mainly with his own manly prowess, his skill with his stick, his invincibility, the might of his legions, and the ultimate doom and destruction that awaited his enemies. The ritual sequence also allowed for the rebuttal of the "enemy" pierrot, who would in turn impress upon his rival his own fearlessness, the power of his men, the many foes he had conquered, and the dire things in store for his opponents. Then the leaders would advance, usually backed by their three best fighters, and the battle would begin. The chantwells would take up the kalinda (here a "battle song") that would enthuse and invigorate the women and men (whose courage was usually fortified with a few shots of rum). As the wounded fell their cry was "*Coule, sang moen ha coule*" ("flowing, my blood is flowing"), and they would be quickly scooped up by the women and sympathetic friends, who would take them away and attend to their wounds, so that they could return to the fray. A typical stick fight may have lasted from 8:00 in the evening till dawn, and they were accompanied by singing, drumming, and/or the tambour-bamboo—bamboo stamping tubes, cut to different lengths to produce different pitches, that were beat against the ground.

The boasting of the stick fighters and the songs of the chantwells were "simultaneously chivalric, aristocratic and proletarian," a complicated, extended, and extensive masculinity ritual, and the calindas that accompanied the match transmitted ideologies through the music. The stick fighter's boasting was also tied to African-derived traditions of obeah and religious magic: rootwork. Language in this context takes on a spiritual and supernatural power; the word itself becomes ritual mask. "Language for the chantwell who reinforced the stickfighter's boast . . . *was power*; the word was magic, its form, incantation, its purpose inspiration and celebration. This aspect would remain in the Calypso . . . and would see a revival in the late 1930's, when singers would recall and revamp old calinda fragments" (Rohlehr 1990, 53). Rohlehr's observations point toward the linkages between linguistic practices and musical forms: the inter-affectivity of word, sound, and power; the ways in which the past continues to (in)form the present; the kaiso epistemology that shapes and is shaped by the development of the music.

The performance of masculinity and ethic of male virility and sexual mastery were also connected to the fighter's prowess with his stick.[14] An early stick fighter's boast went: "I, Lawa [French: Le Roi] with stick, with fight, with woman, with dance, with song, with drum, with everything." This single line pulls together much of the kaiso ideology and performative strategies. The audacity and defiance of the kalinda chants reflected the conditions of daily existence, part boast, part wish fulfillment, wavering between domination and mastery. This was a rhetoric of violent self-assertion acquiring force through the raising of "bad talk" to a high art. Verbal adeptness coupled with a martial art became a central component of masculine role-playing.[15] The stick fight was a crucial component of "manly" identity formation in an economically perilous and socially powerless situation. Interestingly, Elder (1998) cites accounts of accomplished female stick fighters from the nineteenth century: Sarah Jamaica, Boobull Tiger, Techselia, and B-bar the Devil, who were also referred to as matadors, this complicates the relationship between stick-fighting and the performance of gender identity. More frequently, however, women were kalinda singers and members of the chorus, indispensable to and inseparable from the stick fight. Between breaks in the fighting, the women would sing their *carisos*, generally witty, metaphorical songs of praise and derision, at times sexually suggestive and/or explicit.[16]

By the middle of the nineteenth century, the British had adopted a policy of systematically Anglicizing the island, in accordance with their political and economic makeover, and brought with their "civilizing" efforts the "frigid morality" of Victorian England. To the British ruling class the "Jamette Carnival"—with its fighting, drinking, dancing, and lewd songs and behaviors—was the antithesis of decency and respectability. The British were preoccupied with labor discipline and steady industry. In their eyes, the "rude jamettes" were the antithesis of reliable labor and orderly society, they were castigated as ruthless criminals, vagabonds, "lazy niggers," ruffians, unemployed rowdies, and prostitutes addicted to rum, dancing, and indecency. These lower-class elements had co-opted the once refined traditions of carnival. The ruling classes mobilized their rhetoric of morality in conjunction with a discourse of law and order and sought to suppress the jamette celebration. The struggle between the ruling classes and the lumpen-proletariat over definitions of propriety and acceptable forms of behavior was a constant feature of nineteenth-century Trinidad. The British sought to impose what they considered to be a "proper" style on the "primitive" African-based style of celebration, in the same way they sought to inculcate the "apprentices" with the proper work ethic and discipline for semi-industrial production. Both endeavors affected the shape of carnival and calypso well into the twentieth century. Behind the moral indignation lurked the justifiable fear (held over from slavery) that the assembly could get out of control, and the exploited could unite and turn on their oppressors.[17]

In 1881 depression hit Trinidad, unemployment swelled, hardship and poverty were rampant, and class conflicts came into sharp focus. During carnival the previous year, police had succeeded in disarming the stick-fighting bands and had extinguished the torches of the canboulay procession; in 1881 that would not prove so easy. As the police moved on the carnival revelers and masqueraders, riots erupted. The stick-fighting bands, "in the spirit of détente," came together in a class action to fight the police. Armed with their *puis* (*bois*) and wearing pots on their heads as helmets, they met the police in the streets. Thirty-eight policemen were wounded and somewhere between fourteen and twenty-one people were arrested and tried. The Canboulay Riots of 1881 (as they came to be called) were followed by riots in 1883 and 1884, and were met, in turn, with a series of legal maneuvers by the ruling class. The ordinances passed in 1882 and 1883, as noted, sought to make carnival "decent" through sponsorship and surveillance, and systematically outlawed canboulay, drumming, dances, processions, assemblies of ten or more persons, and stick-fighting. The ordinance of 1884 went even further, banning "the assemblage of felons, persons convicted of riot or affray, common prostitutes, rogues and vagabonds to the number of ten or more in any house, building, or yard or other place" (E. Williams 1964; Rohlehr 1990; Cowley 1996).

With stickfighting outlawed, and the men "deprived of their martial activity," the kalindas and lavways of the stick fighters appropriated and incorporated the originally female mode of cariso. "The *kalinda* was suppressed by the Trinidadian government in 1881 as the cause of 'disorderly conduct and rioting in the streets.' As a result the folk switched over to the *cariso* which until then was a female dance-song performed during rest periods between *kalinda* fighting bouts" (Elder 1966, 200). The *picong* (from the French: *piquant*, "insult") and the oppositional mode of the cariso were added to the lavway vocabulary. The ban on stick-fighting led to the sublimation of hostilities through an aggression of the tongue; the figure of the stickman and badjohn gave way to the "man-of-words." However, we must avoid seeing the male appropriation of cariso and the channeling of male aggression into verbal violence as merely a phenomenon of masculine activity and feminine passivity.

Victorian ideals of social reform and bourgeois ideologies of the late nineteenth and early twentieth centuries led to the shrinking participation of women in the public sphere. The canons of respectability being erected by the ruling classes increased social pressure on women and discouraged their participation in behavior deemed indecent. However, women continued to play a vital role in carnival celebrations, eschewing the norms and expectations of the ruling classes, even while accepting some tenets of the ideologies of respectability. The attempts to "domesticate" working-class women coincided with the cooptation and official sponsorship of the rowdy, proletarian carnival celebration. Under the stick-fighting ban, the bands reorganized into smaller "social unions" oriented around the various yards in Port of Spain and San Fernando, where annual "rehearsals" were held for carnival. These yard rehearsals were the predecessors to the tents that would emerge in the early twentieth century and become signal features in carnival and calypso.

The years immediately following the 1881 riots saw concerted efforts by the planter class to censor both East Indian Hosein festivals[18] and the Creole Carnival. "The reaction of the upper classes to the participation of the free colored and the ex-slaves was to withdraw from participation and subject to the institutions to the venomous fires of press, pulpit and state" (Quevedo 1983, 55). The fear was that these festivals were thin smokescreens for imminent rebellion of peasants, workers, and the urban unemployed, and the specters of urban revolt continued to haunt the ruling-class imaginary. At the same time, the growing local bourgeoisie and middle classes were beginning to push for a more representative government and were chafing under their politically neutralized position. Class pressure from below forced the elite to attempt to reassert their hegemony and the merchant class began to sponsor carnival song and costume competitions as a means of controlling and surveilling the celebrations. Control of carnival simultaneously allowed for the spread of the middle-class power base and suppression of the more radical and dangerous elements of the jamette festivities.

The spread of primary education and English literacy (beginning in the 1870s) helped disseminate and reinforce both the primacy of the English language, metropolitan values, and ideologies of respectability. The cultural imposition of bourgeois education resonated with lower-class aspirations of self-improvement and uplift and, understandably in a situation of poverty and deprivation, striving for middle-class status was woven into the fabric of Caribbean societies. Crucially tied to these aspirations was the "quest for language" that had been under way since slavery. The splitting up of the enslaved from other members of their respective ethnic groups complicated direct lexical and syntactic transmission, while at the same time providing a common cultural base as well as a common identity for pan-African linguistic development. Many West African languages are related at their roots, and the process of enslavement and acculturation, while in some ways depriving the (Creole) slaves of their mother tongues, provided the basis for the synthesis, recombination, and transformation of African cultures. The deep grammatical structures at the base of the varied West African tongues were brought to bear upon the European languages of their owners, and the transformations of masters' tongues became the *lingua franca* of resistance. And, perhaps more importantly, as Maureen Warner-Lewis points out, African linguistic antecedents with "the high proportion of sung rather than spoken language retention testified to the remarkable role of melody and rhythm in stimulating and sustaining historical memory" (1991, 79).

The love of "fine speech," the quest for "more splendid language," linguistic creativity and improvisation, and grandiose utterance certainly had African provenance. The aesthetic pleasure in the play and display of words was easily incorporated into verbal contest. Eloquent speech was wrapped up in the whole interpenetrated cultural complex of music, dance, and song, and the language of the slaves was necessarily masked and "double-voiced"—that is, both ornamental and functional, aesthetic and aggressive, an instrument of diversion and display as well as the standard vehicle for communication. By the late nineteenth century the kaiso was a Creole blend of standard English, lofty metaphor, and cosmopolitan references combined with vernacular humor, quotidian happenings, and "scandalizing practices." These musical/linguistic traditions were first translated into French Creole, and then into the "prestigious" new language, English. Around the turn of the century, the singing of carnival songs in English gradually replaced the old patois lavways and calindas (Atilla dates the first entirely English kaiso to 1899). The complexities and tensions that derived from cultural plurality, the long history of cosmopolitanism, constant immigration, and intense class/caste stratification resulted in a linguistic and cultural "ambivalence" felt by the lower classes, an "unstable relationship to their own reality" (Glissant 1989). Perhaps, the ancient pan-African fondness for linguistic expressiveness (the "man of words"), transplanted to the Caribbean "sea of languages" and the diversity of word sounds and signifier/signified combinations and possibilities inherent in such a creole situation explains the central significance of pun, rhyme, and wordplay in the West Indies in general, and in Trinidad in particular. As Eduoard Glissant has said, "Creole is originally a kind of conspiracy that concealed itself by its open and public expression" (1989, 124–25).

The former slaves' appropriation and re-signification of the masters' linguistic tools also paralleled the changing instrumentation and accompaniment of carnival songs. As the era of the Oratorical or *Sans Humanité* calypso began (around 1900), and the quest for finer speech and linguistic power accelerated, the tambour bamboo and traditional percussion increasingly found itself in competition with the string bands—of Venezuelan/South American extraction—as the accompaniment of the new-style kaiso. The introduction of the string bands is also a sign and symbol of the burgeoning middle-class penetration into the jamette carnival, as the string band sounds were deemed more "appropriate" than the rowdy tamboo bamboo. Another facet of the middle-class desire to restore decency to carnival and to censor and control the music is that they themselves (with their well-publicized scandals) were often targets of kaisonian scorn—and like any "respectable" class, they resented the kaisonians gossiping on "white people scandal."

The Oratorical/Sans Humanité style emerged from the convergence and creolization of the styles and modes of the male calindas, female carisos, the competing instrumentations and rhythms the traditional drum/tamboo bamboo complex and the string bands. The melodies derived from African (particularly Yoruba/Shango) religious chant, kalinda tunes, and the old practice of "lining out" hymns and psalms (in the late nineteenth century, masses were given in French Creole, not Latin)—which leaves meters open, resolves stresses in uneven lines, and promotes the practice of intoning on single lines and notes. These chants and "lining hymn" melodies were fused with the modal or minor-key calindas (usually in *Mi, Re* or *Lah* minor), indicating a "transfer of function in respect of identical melodies... the socio-historical evidence points to the coexistence of *shango, kalinda,* [shouter/baptist] and *kaiso* in the same locales and, furthermore, to the interchange of roles by the same performer—from shango habitué, to shouter soloist, to kalinda chantwell and kaiso bard" (Warner-Lewis 1991, 145). Warner-Lewis's comments point out the complex interrelationships between the sacred and the secular, a line regularly crossed in black Atlantic traditions, as well as the role of musicians and performers as the "wearers of many masks." The name of the genre, Sans Humanité, seems to be a retention from the old stick-fighting lavways, as a stock ending to the kalindas.[19]

The mode of performance of the Sans Humanité was that of a competition or duel between singers who would improvise lines of *picong*, and "give fatigue" or sing war on one another. Atilla explains: "The picong was the weapon of war or friendly rivalry in song between kaisonians. Reminiscent of the days of slavery, it perpetuated the custom of barbed wit, biting satire and ridicule directed at one another, and of self-praise on the one hand, and attacks on one's conferees on the other" (Quevedo 1983, 27). There were two basic verse forms in the kaiso, the "single tone" (four-line stanzas) and the "double tone" (eight-line stanzas). The rise of the Oratorical calypso gave prominence to the double tone kaiso, and its debate/challenge form was also influenced by the prominent rhetorical traditions of the middle class (particularly lawyers and politicians), whose increasingly vociferous agitation for political influence led them to identify with popular causes and more direct engagement with the people. The calypsonians, in their own quest for power, imitated the lofty speech of the bourgeoisie, appropriating and restructuring it to the needs and modalities of black performative and musical traditions. The kaiso expanded its topicality in response to the broader verse structure, and strove for a loftier expression and improved lyrics, moving away from the primacy of picong.

Just as the rhetorical traditions of the middle class were re-signified by the singers, the string band instrumentation, too, was coopted by the masses. The 1883 Musical Ordinance and the 1884 Peace Preservation Ordinance, passed to suppress African and African-derived instrumentations and performative elements, led to their integration and transformation in the string bands; the percussive principle was transferred to different instrumentation. However, folk forms are notoriously conservative, and the grassroots did not simply give up the old forms of percussion and accompaniment. For a period the string bands and the tamboo bamboo were in confrontation, if not opposition. This tension between the forms was class-based; the Oratorical tradition in English was in competition with the rude jamette calinda, in the same way the string bands were in competition with traditional percussion. The tension was abated by the merging of the forms: the Oratorical style was simplified and shaped (largely by Lord Executor) into a storytelling form, while the old single-tone picong (itself derived from the earlier calinda/cariso fusion) expanded its repertoire while still remaining rooted in its folk form with themes of boasting, sexual scandal, and vituperation. The changing and competing forms of the music were also a reflection of the changing social climate in Trinidad and the changing social functions of the music.

By the last decade of the nineteenth century, the reign of King Sugar in Trinidad was coming to an end. Competition from larger sugar producers like Cuba and Brazil, as well as competition from beet sugar producers in Europe and Asia, made it increasingly inefficient to produce sugar in "backwater" and technologically backward British colonies like Trinidad. Despite the sagging economy, migration (both internal and external) to urban centers continued unabated throughout the early 1900s. The large and entrenched lower-class population was augmented by rural migrants, small-islanders, and until the end of indenture in 1917, East Indians. Unemployment, underemployment, crime, lawlessness, unrest, and urban squalor exacerbated class tensions and lower-class disaffection, and culminated in the conflicts associated with carnival in the 1880s. However, migrations to urban areas and larger towns continued due to the fact that the towns offered greater opportunities (albeit limited) for employment, mobility, and social amenities unavailable in the countryside. The modern calypso emerged out of the slums, shanties, and barrack yards of Port of Spain, San Fernando, and other towns in which these social and cultural forces met.

The calypso tents evolved from pre-Lenten yard rehearsals around the turn of the century. The early tents were informal gatherings, constructed through "gayap" (often maintaining and reinforcing the old boundaries and rivalries of the stick-fighting yards). Chantwells were hired by masquerading bands to perform in a similar capacity as their previous roles in the stick-fight ritual. As the tent became an institutionalized feature of carnival, the old social unions became "syndicates," and the descendants of the stick fighters and old Patois chantwells were transformed into calypsonians. This was a gradual process that also reflected the increasing cooptation and "mainstreaming" of carnival in order to better assert control by the ruling classes. Erroll Hill elaborates: "The social unions begot the calypso tent, the most deliberate and contemplative medium for the expression of Carnival values. In this dialectic of masks, sticks, skits and songs Classic Calypso was born" (1989, 63).

The calypsonians continued the stick-fighting tradition of elaborate and evocative sobriquets; their elaborate naming practices also reflected their flamboyant use of language. The early stick fighters took names that indexed and identified their skills and the blows and parries they were known to deliver. There was Myler the Dentist, "who could extract a tooth with a single blow"; Cut-Outer, a legendary badjohn; Johnny Zee Zee, and Gumbo Lai Lai. The calypsonians continued these traditions with even more grandiose names: Lord Executor, "Chinee Patrick" (of Afro-Chinese descent, who was also known as Oliver Cromwell and Lord Protector), the Duke of Albany, Pharaoh, Ivan the Terror, the Inventor, and, later, Atilla the Hun, the Growling Tiger, the Roaring Lion, Lord Caresser, Lord Beginner, Lord Destroyer, Lord Invader, Dictator, Small Island Pride, Lord Iere, and King

Radio. Significantly, there were even several female calypsonians, such as Lady Iere, Lady Trinidad, Lady Macdonald, and Lady Baldwin.

The calypsonians, through the extended Sans Humanité/Oratorical form (sung in the favored traditional minor modes of the calinda) created a new urban music, recycling and re-fusing older mediums and practices with new ideas and instruments. Like the names they sported, their songs spoke of their supernatural powers, their invincibility, their sexual encounters, and prowess. As calypsonian Small Island Pride sang: "And I jumping up like / I alone go collapse the city / With my razor tie onto me poui / I like a badjohn in the eighteenth century." The singers made stories and fictions out of everyday life, relating current events; at the same time, their songs contained pointed social commentary and criticism about the living conditions, racism, inequality, male/female relationships, and the problems that confronted the people in their everyday lives.

Largely unemployed during the carnival off-season, calypsonians were stigmatized by the authorities as lazy rowdies and rum-drinkers, living off the wages of prostitutes and loose women. Old stereotypes of slavery days found renewed currency in the early twentieth century. In rum shops ("that great breeding ground of much of the folk-urban music of the new world diaspora"), yards, and general stores, calypsonians would ply their trade, rehearse their songs (often teaching themselves and their chorus at the same time), and practice "giving fatigue" (exchanging insults). Their marginal position within Trinidadian society at the bottom of the social ladder (although some calypsonians, including Executor, were originally from the middle class or working-class elite), gave a unique resonance and insight to their lavways, and made their music a stubborn node of resistance. Atilla explains: "The kaisonians . . . sprang from the working class and shared the workers' life and attitudes and his class viewpoint erupted in the kaiso" (Quevedo 1983, 85).[20]

In 1903 mounting tensions between the conflicting groups in Trinidadian society were to come to a head. Middle-class entry into and cooptation of carnival had resulted in an uneasy peace, a fairly well-controlled carnival that mediated between the early elite masquerade and the rowdy jamette celebration. The peace was not to last. The middle class used carnival as a means of creating a community of interests between themselves and the exploited classes, and would attempt to transfer this "identification" into the sphere of politics. The issue that lit the conflagration was water rationing. The middle class, aspiring to political power, resented the rationing practices of the state-appointed board and organized demonstrations outside the Red House (Trinidad's seat of government), where the issue was being debated. Their protest was a reflection of their growing impatience with colonial rule, and in the process of their demonstration the lower and working classes were drawn into the melee. The worst riots in Trinidad's history erupted; the Red House was burned to the ground, and police killed sixteen rioters and wounded forty-three. The Water Riots of 1903 were an explosion of the pressures seething beneath the surface of Trinidadian social life. And, as is often the case, it was the working classes that paid the price, rather than the bourgeois instigators. As Eric Williams said: "The water agitation was started by the disenfranchised middle and upper classes, though it was the ordinary citizens who got shot down on Sackville Street or in Woodford Square" (1964, 186). The unrest also demonstrated to the imperial powers-that-be that political stability on the island could only be ensured with the active participation of the middle and upper classes (white and black); some concessions toward a more representative government had to be made. The whole affair articulated many of the patterns that would repeat throughout the history of the colony, and provided further impetus for the repression and surveillance of the masses. The Water Riots were immortalized in the calinda-like chorus that became a carnival lavway in 1904: "Fire brigade, water the road / Mama, Red House burning down."

Throughout the first decades of the twentieth century, carnival—in costumes, ornamentation, and musical accompaniment—became more elaborate, as did the tents that were to become the centers of the celebration. The newly emergent syndicates solidified the connection between the "mas" (masquerade) and the tent, and spread the institution throughout the island. The tents, which charged admission, created a centralized location for economic exchange, and introduced a structured profit margin into the informal economy of the old mas. Railway "Chieftain" Douglas, chantwell for the Railroad Millionaires, was central to the establishment of the tents as cultural centers and moneymaking enterprises and at the same time central to transforming the musical form itself. Atilla recalls: "Before Chieftain Douglas, the general musical pattern in kaiso followed the minor key... Douglas initiated a new vogue not only by the fact that he embraced the major key but also by intensifying the trend toward comprehensive topicality in the kaiso. Prior to the development of this trend, the kaiso concentrated mainly on picong" (Quevedo 1983, 27).

In 1921 Douglas opened the Railroad Millionaires tent, and was the first in a long line of tent manager/calypsonians. His tent was well constructed and well-lit, he rented chairs, printed tickets, charged variable admission for seating and standing room, and his shows started promptly at 8:00 p.m. and ended at 10:00 p.m. Douglas was not really partial to the jamette aesthetic or their idea of fun. He preferred the English-language calypso, composed most tunes in major keys (rather than the favored minor, a nod to bourgeois notions of "propriety") and downplayed the old-style calinda. Douglas actively sought to attract a middle-class audience and corner the middle-class market. His tent was "high class" and the old-time picong and improvisation (in more restrained form) were reserved for the end of the show.

Despite class pretensions and commercial aspirations, however, Douglas provided an important forum for calypsonians and stimulated the further development of the tent as a vital space of cultural expression. The conversion of the informal economy of the old mas into a professional capitalist venture corresponded with the emergence of "professional" singers. Douglas's advancements paved the way for more explicitly commercial ventures and he early on recognized the potential of the tent as a base for the development of a local entertainment industry. His successes sparked the formation of other tents and competition between and within the tents. The increased professionalization and competition (between both tents and performers), combined with added monetary incentive, further accelerated the quest for "more splendid language," and an equally expressive musical accompaniment.

After World War I the sponsorship, patronage, and surveillance of the middle class became even more thoroughly entrenched. The bourgeois ideologies of respectability would continue to be imposed upon the masses and found its way into the tents. Police, selected for their fluency in patois, would patrol the tents to make sure no obscenities, politically sensitive scandals, or potentially incendiary lyrics were uttered. A Carnival Improvement Association was founded, and middle-class patrons offered prizes for the best bands, songs, and costumes. "The proud aim of all these people was to abolish the Ole Mas of the unwashed and to put in its place the pretty Mas of the respectable" (Rohlehr 1990, 97).

The calypsonians were open to the patronage, and, the surveillance of the tents and the increased competitive atmosphere led to innovations in the calypso. Whereas old kaisos tended to be recycled from previous tunes and fit with new lyrics, the new tent environment demanded more rapid innovation; new songs were composed while the musical vocabulary was expanded. The calypso was simultaneously extended outwards to embrace new ideas, idioms, and audiences, and inwards, digging deeper into older modes and folk resources for inspiration and innovation. The growing professionalization of the calypsonian as artist paralleled increasing middle-class interest in and profitability of the music; similarly, the increased use of English-language lyrics reflected both the gradual replacement of patois by English as the language of national identity and the growing mass audience of calypso. The Sans Humanité calypso was to reach its peak in the post-WWI tents.

After some seventy years of continuous operation, the Indian indenture system was brought to an end in 1917. The immediate response of the ruling class was the passage of the Habitual Idlers Ordinance (1918), a strict vagrancy law subjecting "habitual idlers" to arrest, imprisonment, and forced labor if they could not offer proof of regular employment. This period of growing labor unrest continued through the 1920s, and came to a head in the following decade. Trinidad was mixed economically and was one of the wealthiest islands in the region, boasting a substantial middle class. However, in the worsening postwar economy, rampant inflation, the agitations of organized labor, and rising racial violence (aimed particularly at returning servicemen), and increasing agitations by workers and the Labor Party all contributed to the strikes and tensions of the period.

These rumblings from below were met with forceful reassertions of power by the crown colony government, which cracked down with brute force and legislation, passing the Seditious Publications Ordinance in 1924. The bill banned a wide variety of publications and papers, targeting those with Marxist, pan-African, and especially Garveyite leanings. Black working-class consciousness was being reinforced through appeals to race consciousness and pan-African solidarity. Marcus Garvey's UNIA was having a tremendous impact on the black population of the West Indies and beyond, and in the region Trinidad was a thoroughly organized UNIA center; only Cuba had more UNIA chapters in the Caribbean.

At the same time, increasingly militant labor organizations, like the Trinidad Workingmen's Association (TWA), were posing acute ideological challenges to the status quo, in conjunction with the Garvey movement. The colonial authorities were all too aware of the links between the agitations of organized labor and the UNIA. In the 1920s the Garvey movement was having an electrifying effect on peasant and proletarian masses in the Caribbean and the United States. Garveyism, pan-Africanism, trade unionism, and nationalism all suffused the workers movements with a "new consciousness." A "new Negro" was on the scene in the West Indies. The Seditious Publications bill was a sweeping piece of legislation calling for censorship of ideas and publications, any which could be said to be advocating disloyalty to the crown or black and working-class solidarity. The *Negro World, Crusader, Messenger, Revolutionary Worker*, and the constitution of the UNIA, along with a whole host of other Marxist, Leftist and black publications were banned in the next two decades. The competition over social places and between competing ideological spaces was finding fuel in the labor movement, and the fires of discontent that flared in 1903 and 1919 would reignite in the 1930s.[21]

The general unrest that had been simmering for much of the previous decade came to a boil in the 1930s. "Class war evolved out of racial conflict and complicated the situation to a bewildering extent" (Elder 1964, 128). Depression-era Trinidad witnessed labor uprisings, strikes, massive unemployment, and a shrinking economy (the same socio-economic patterns and general unrest that occurred throughout the Caribbean in this period). An intellectual and middle-class movement (paralleling the Harlem Renaissance, Negritude, and Afro-Cubanismo movements) precipitated and fomented anticolonialist sentiments and combined with a heightened nationalism, strains of pan-Africanism, and working-class struggle (the Garveyite impulses found renewed vigor with the Italian invasion of Ethiopia; listen to Tiger's indictment in "The Gold in Africa"). A dialectic of militant working-class activity and middle-class reformist agitation had emerged. In this context the calypsonians were both chroniclers and critics, mediating and masking racial and class tensions through the kaiso. The double-voiced nature of calypso utterance, at once accessible and covert, enabled it to remain the vehicle of popular expression in an audibly entangled context of racial conflict, class struggle, and colonial rule. As Inventor sang: "Class legislation is the order of this land / We are ruled with an iron hand."

In 1937 wildcat strikes in the oil fields in the south, led by Uriah "Buzz" Butler, a charismatic and millenarian labor leader who combined radical working-class politics with Baptist ideology (he founded the Butlerite Moravian Baptist Church and used that as the center for his political activities) and enjoyed wide popular support. The oil-field strikes led to rioting and violent confrontations with the authorities, in which twelve civilians and two police were killed. Protesting reduced wages, squalid living conditions, and lack of worker representation, the demonstrators were met with massive resistance from the ruling government, despite the relative prosperity of the oil industry. The calypsonians, most of whom supported the Labor Party and the newly Butler-organized Trinidad Citizens League, vividly captured these events in their music, as they themselves were facing a similar situation of repression in the midst of prosperity. Butler escaped during the uprising and went into hiding for three months, only to emerge to testify before a colonial commission investigating the riots and promptly be arrested. The events were immortalized in calypsos by Attila like "Where Was Butler?" and "The Strike": "Fyazbad was like a battlefiel' / Police surrounded by a ring of steel / With blood an' carnage litterin' the scene / An' pandemonium reignin' supreme." In another verse of "The Strike," Attila wryly critiques the censorship of the colonial authorities. After stating that he was innocently at the scene of the riots only to get material for a calypso he goes on to say: "But I wouldn't tell you friends all that I saw / For I'm afraid of the Sedition Law."

As calypsos became more political, mirroring the growing labor unrest and the perpetual rebellion of the unemployed lumpen and jamette in Port of Spain, the government resorted to draconian measures to stop the music of the people. Atilla states: "Caught in the cross-currents of an ever-changing society, the kaiso could not be denied its social role—and although hemmed in by prejudice, it had become a rallying point for the oppress [sic], the aggrieved and the underprivileged" (Quevedo 1983, 53). Just as kaiso supported and sustained its enslaved creators, it came to the aid of their descendants to document the travails of the working poor, the colonial politics of intrigue and exploitation, and to argue against the censorship and sedition laws. King Radio, referencing the "heavy manners" of the colonial authorities as well as recent events in the oilfields, sang: "They want to licen' me mout' they no want me to talk / Ai-Ai, I ain't Butler / They want to licen' me foot they no want me to walk / Ai-Ai, I ain't Butler."

The Decca Mafia

In 1934 Attila the Hun and the Roaring Lion set sail for New York City where they recorded some thirty to forty records accompanied by Gerald Clark and his Caribbean Serenaders.[22] This trip had a massive impact both within and Trinidad and the United States; it was so successful that for the next decade calypsonians would be recorded annually in both New York and Trinidad. Aspiring calypsonians on the island glimpsed the opportunities that performing kaiso could present; entrepreneurs recognized the profits beginning to accrue in the burgeoning calypso market; and it launched the first calypso boom in the United States (popular vocalists Bing Crosby and Rudy Vallee appeared on the radio with Atilla and Lion).[23] Harlem's ascendance as the cultural capital of the African diaspora coincided with the rise of Garveyism (mass movement), West Indian emigration, and the rise of the culture industry (mass media). By 1940 West Indians made up nearly one-quarter of Harlem's black population.

Attila and Lion's trip was organized and financed by Eduardo Sa Gomes, a Portuguese businessman from Trinidad who saw the potential profits in sending calypsonians to record in the United States and making the calypsos of the carnival tent available year round. Sa Gomes reaped the principal benefits from recording the calypsos. He had a chain of stores throughout the Antilles and in South America that sold radios, musical instruments, and 78 rpm recordings, which not only disseminated Decca product throughout the region but also helped enable the stylistic cross-fertilizations of genres and styles in the new and prestigious "recording industry" and the mass-mediated opportunities afforded by recording and radio. Sa Gomes was the sole distributor for Decca, Brunswick, Continental, American, and a whole host of other labels. "The trip and the sales were such a success that SaGomes continued sending local singers to New York City annually after each Carnival season. SaGomes greatly expanded and effectively cornered the calypso market in Trinidad" (Shapiro 1979). By the late thirties the market had become so promising that Decca, Bluebird, and RCA sent mobile recording units down to Trinidad. Local consumption as well as international attention turned the kaiso into an important local commodity and export. Sa Gomes had realized the marketability of the calypso, and was to carry "Railway" Douglas's commercial vision to new heights and into new territories.

In 1935, Sa Gomes sent Atilla, Beginner, and a young calypsonian known as the Growling Tiger to record for Decca in New York. This was the (unofficial) beginning of the "Decca Mafia," a loose configuration of the top calypsonians of the day that was to reign supreme for the next ten years. They were dubbed the "Decca Mafia" because of the sheer volume and quality of their output as well as their uncontested dominance of the calypso scene in Trinidad. Between 1935 and 1940, Decca emerged as the major label with an interest in recording calypso. The company was followed by other labels like American, OKeh, and Bluebird, all of whom hoped to mine the Caribbean folk traditions and produce an international hit that would recover and recoup the (actually quite minimal) costs of the expenditure.

It is significant that the opportunities for calypsonians to record and become professional entertainers (in an international market) coincided with increased surveillance from the colonial government and deepening penetration of US capital in the Caribbean. The 1930s witnessed the growth of opportunities to record calypsos, and at the same time the intensification of calypso censorship. All calypso lyrics had to be reviewed by the Censorship Board for approval prior to recording. Any song deemed obscene, seditious, too political, or in "bad taste" was banned (as the episode at the beginning of this chapter illustrates).[24]

The growing accessibility of radios and gramophones stimulated a demand for calypso in Trinidad and elsewhere. Trinidadian folk music was recorded as early as 1914, but by the 1930s the recording of Caribbean folk songs and calypsos had created a viable market and competition between American recording labels increased.[25] The large West Indian population in the United States, especially New York City, had been growing since the first wave of migrations in 1910. This growth was further stimulated by wartime opportunities, and national radio broadcasts by calypsonians took the music to a much wider audience. Although the majority of the recordings were sold in the Caribbean and Latin America, with the beginnings of recorded calypsos in the twenties and thirties the form and function of the music became popular entertainment for a broad audience of blacks in the West Indies and Latin America, West Indians in New York, African Americans, and whites.[26] Calypso's popularity grew immensely during the 1930s, and many of the recordings have a "domesticated" and genteel quality far removed from the rowdy tents.

From the earliest moment when calypso moved from the streets to the tents, commercialization and marketing went hand in hand with musical and stylistic innovation. The increasingly cosmopolitan calypso drew upon various circum-Caribbean and pan-African musical resources. A cultural expression in continuous black Atlantic circulation, kaiso is a transcultural and "entangled" musical form par excellence. The coming of the recording industry (itself a product and vestige of the increasing Americanization of the region as the imperialism of the burgeoning entertainment industry sought not only raw materials but also new markets) affected calypso in other ways.[27] Agents for the labels actively encouraged calypsonians to recall and revamp old tunes, melodies, and folk songs, stimulating a revival of old calindas, shouter's hymns, shango chants, obeah melodies, and other folk forms and themes. Calypsonians vied with one another in recycling and remembering old tunes, which were then recorded intact, given new words, or presented in their half-remembered and fragmented states.[28] This rootwork served to further complexify the calypso as older modes were reemphasized and blended with the modern sounds of calypso instrumentation and compositional styles.

At the same time, true to the history and cosmopolitan nature of the music, the expanding external market for calypso led to the incorporation of elements from other genres. To the Afro-Latin syncopation that formed the musical/rhythmic base was added the sounds of jazz and swing, vaudeville, Tin Pan Alley, and Hollywood–style show tunes; and the folk melodies of British Guiana, Venezuela, and the nearby islands continued to inform the music. Thus, by 1934 when Atilla and Lion first went to New York to record, the music was already a rich blend of "urban sophistications and folk idioms." The innovations of the "Old Brigade," first led by Executor (who began singing in 1896) and including singers like Douglas, Black Prince, Atilla and Beginner, along with the creativity of the "new school," the younger generation of skilled singers like Lion, Tiger, Caresser, Invader, and Destroyer made the thirties a watershed, in Rohlehr's words, "where tradition confronted change and the tributaries of calypso ran off in all directions from a still discernable main stream" (1990, 126). It was truly the "golden age" of calypso.[29]

The thirties were the age of the great narrative/oratorical and Sans Humanité calypsos, and the calypsonians were busily drawing their musical inspiration from any and every aspect of Trinidadian life. Politics, contemporary events, economic conditions, cricket matches, fatal accidents, international affairs, religion, the scandals of the middle class, and, of course, gender relations, were all topical features in the storytellings of the calypsonians. "Stark social realism co-existed with fantasy, folklore and the marvelous in the calypso of the 1930s. It was an intersection of the ordinary with the extraordinary, that created the milieu of fantasy, excitement and melodrama" (Rohlehr 1990, 172). The harsh and mundane lives of the calypsonians and the jamette class they represented were in sharp contrast with the rich poetic language and "good life" ideology of the singers. The facts of their socio-economic positions and political impotence diverged from the wild fictions of natural disasters and calamities the calypsonians frequently claimed responsibility for. As the Roaring Lion sang in "War": "The earth is trembling and tumbling / and heavens are falling and all / Because the Lion is roaring."

However, the plight of the people—that "proto-proletariat at the rotting edges of the cities"—was too serious, their predicament too uncertain for these singers to indulge in pure fantasy, romanticism, or make-believe.

Certainly, wish-fulfillment, transference and magical thinking were all part of this musical milieu, but these features were absorbed, adjusted, and rearticulated to fit the psychological and cultural needs of the people and were never allowed to obscure the reality of their situation. This context of "hunger, unemployment, economic depression, worker militancy, desperation, struggle, and sheer survivalism" is the cultural environment from which the calypsos of the 1930s emerged. In 1935 Growling Tiger composed the famous calypso "Money is King," with the refrain: "If haven't money a dog is better than you." As Tiger (Neville Marcano) describes the genesis of the song: "I was looking at the economic situation. I used to see cocoa proprietors come into a shop on Fridays and Saturdays, sit on the counter, and order anything they wanted from the shelf. I said, these fellows are like kings. I saw people arrested as 'habitual beggars' while dogs could easily take up bones and bread" (Shapiro, 1979).

Tiger's song eloquently brings out the conditions and contradictions of colonial society in Trinidad. An anecdotal verse in the song captures class stratification, ethnic conflict, and economic exploitation, vividly illustrating and encapsulating a lyrical encounter between a Chinese shopkeeper and a "college man" (presumably educated for middle-class professions that were not extant or were in short supply). The college man asks for store credit toward a meal ("to trus' him acra and float"—fish and bread), and the "Chinee" man deftly denies his request (i.e. no money, no food), parrying from his uneducated class position ("you college man, me no know A-B-C"). Each stanza of the song adds new layers of complexity and analysis. He sings about "De worm in de man's belly" referencing the squalid quality of life in the barrack yards: malnutrition and the impoverished and unsanitary conditions that are the breeding ground of internal parasites. Many of the intricacies and realities of class orientation and ethnic identification among the underprivileged are elegantly captured in this calypso.

This cultural and economic context also provides the frame for the calypsonians' representations of male and female relationships. That the western bourgeois ideals of patriarchy and gender roles, the structural counterparts to the discourse of "respectability," made their way into calypso reveals the way marginalized peoples on the fringes of the economy still come to share some of the ideals of bourgeois society. The bourgeois ideal of the male as "bread-winner" and the female as "faithful domestic" was clearly incompatible with the "jamette" reality of colonial Trinidad. The stable nuclear family, indispensable for the reproduction of bourgeois values and patriarchy, had long been altered or shattered by the slave system. The staid bourgeois homestead had little resonance with the urban dwellers in barrack yards and shanties. Traditional patriarchal gender roles were inapplicable to disenfranchised women and men, whose only resource was their labor, in a period when the labor market was contracting, wages notoriously low, and unemployment and underemployment were cyclical epidemics. Tiger, discussing gender and poverty, continues: "When you try to caress her she will tell you, 'Stop' / I can't carry love in the Chinee shop."

In this context, male/female relations became a central site for the mediation of gender conflict, class tensions, and ethnic strife. The calypsonians' age-old representations of themselves as "sweet men," "dandies," and "players" was (hypocritically) juxtaposed with the abstract morality they attempted to impose on women, who were consistently represented as disloyal, gold-digging, immoral, and greedy. The sexual freedom that the singers celebrated and cherished was denied the women of the community. In a situation where male dominance, in accordance with western bourgeois ethics, was impossible, the stigmatization of the feminine and symbolic control over women's identities and behavior comes to take the place of actual power. This is evidenced in the satirical calypso dialogue between Lord Beginner's "Always Marry a Pretty Woman" and the Roaring Lion's response, "Ugly Woman." The two songs debate the virtues of marrying a pretty girl versus marrying a woman "uglier than you." In the former, the pretty woman stands for all the idealized feminine virtues and ugly women are represented as "coarse, barbarous, and rough," apt to cause a man's downfall. By contrast, in the latter it is the pretty woman who represents all the evils of femininity—scheming, demanding, fickle, faithless, etc. Although both are clearly written with humorous intent, they speak volumes about gender perceptions and relations in Trinidad in the 1930s.

Calypso lyrics are filled with tales of marital infidelity, emasculating prostitutes, dangerous women, and sexual promiscuity, as well as plenty of advice and instruction to men on how to handle these women. Male/female conflict in calypso was a logical outcome in the context of survivalism and the economic locations of the Trinidadian lower classes. Calypsos revealed the incongruity of bourgeois ideals and mores and the lived worlds of the consistently marginalized.

The history of calypso reveals the continuous dialogues, debates, conflicts, and conversations that shaped the music, as carnival became a national festival and calypso a national music. Race and class conflict, gender roles, poverty and hardship, and the joys and pains of Trinidadian life all found expression in and were mediated by the form. Kaiso epistemology played an important role in articulating both national identity and pan-Caribbean selfhood in diaspora, creating usable identities in an audible public sphere. The music's history of local, inter-island, and international exchange, interchange, and cross-fertilization, its recyclings and re-presentations open a telling window onto African and Afro-diasporic processes and practices of cultural expression and link the calypso with the wider body of black traditions of musicking and the "audible entanglements" that inhere. The complex web of alliances, allegiances, affirmations, appropriations, and identities—formed out of the necessities of survival and cultural creation in the slums and barrack yards—reveals the myriad and complex ways the musical tradition moves and gets moved, and the modes in and through which it gets constructed, reconstructed, and continuously re-created, in theory and in practice: rootwork. Kaiso was a masked utterance of the urban working classes of Trinidad, which through the dialogic strategies of "mastery of form" and the "deformation of mastery" in the early twentieth century emerged from a "folk" form to a "national" music, cosmopolitan in depth and international in acclaim. We shall encounter these dynamics and paradoxes in the chapters that follow as these "national" musics form the "dark side of empire." San Humanité.

2. "Cuba Libre"

Clave Consciousness and Montuno Aesthetics 1945–1955

In 1947, on his way to New York to explore the possibilities of treatment to restore his lost eyesight, Cuban composer and *tresero* Arsenio Rodriguez lodged temporarily in Tampa, Florida, where he experienced Jim Crow and the racial segregation of the US South firsthand. While in New York, the mass migrations of African Americans from the rural South and people of African descent from the Caribbean were expanding the cosmopolitan nature of the city and exploding the image of the US South as the "scene of the crime" compared to the opportunities in the North (there had been race "riots" in Harlem in 1935 and 1943). Upon returning to Havana in 1950, Arsenio composed the song "Aquí Como Allá" ("Same Here As It is There"): "En África y en el Brasil / igual en Cuba como en Haiti / igual al Sur que en Nueva York/ el Negro canta su dolor." The story behind the composition of the song is significant for several reasons. Arsenio was one of the most important innovators of Cuban music in the twentieth century; at the same time, he always stressed his African heritage as well as his Cuban nationalism. The song itself reveals not only a commitment to social justice, but also, by drawing direct linkages to the collective plights of people of African descent both on the continent and in the "new world," the song outlines the contours of the African diaspora, the indignities and solidarities of a shared history, the legacy of slavery, and discrimination, as well as a notion of black unity. Arsenio was sounding the entanglements of music, race, nation, and ethnic identity.

The music of Cuba has been central both to the construction of a Cuban national identity and important internationally. From the concert halls to the nightclubs and from Congo to Colombia, Cuban musics and musicians have played a vital role in the creation, dissemination, and influence of many new styles in the twentieth century through imitation, creative appropriation, indigenization, and influence. The rhythms and sonic force of the music of Cuba have had a global impact disproportionate to the size of the island (the largest in the Caribbean). The long intertwined histories and cross-fertilizations of musical styles in the Caribbean, the country's close ties with the United States, and the recording industry are certainly responsible in part for the exemplary status of Cuban music. However, it is the grooves of Cuban music and its cosmopolitanism that made it a simply irresistible force. The influences and reverberations are clearly discernible in diverse forms such as calypso, jazz, highlife, juju, and especially the Congolese "rumba." The son/rumba complex of Cuba has left decisive imprints on the "Atlantic sound."[1]

From the early recordings of the first decades of the twentieth century to the recording ban of 1961 (instituted after the Cuban Revolution), the musics of Cuba exerted tremendous influence on popular cultural styles throughout the African diaspora and beyond. By exploring the development of the music of Cuba as well as the entangled modalities of ethnicity, nationalism, and blackness, we can see not only the continuous renovation, reinvention, and rootworking of the tradition at the heart of the music, but also the deep interrelation of expressive forms, transcultural creativity, and the ways in which the iconicity of styles in Afro-diasporic culture is made manifest in their continuous transformations.

The history of Cuban music in the twentieth century invites theorizing of the polyrhythmic nature of historicity and Afro-diasporic consciousness, and the intermeshed complexities of commodification and popular culture. At the same time, the rhythms and musical forms of "Cubanidad" have always rootworked earlier rhythms and styles, linking histories with its cosmopolitan and protean style. Race, nation, history, and capital are interwoven into the son/rumba complex and clave consciousness. Locating the music within the changing contexts and shifting contours of a rapidly transforming Cuban society, we can see (as in the previous chapter) the role music plays in articulating diverse sounds and sentiments and its simultaneous oppositionality and cooptation due to the factors of its creation and dissemination. The evolution of these forms—in contexts of migration, urbanization, and political upheaval, combined with their ascendance to national symbol—inform the peculiar positionality of blackness in Cuba. As Ortiz has said, "the real history of Cuba is the history of its intermeshed transculturations" (1995, 98).

"El Cerro Tiene La Llave"

The popular music of Cuba, while African at its core, has always been a hybrid formation, the result of "intermeshed transculturations." Like Trinidadian calypso, relations of production under racialized slavery in Cuba both forced and enabled the transformation of ethnicity into race, and music played a vital role in this process. Music was a stubborn node of resistance and affirmation in the face of dehumanization and exploitation. The songs and rhythms provided a vehicle for remembering Africa and creating "living room" for the enslaved and their descendants. The essence of the music is reflected in the development of the *son/rumba complex*: not only the continuum of musical styles (rumba, son montuno, guracha, cha-cha, mambo) but also their interrelationships and increasing interpenetration in the twentieth century. The key that unites this continuum is clave, a rhythmic consciousness in which "the feeling of polyrhythm [is] submitted to the unity of tempo" (Carpentier 2001, 225).

Clave is the fundamental rhythmic organizing principle of Afro-Caribbean music in general, and the root of Afro-Cuban music in particular. Clave is the centrifugal force in Afro-Cuban music, consisting of five strokes whose drive derives from complementarity in opposition. Clave creates a rhythmic counterpoint, the central concept is that two cells that make up clave are held together in a binary structure generating "a cycle of tension-and-release": unity in difference. "Clave is a two measure pattern in which each measure is diametrically opposed. The two measures are not at odds, but rather, they are balanced opposites, like positive and negative, expansive and contractive, or the poles of a magnet. As the pattern is repeated the alteration from one polarity to the other takes place creating pulse and rhythmic drive" (Amira and Cornelius 1992, 23). The word itself means "key," "clef," or "key-stone." Clave is both the rhythmic pattern itself and the underlying principle that (in)forms all Afro-Cuban music. Clave is the foundation.[2] As musicologist Ronald Erin explains: "Afro-Cuban rhythms form the most identifiable feature of Cuban music. Though the rhythmic patterns present a unified complex, this complexity is an outgrowth and the elaboration of the primary building block of Cuban music: the unit of the clave" (1984, 4).

In Cuba, essential rhythmic elements and generative principles from sub-Saharan Africa were rearticulated, notated, and wed to European harmony. Clave unites the musics of Cuba in the son/rumba complex, the 2-3 or 3-2 rhythmic pattern that organizes the polyrhythmic texture of the music. "In a sense, the Cubans standardized their myriad rhythms, both folkloric and popular, by relating nearly all of them to the clave pattern. The veiled code of African rhythm was brought to light due to the clave's omnipresence. Consequently, the term *clave* has come to mean both the five-stroke pattern and the total matrix it exemplifies . . . the rhythmic matrix is the *clave matrix*" (Peñalosa 2009, 88). A timeline pattern that gives both direction and orientation to musicians and dancers, clave at the same time coordinates the different rhythms played by the various instruments and sung by the vocalists. The clave quite literally keeps time, marking both the what and the where of the groove in time and space. Performers and dancers must have an internal (embodied) "metronome sense" (Waterman 1952) of the clave in order to make sense out of the music. This clave consciousness is both the ontological and phenomenological root of Afro-Cuban musicking. Clave "decodes" the rhythmic structure; it is felt and understood. The actual pattern does not necessarily need to be played for music to remain "en clave." Foregrounding both the cognitive and emotive aspects of the music, clave is the key to understanding rhythm and musical memory in Cuba. The circular asymmetry of the rhythmic pattern performs an integrative function that is both musical and historical, connecting the rhythms and styles of the son/rumba complex with the pleasures and meanings made in and through the music, and articulating the historical development of Afro-Cuba.[3]

Although one of Columbus's earliest "discoveries" in the New World, the island of Cuba remained largely undeveloped until the late eighteenth century. Havana had been an important shipping port since the sixteenth century, but the backward nature of Spanish commercial enterprise coupled with royal monopoly (and the much more lucrative interests on the Spanish Main) meant that the island developed little internally. Due to the "malaise of empire" contraband trade was widespread, and not until the early seventeenth century did the population of the island begin to stabilize and reorient its economy around agriculture. The slow growth of Cuba mirrored the gradual decline of the Hapsburg Empire, and inter-imperialist rivalries only served to further undermine Spain's tenuous hold on her New World possessions. In the early eighteenth century the expansion of the tobacco market provided a modest boost to the Cuban economy (particularly through trade with France); however, unequal exchange with the metropolitan powers still kept the prosperity of the economy relatively low (Pérez 1988).

However, between the late eighteenth and early nineteenth centuries Cuba would undergo a period of profound and rapid change. The economy and society of pre-plantation era Cuba was largely devoted to the production of tobacco, cattle ranching, and small-scale sugar cultivation; and though Havana remained an important port, much of the island remained underpopulated and relatively outside the developing global market. Although the British only occupied Havana for ten months, their presence was one of several significant historical convergences that would fundamentally reshape the island. The British presence stimulated trade in goods and slaves, with some 10,000 Africans entering the island in a ten-month period between 1763–64 alone (Knight 1970, 7). At the same time, important shifts in international trade, the administrative and economic reforms of Charles III, the consolidation of most of the arable land in the hands of a few landholders, and technological and agricultural advances combined to create the conditions of possibility for the great sugar kingdom that Cuba was to become. Ned Sublette states: "In marked contrast to the other territories [of the Caribbean], whose slave importations had already peaked, between 75 and 90 percent of the slaves brought to Cuba came *after* 1790" (2004, 111).

At the time of the outbreak of the Haitian Revolution in 1791, Haiti was the world's premier sugar producer, most profitable colony, and the "jewel" of the Antilles. The mass production necessitated a mass labor force, and in 1791 there were some 450,000 slaves on the island, nearly two-thirds of whom had been born on the African continent. This was an African revolution in the Caribbean Sea, and the only truly successful slave rebellion in modern history. The formerly enslaved Africans successfully defeated the forces of the French, British, and Spanish to take control of the island. In 1804 Ayti declared its independence, becoming the second independent nation in the Western hemisphere; they were truly the "avengers of the new world" (Du Bois 1999). The loss of Haiti dealt a devastating blow to French imperial ambitions in the circum-Caribbean, and would have profound geopolitical, economic, ideological, and cultural effects that would reverberate throughout the region. The specter of Ayti loomed large in the imaginary of both the planter classes and the slaves, while the loss of the most profitable sugar colony would open up a critical economic space in the world sugar market into which Cuba would be inserted.[4]

Although slaves and sugar were introduced to Cuba in the sixteenth century, it was not until the late eighteenth and nineteenth centuries that African slaves became the sinews of Cuba's sugar empire. The ascendance of the plantation complex and the transformation from *trapiche* to *ingenio* (from small-scale operations to an industrialized mode of production) would have dramatic effects on the island. In 1790 Cuba exported 15,423 tons of sugar; by 1840 that figure increased to 161,248 (Moreno Fraginals 1978, 44). With the massive increase in sugar production came an equally massive increase in the number of slaves. In 1774 Cuba had 43,333 slaves, by 1817 there were 199,145, and by 1846 the slave population stood at 323,759 (Pérez 1988, 86).[5] The labor-intensive conditions of industrialized sugar production beginning in the early nineteenth century required large capital outlays and a large (captive) work force. The requirements of cultivation and manufacture necessitated close coordination between all aspects of the production and distribution process.

> The rapidity with which the cane must be ground after cutting and milled in an unavoidably brief space of time gave rise to the need for having on hand plenty of cheap, stable, and available labor for work that is irregular and seasonal. The intermittent concentration of cheap and abundant labor is a fundamental factor in the economy of sugar production.... This urgent agricultural-chemical nature of the sugar industry has been the fundamental factor in all the demogenic and social evolution of Cuba. It was due principally to these conditions governing the production of sugar that slave-trading and slavery endured there to such a late date. (Ortiz 1995, 33–34)

With the rise of the great *latifundias* and sugar mills, an advanced industrial sector emerged in Cuba on a semi-feudal socio-economic base. Moreno Fraginals (1978, 3 vols.) presents the most exhaustive and insightful analysis of the technical, economic, political, and social aspects of sugar production. Charting the "road to the plantation" from the early trapiches to the full-blown socio-economic sugar complex of the nineteenth century, his research further demonstrates that the development of a full-fledged factory system and the proletarianization of a semi-rural, industrial labor force occurred in the Caribbean prior to similar developments in Europe. Following Williams (1984), among others, we can say that it was the machete that made the machine. The rapid growth in sugar production owed itself to a combination of multiplier effects: the island's ecology, virgin soil, and plentiful forests, the world economy, local initiative, foreign capital penetration, and plentiful cheap labor. Machetes and machines, white sugar and black slaves, combined and uneven development in the orient and occident became structural features of the contrapuntal nature of Cuban society.

Ecology and coastal geography played a large role in determining the modes and relations of production as well as commodities produced. In the east (*Oriente*), small-scale tobacco cultivation predominated, generally the province of small, independent (largely white and mestizo) farmers (*guajiros* and *peones*). In the west, on the plains and plateaus of Havana, Matanzas, Cienfuegos, and Sancti Spíritus, large-scale sugar production and the plantation complex dominated. These different modes of production and demographic compositions led also to the development of different forms of social organization and cultural identification and aesthetic expression. In the east, a more distinctly local culture emerged due to its relative isolation. In the west the combination of sustained African importation and the cosmopolitanism of busy port cities led to continuous outside and circum-Caribbean influences in the cultural development of the region. This counterpoint between east and west, sugar and tobacco, slave and free labor, black and white, industrial and artisanal production marked the character of the island, and produced competing discourses of *Cubanidad* (which, as we will see, came to be tenuously resolved through musical developments, cultural and political nationalism, and the contradictions of capital).

Afro-Cuba

With the massive expansion of the sugar industry and the development of the "saccarochracy" (Moreno Fraginals 1976) came a massive influx of slaves. The slave trade reached its peak in the first three decades of the nineteenth century. Over the course of the Atlantic slave trade, Cuba received somewhere close to one million captives, the majority of whom came within the last thirty years of slavery, between 1835 and 1865 (it is estimated that some 400,000 slaves entered during this thirty-year span). Throughout the first half of the nineteenth century, slaves born on the African continent predominated, making up between 75 and 80 percent of all slave imports, and never less than 50 percent (Bergad 1995, 74). In 1841 African-born captives made up almost 40 percent of the island's entire population. As a result most members of the Afro-Cuban population were direct descendants of the *bozales* (literally "muzzled ones"), as African-born slaves were called. The brutality of the slave regime and the inhuman conditions of labor particularly on the large sugar plantations necessitated that between 10 to 12 percent of the population had to be "replenished" annually. "Fresh" Africans were continually introduced to the rhythms of the plantation complex, bringing with them their memories, cultures, and ethnic paradigms.

Africans enslaved in Cuba came from a wide area of catchment; over the duration of the Cuban slave trade, a number of different ethnic groups arrived on the island, depending upon availability, planter preference, and the internal dynamics of African continent. Even prior to the slave trade, the people of West and West Central Africa had complex but stable group identifications. "While African ethnicities were never isolated or rigid constructs, neither was the complex of traits that constituted a group typically located in the context of a binary opposition with a singular Other. Rather it was a multiply-defined, shifting framework which people expressed through cultural practices and in dynamic relationships with those they considered like themselves, or Same, or a shifting Other" (Van Norman 2005, 180).

The social dis-integration and disruption that resulted from the ravages of the slave trade and European colonialism further complicated African "ethnic" identities. Many slaves were identified "ethnically" by their ports of embarkation rather than the point of capture; other nomenclature covered geographic areas that contained a wide variety of groups, and many of the recognized "ethnic" designations (both on the continent and in the New World) were of relatively recent provenance as a result of social dislocation and cultural reorganization stemming from the slave trade.

At the same time, in the context of racialized slavery, ethnic identifications took on a certain fluidity that served to reinforce social formations according to "traditional" African arrangements. Determining ethnicity becomes more intricate under the conditions in the New World, as any number of factors may intervene: extended families, fictive kinship, elective affinities, numbers, pragmatism, prestige, social mobility, survival, sustenance—all could play different roles in ethnic identification. However, in Cuba, due to the late flourishing of the plantation complex, the sheer numbers of enslaved Africans entering in a relatively short period of time, the long duration of slave trade (into the 1860s), and the dense concentrations of various cultural groups in *centrales* and in the urban areas, core cultural codes were maintained and re-created, and ethnicity was gradually transformed into "race." The areas around the sugar mills (centrales or ingenios) were more like industrial towns than simple plantations, and Cuba had a large urban enslaved population. Both circumstances facilitated cross-cultural mixing and ethnic retention. The enslaved and their descendants were still able to preserve a deep, underlying Africanity. Ortiz (1975) lists over one hundred distinct African "ethnic" groups existing in Cuba in the nineteenth century, and at the turn of the twentieth century at least fourteen distinct "nations" could be identified.

Hundreds of thousands of *bozales* entered the plantation complex quite literally watering the cane fields with their sweat and blood. Some 80 percent percent of Africans arriving in Cuba in the nineteenth century were destined for the *centrales*. Religion, music, dance, language, and other cultural practices served important integrative functions in the making of the slave community, reinforced by spatial proximity and material conditions. The constant arrival of new "country" men and women reinforced and reinvigorated traditions, while adapting them to the changed circumstances of New World slavery.

> The commonality of ancient language base and woodland tradition promoted the movement and exchange of people, goods, and ideas and aided in the formation of fundamentally similar concepts about God ... and the universe.... This centuries old familiarity was to play an important role in easing the pains caused by the forced proximity to slavery and the resulting fusions so necessary for survival. This fusion was made less painful because musically a large part of West Africa forms an indivisible whole with Bantu Africa. The Music of all these peoples is essentially one and the same. Both language and music are expressions made in the same medium—sound.... In the Americas, African music has proven to be far more permanent than African language and has even helped to preserve language. (Mason 1992, 2)

As various African ethnic groups became "black" slaves, sharing underlying cultural traits and African antecedents facilitated the creation of a distinctly Afro-Cuban culture. African slaves in Cuba organized themselves in *cabildos*, according to *nación*, as a means of both group survival and cultural preservation. The cabildos were simultaneously religious fraternities and mutual aid and self-help societies that facilitated the retention of important cultural traditions and languages, organized religious observances, and social events. As African languages were fading from everyday conversation, in the cabildos music, dance, and religious ritual conserved vital aspects of African cultural heritages and memories. While the cabildos were mainly an urban phenomenon, similar processes of cultural conservation and condensation were at work in the centrales, where the clustering of ethnic groups occupationally and spatially in the sugar mills and the *barracónes* provided enslaved Africans with opportunities for cultural reinterpretation and retention. Of the many ethnic and linguistic groups brought to the island over the course of the slave trade, four groups stand out for their identifiable and lasting contributions to Afro-Cuban music and black culture in Cuba: Carabalí, Arará, Kongo, and Lukumí.

The ethnic designation *Carabalí* referred to a number of distinct ethnic groups—Ejagham, Efut, and Efik peoples—inhabiting the Cross River delta (Old Calabar) in Southeastern Nigeria and Cameroon. In Cuba (in an interesting "calibanization") the *r* and the *l* of Calabar were reversed, to coin the generic grouping Carabalí (also known as Brίkamo). In the port districts of Havana and Matanzas—and, significantly, nowhere else in the African diaspora—the Carabalí recreated their "leopard" societies (*Ngbè* and *Èkpè*), called *Abakuá*.⁶ The society was only for men, also referred to somewhat disparagingly as ñáñigos, and although hermetic, they exercised an important role in Afro-Cuban music and Cuban popular culture through folklore, songs, dress, and music. With the emergence of the *AfroCubanismo* movement in the 1920s and 1930s, Abakuá became a national symbol. Many important musicians were initiates, and many who were not made reference to the societies through the use of Abakuá rhythms and in lyrics.⁷

The Arará were Fon-Ewe speakers from the kingdom of Dahomey in modern Benin. The name itself is a linguistic corruption of Allada, the ancient capital of Dahomey. Large numbers Arará entered the slave trade in the eighteenth century as the western Yoruba speakers consolidated their power in the region. Large numbers of these people ended up in Haiti when the sugar colony was at its peak, just prior to the revolution. There they brought their religious practices and belief systems and had substantial impact on Haitian *vodun*. Many also ended up in Cuba, and the earliest Arará cabildos date back to the seventeenth century. Arará continued to arrive throughout the duration of the slave trade, however in smaller numbers than other ethnic groups. Close cultural contact with Yoruba speakers on the continent and in Cuba enabled them to preserve distinctive religious and ritual practices (although many of these were adopted and/or enfolded into Lukumí liturgy: the Yoruba-Dahomey complex).⁸

The Lukumí are one of the most important African ethnic groups in Cuba. Originally there was no inclusive reference for all the heterogeneous ethnic subgroups of the kingdom of Oyó, in what is now Nigeria. The term "Yoruba" dates to mid-nineteenth century colonialism as a common designation for people of the kingdom (Egba, Ijebu, Ekiti, Iyesa, Anago, etc.)

who, while sharing a common religious beliefs and a mutually intelligible language, did not see themselves as a single ethnic group. In Cuba these Yoruba-speaking peoples were known as Lukumí (Lucumí) from the Yoruba "Oluku mi," meaning "my friend." With the fall of the powerful kingdom of Oyó to the Hausa from the north, in the early nineteenth century the Lukumí began entering the slave trade in massive numbers—just as Cuba's sugar complex was peaking (Law 1977). After 1830 the Lukumí became the dominant ethnic group in Cuba, as whole sections of their society were uprooted and enslaved, leaving a lasting imprint on Afro-Cuban culture. The religion, songs, and liturgy of Santeria and the rhythms of the sacred bata drums would be incorporated into popular music and culture over the course of the nineteenth and twentieth centuries.[9]

All of the captives who came to Cuba from West Central Africa, what is now the region around Congo and Angola, were referred to as "Congo."[10] The Kingdom of Kongo was involved in the slave trade from its very beginnings to the very end; as a result Kongo supplied more slaves to every part of the New World than any other region. From 1519 to 1867, West Central Africa contributed some 44.2 percent of all enslaved Africans making the middle passage (Warner-Lewis 2003, 10). Throughout the New World the imprint of Kongo culture is strikingly visible. As the first and last victims of the slave trade, Kongo culture played a vital role in the transculturations that created Afro-Cuban culture, affecting language, music, dance, and religion in profound ways.[11]

Linguistically, Congo syntactic features are intercalated in Afro-Cuban Creole Spanish, and Congo has contributed the greatest number of words to the Afro-Cuban vocabulary. Similarly, the names of the drums most associated with Afro-Cuban music, the conga and the bongo, as well as the musical style rumba are clearly of West Central African derivation. The religion of *Palo Mayombe* (also referred to as Palo Monte) is of Congolese origin. Lastly, the two most important Afro-Cuban musicians of the twentieth century, Beny Moré and Arsenio Rodriguez, were of Congolese descent and spoke of it often in their songs.

The slave trade to Cuba ended in the 1860s, and slavery was finally abolished in 1886. Over the course of the slave trade, many ethnic groups came to Cuba; however, by the end of the nineteenth century the vast majority of Afro-Cubans identified themselves as Arará, Carabalí, Congo, or Lukumí. The waves of succession, times and points of entry, age and gender ratios, demographics, mortality, and occupation all affected the "intermeshed transculturations" and audible entanglements that formed Afro-Cuban slave culture and music. The predominant cultural template in Afro-Cuba was laid down by the Kongo and the Lukumí. The Bantu speakers of West Central Africa came continuously throughout the duration of the institution, thus establishing and reinforcing the Kongo "cultural template" of Afro-Cubana (as amply demonstrated by the linguistic evidence). The Lukumí arrived from the height of the plantation complex till the end of slavery, in such numbers as to seemingly overshadow the other ethnic groups on the island. In many ways, Afro-Cuban culture is a contrapuntal relation between the Congo and the Lukumí, a dialogical interaction between a Yoruba superstructure and a Congo base.

Nationalizing Blackness

After having defeated Spain in 1898, Cuba found itself under the heel of what Jose Martí famously referred to as the "giant with the seven-league" boots. With the introduction of the Platt Amendment in 1901, which ceded the right to the United States to intervene in Cuban affairs as they saw fit, Cuba was granted "independence," and the fate of the island became inextricably tied to US capital interests. During the war, black Cubans served as generals (Maceo, Gomez, Banderas, etc.) and soldiers (often referred to as *Mambises*), who were overrepresented in the ranks of the liberation fighters (some estimates put their numbers as high as 80 percent of the total fighting force after 1895). Despite, the sacrifices made on behalf of the new republic, Afro-Cubans found themselves still disenfranchised and unrecognized for their efforts in the battle to win both their freedom and the liberation of the island. With the "Americans" came Jim Crow, and North American racism was grafted onto the discrimination the formerly enslaved and freed people of color had experienced at the hands of the Spanish and the Criollo elite. Economic advancement and social mobility were severely circumscribed under the new order, and increasing "white" immigration from Spain (subsidized by the new government) made the precarious situation of Afro-Cubans all the more acute.[12]

Afro-Cubans, chafing beneath the racism and exclusion, began to organize independently and agitate for more representation in the government and participation in the country they had helped to liberate. In 1907 black Cubans formed their own party (made up largely of former officers of the revolutionary army and the black petty bourgeoisie), which became the Partido Independiente de Color the following year. After an unsuccessful bid at electoral politics (then-president José Miguel Gómez outlawed the formation of political parties along racial lines), in 1912 the Independientes organized an armed uprising in Oriente. After briefly taking the small town of La Maya in the province Alto Songo, the government and the white Cuban citizens responded ferociously. An all out "race war" (*la guerra de razas*)[13] erupted and hundreds of Afro-Cubans were slaughtered indiscriminately (with the tacit approval of the US government, which had stationed battleships in the harbor to "protect US interests"). The history was chronicled in the music and the events were memorialized in the song "Alto Songo" (made famous in the 1950s by the Afro-Cuban trumpeter/bandleader Félix Chappotín): "Alto Songo, se quema La Maya / Alto Songo, que venga la bomba."

In the wake of the race war in Oriente, Afro-Cuban religions and cultural expressions came under increasing scrutiny and repression. As we have seen with virtually all Afro-diasporic forms, the culture of the black enslaved and their descendants in Cuba was alternately tolerated and outlawed from the beginnings of the slave trade through the early twentieth century. In the mid-nineteenth century most of the repressive focus was on religious rituals (Santeria and Palo) and the secretive ñáñigo societies. After the "War of 1912" the government began to crack down on both secular and religious expression (a line always "worried" by African and Afro-diasporic practices). Cabildos were raided, drums were confiscated and/or destroyed, *comparsas* (carnival street music, much like contemporaneous events in Trinidad) were prohibited, and a number of lurid stories began to appear in the popular press regarding atavistic "dark rites," "human sacrifice," and other barbarities attributed to the inherently savage nature of the formerly enslaved and their descendants.[14] At the same time, since the colonial era, the majority of the musical performers on the island had been Afro-Cubans, and African-derived elements had been incorporated into "white" Cuban music since at least the early nineteenth century, while Afro-Cubans (free and enslaved) had become fluent in European-styled musics. As a result, the music of Cuba, from the stage to the concert hall to the street rumba, had a marked Afro-diasporic and cosmopolitan accent. While Afro-Cubans themselves faced hostility and discrimination, Afro-Cuban music and culture became an inseparable aspect of the national culture. Artists and intellectuals began "using music and other forms of artistic expression (dance, plastic arts and writing) to experiment with new types of urban and national identities" (B. White 2002, 675).

In the early twentieth century, US capital began deepening its investments in Cuba. In the late 1920s North American mills were manufacturing more than 80 percent of all the sugar produced in Cuba and by the 1930s the United States had invested more in Cuba than any other foreign territory (Benjamin 1977, 19–20). Despite its nominal independence, Cuba had become a satellite of the United States. However, beginning in the 1920s, cracks began to show in the façade as sugar prices fell and economic hardship began to grip the island. This was also a period of a dramatic upsurge in nationalist and anticolonial sentiment throughout the Caribbean. Mass movements, mass migration, mass media and communications, and mass culture all stimulated and transmitted a "nationalist" awareness during the inter-war period.

Labor agitation and strikes erupted throughout the region following closely on the heels of the radical revolutionary uprisings that had begun in Mexico (1910), Russia (1917), and Nicaragua (1927), and the class struggle took on distinctly nationalist overtones. At the same time, Marcus Garvey's UNIA movement was growing, responding to the plight of blacks throughout the diaspora. Tony Martin states that "Cuba had more branches (52) than any other territory in the West Indies, and indeed any country other than the United States" (Martin 1983, 59). In addition, there were mass migrations of workers throughout the Caribbean in search of work opportunities. In Cuba, railroad and highway construction both provided work opportunities and enabled the movement of workers, helping integrate regional cultures across the island. Within these movements developing in the 1920s we see the regional unification taking place in the music, the "rumba-ization" of the son and the "son-ification" of the rumba as differing regional sounds and rhythms were brought together and transformed into "national" musics. "Though the son emerged about the same time as the guaguancó, it emerged on the opposite end of the island, so the latter was more rawly African and the former more creolized" (Sublette 2004, 334). The music of Afro-Cuba was at once a marker of authenticity (the *roots* and resilience of Afro-diasporic culture) and cosmopolitan modernity (the flows and *routes* of musical production in the circum-Caribbean).

In Cuba as people, musics, movements, and ideas began to move intra- and internationally on a large scale, culture became the terrain of nationalist political struggle. "Jazz, blues, samba, tango, son: a hemispheric musical revolution was in progress spurred by new media [recording and radio]. . . . The music of the underclasses was for the first time directly available to vast numbers of potential consumers. This had a profound effect on every country and ultimately would constitute a major means of empowerment for black people" (Sublette 2004, 369). The intellectual classes on the island,—responding to the post–World War I currents sweeping through the region, inspired in part by the Harlem Renaissance and the emerging Negritude movement in the Francophone Caribbean—began looking inward to their own society to create an "authentic" version of "Cubanidad" to contest both North American imperialism and Spanish cultural hegemony. Scholars, artists, and writers like Fernando Ortiz, Lydia Cabrera, Alejo Carpentier, Nicolas Guillén, and Wilfredo Lam, among others, began researching Afro-Cuban culture and creating works based upon or derived from Afro-Cuban themes, refashioning culture in the service of nationalist expression under US domination and in the context of world depression.

Afro-Cuba was in vogue from the minstrel stage to the conservatory. To qoute Robin Moore: "In this way, musics such as rumba and *toques de santo*, which even ten years earlier had been prohibited by presidential decree, gradually attained tentative acceptance in the public sphere" (Moore 1995, 133). Despite the gradually expanding appreciation among intellectuals and growing sectors of the general public for the arts and culture of Afro-Cubana, Afro-Cubans themselves still faced rampant discrimination, segregation, and unequal opportunities. As Alejandro de la Fuente has said: "Afro-Cubanismo and the ideology of *mestizaje* were thus open—like Martí's ideal republic with and for all—to disparate interpretations. The invention of a 'Cuban race' and the representation of the country as a mestizo land in which everyone had some African ancestry worked in contradictory and not always predictable ways" (de la Fuente 2001, 187). Nonetheless, the music of the black working classes of the urban slums and towns continued to innovate and revitalize itself to respond to the changing needs and circumstances of the people who created it.

The groove of the music of Cuba was born of the transculturative interaction of diverse African traditions and Iberian influences, expressing what Bob White (2002) calls a "rooted cosmopolitanism," expressly African yet at the same time partaking of a variety of cultural influences and responding—simultaneously—to the changing contexts of urbanization, nationalism, colonialism, and coloniality. "Afro-Cuban music is particularly revealing because it represents a form of cultural practice that is expressly African yet profoundly cosmopolitan" (678).

"La rumba"[15] combined percussion, dance, and poetry in a highly stylized yet spontaneous musical/dance form. As the various ethnic groups became "black," the rumba—born initially in the barracón where slaves of various *naciones* held their Saturday or Sunday dances (and closely related the *yuka* and *makuta* dances of West Central Africa)—became the dance of the Afro-Cuban workers, synthesizing the aesthetic contributions of the various African groups. In the rumba, rhythms of Africa were syncopated with those of the *zafra* and the sugar mill, the loading and unloading of trade ships, and the practice of everyday life. As the music of the black proletariat, rumba was one of the first industrial art forms, a work of art in the age of industrial/agricultural production. Time, labor and work discipline inflected the rhythms and stylizations of the rumba. The form has always been closely associated with manual labor and the black underclass. The port cities and towns were vital in the creation and spread of the rumba, and the Abakuá were instrumental in its development, as the societies controlled the distribution of work on the docks. Also, many of the primary instruments used in the creation of the rumba were re-appropriations of the tools of labor and means of production, "techno-interventions" (or "readymades") by the black proletariat, converting packing crates into percussive instruments (*cajones*) when African percussion instruments were outlawed, and barrels into drums, and creating claves (the paired sticks used to keep the rhythm) from the hardwoods used in shipyard construction.

The modern forms of rumba originated in the mid-nineteenth century, but were fully developed in the first quarter of the twentieth century. Robin Moore explains: "'Rumba' as a complex linguistic sign is perhaps best understood as comprised of both specific associations with music and dance styles and broad, historically derived associations with Cuba's black underclasses, their attitudes, lifestyles and culture" (Moore 1995, 170). Rumba refers to the style, rhythms, and context of performance.[16] There are three dominant types of rumba: *columbia, yambú,* and *guaguancó*. The guaguancó is a couples dance, the climactic center of which is the *vacunao*, a symbolic game of sexual pursuit between male and female dancers. The yambú, from which the guaguancó was derived, is a slower-tempo couples dance more stately, reserved, and sensual than the guaguancó. The columbia is the fastest and most aggressive rumba style danced competitively by men. Columbia has a wide vocabulary of kinesthetic movements blended from the diversity of the ethnic groups of the enslaved. The dance itself was derived from the Congo pugilistic tradition of *mani*, a fighting dance/game related to other Afro-Caribbean arts like Brazilian capoeira and "knocking-and-kicking" in the Anglophone Caribbean. Although the dance is traditionally the province of males, Cabrera (1954) cites several accomplished female *columbianas*. These three genres of rumba were the predominant styles in the twentieth century. As former slaves moved off the plantations after emancipation and into the cities, the rumba took on a decidedly urban feel, a quickened pace, and heightened rhythmic tension: "the music changed because the musicians changed" (Baraka 1963). In sound, song, and dance, la rumba poeticized, historicized, and mobilized tradition.

Musically, rumba is typically played on three drums: the *tumbadora* (the lowest-pitched drum), the *salidor* (middle-pitched), and the *quinto* (the highest-pitched), which does the "talking" in the rumba ensemble.[17] The two lower-pitched drums share the *tumbao* (or primary groove), while the quinto improvises in response to the dancers and singers. The rumba is a dialogic enactment of structure and freedom (Crook 1982); the form and nature of the tradition invite participation as modalities of socialization and resistance, at once spontaneous and cooperative, lyrically drawing elements from daily life, popular history, folklore, and current events, and musically combining the rhythms of Africa and the Americas in the service of the groove. "Clave consciousness" came about in and through multi-mediated streams of creativity and imagination expressed in the musical and choreographic iconicity of style in Afro-Cuban musicking. Clave here is both metric and metaphorical; the 3/2-2/3 structure vacillates backward and forward through space and time—history made meaningful and feelingful through the groove. Rumba is above all party music.[18]

If the rumba was the first industrial art form of Afro-Cuba, the son was Cuban blues, the musical and geographic Cuban counterpoint and counterpart to the rumba of Matanzas and Havana. Born in the countryside of Oriente, son moved west into the cities around the turn of the twentieth century with the soldiers of the Permanent Army (Urfé 1981). *Son* was a complex of musical and aesthetic elements and genres, composed of African and European influences, played and innovated by and for Afro-Cubans, and went on to become the quintessential *Cuban* national musical form, the acknowledged sound of Cubanidad: "Eso es mi son cubano cubano." The son combined African rhythms, percussion, and antiphonal singing with Spanish guitar and language, and was deeply influenced by the Afro-French culture of the eastern side of the island.

Oriente did not witness the proliferation of the *ingenios* and *centrales* and the tremendous expansion of the sugar industry as did the western side of the island, and thus did not have a massive influx of Africans in the nineteenth century. However, there had been Africans in the region since the sixteenth century, and the black population was augmented and further hybridized by the Haitian refugees. As such the culture of Oriente by the late nineteenth century was thoroughly creole. The *son oriental* was country music, rustic and simple, requiring few musicians and instruments. Its portability facilitated its spread from the *monte adentro* to towns and cities throughout the island. A transculturative form par excellence, son combined African and European elements in flexible and novel ways that gave it a distinctly Cuban character as well as an adaptability that enabled the form to incorporate and amalgamate a variety of older and contemporary styles, all unified by the clave. In the course of the development of the son/rumba complex, Stephan Palmié elaborates: "the two traditions, not only merged into a larger complex of partly overlapping conceptions and practices, but came to offer functionally different forms of historical experience and contemporary sociality" (2002, 27).

The liberation of the drum and the ascendance of the son/rumba complex to a national art form began under the reign of Gerardo Machado, the president of Cuba from 1925 to 1933. Machado (to an extent) promoted son, a political appropriation of the music of the working classes, while at the same time he continued the persecution of African peoples and culture on the island. As son spread, it was interpenetrated with other styles and genres; uniting Oriente and Occidente, the musical form became emblematic of Cuban-ness. The innovations of son were contemporaneous with the development of rumba, and as Ned Sublette explains: "when the son arrived in Havana, it took root in the same *ciudadelas* and *solares* where the rumba was already firmly entrenched" (2004, 335). In the barrios of Havana, son (like rumba) was associated with the urban, black underclass and accordingly stigmatized. But son in Havana was transformed from its rural incarnation and took on an urban sophistication and an added rhythmic complexity, which distinguished it from its rustic origins in Oriente. Blended with the rhythms of the rumba, son achieved a stylistic diversity and cosmopolitanism—a unique sound that registered both rooted authenticity and modernity. In this sense, Afro-Cuban musicking was a sister to the jazz that was developing contemporaneously in the United States.

With the rise of the recording industry, radio, and the spread of music publishing, the popularity of son increased exponentially throughout the island and beyond. Radio in particular became crucial to the commercial viability of local orchestras. In the 1920s son was increasingly embraced as *the* music of Cuba. US recording companies—Brunswick, Victor, Decca, and Columbia (unsurprisingly, the same record companies actively recording Trinidadian calypso)—were vying for access to the "exotic" sounds of Cuba. At the same time, Afro-Cuban musicians and dancers were absorbing the sounds of the diaspora while dealing with conditions of colonialism and coloniality. Competition between record companies actually fostered aesthetic developments. The emergence of the storied sextetos of the 1920s was directly tied to the recording industry. Sexteto Habanero and Sexteto Nacional, recording for Victor and Columbia respectively, became the most important bands of the era (Blanco, 38). The popularity of son was also due to the aforementioned Cuban intelligentsia's growing interest in Afro-Cubanismo. "In the 1920s son caught on and everyone wanted to dance son. The old people still danced the danzón, but many of the old forms—guajira, guaracha, criolla, changüí, sucu-sucu—first they became guajira-son, changüí-son, and then pretty soon everything was just son" (Linares, qtd. in Sanda Figueredo 2001). Son was to become an approach to playing, a feeling and space of improvisation, expressible with and through other genres and styles, a dimension and extension of the clave consciousness and montuno aesthetics[19] at the heart of the music of the circum-Caribbean.

The 1920s witnessed several crucial developments in the creation of the modern son. The son began with rudimentary instrumentation distinguished by the tres, a small six-string guitar with the middle pair of strings tuned in unison and the outer pairs of strings tuned in octaves, and the bongo, the double-headed drum that with the claves (sticks) guides the son ensemble (bongo is the rhythmic core of son in the same way the tumbadoras are the soul of rumba). The tres and bongo were typically accompanied by voices, guitar, maracas, and a bass instrument, in early ensembles either a *botija* or *marímbula*, and in later ensembles the string bass. The tres plays repeating figures called *guajeos*—"endlessly repeating figures" (several scholars have pointed to the similar sonic role of mbira and sanza in West African traditions)—while the bongo kept the steady rhythm known as the *martillo* orienting the ensemble with the guided precision of the clave. Most of the early son groups were trios or quartets, but in the 1920s these groups were reformed as sextetos, and later septetos with the addition of trumpet sometime in the mid-twenties. The incorporation of the trumpet into the son ensemble was a reflection of both the close cultural and geographic proximity to New Orleans and circum-Caribbean musical developments that were occurring simultaneously. The use of trumpet in the ensembles was also an indication of the powerful role of the growing entertainment industry of the United States. The "golden age" of the son coincided with the reign of Machado, the rise of electronic recording, the exceptional expansion of radio—by 1923 there were thirty-four stations regularly broadcasting in Cuba (Mota in Robbins 1990), and the growth and development of US recording companies. Parallel with the rise of "race records" and the beginnings of recorded calypso, soneros would travel to New York to record, and record companies began traveling to Cuba to record *in situ*. With the deepening penetration of US capital and the beginning of Prohibition in the United States, Cuba became a popular destination for tourism, and a hub of gambling, prostitution, and organized crime. "In about thirty years, son had gone from an obscure regional performance genre to something that could be played by any number of ensemble types, in any number of settings; it had been used as the 'root' in the cause of cultural nationalism;[20] and it had become an international pop music phenomenon, occasionally under its own name, but more often as rumba" (Robbins 1990, 187).

In many ways it was Septeto Nacional, led by the bassist, vocalist, and composer Ignacio Piñero, that led the musical revolution in Cuban popular music.[21] Formed in 1927, the band was named for the fact that it contained musicians from all over the island. The choice of name was an expression of a developing sense of national identity, cosmopolitan modernity, and black pride. A tradesman from the barrio of Jesús María in Havana (a cauldron of Afro-Cuban creativity), Piñero was intimately familiar with the vast repertoire of Afro-Cuban music. He was Abakuá and infused his son compositions with the rhythms of rumba, as well as blending son with older genres like guajira, bolero, changuí, and guraracha. The tempos were faster, refracting everyday life and urban sensibilities through cosmopolitan swing and danceable jams. His arrangements were musically complex and sophisticated, while rooted solidly in the groove; his lyrics were pointed and topical; and the whole sound was linked together by the insistent rhythm of the clave. His compositions explored the range of the son/rumba complex; songs like "Echale Salsita,"[22] "Suavecito," and "Sóngoro Consongo" influenced the development of Afro-Cuban and Cuban-derived musics throughout the twentieth century. With the development of son and the spread of its popularity, the music of the black working classes became a symbol of Cubanidad and an international phenomenon, embodying the transcultural nature of Cuban national popular culture, and its polyrhythmic interrelation with the musical spectrum of the circum-Caribbean.

While the commercial popularization and national appropriation of son began under Machado, it coalesced in the 1930s and 1940s under the Batista regime. One of the most important innovators of Afro-Cuban music from this period was the blind tresero and multi-instrumentalist Arsenio Rodriguez ("El Ciego Maravilloso"). Born in the province of Matanzas in 1913, his family moved to Güines, a sugar and agricultural municipality outside of Havana, and he lost his eyesight as a child soon after. Arsenio was born and raised during the height of the government repression of Afro-Cuban traditional practices and the crystallization of modern son. His grandfather was from West Central Africa, and from an early age he was immersed in many of the sacred and secular traditions of Afro-Cuba. The son montuno and musical approach he developed was built upon the foundation of his African cultural heritage; many of his lyrics expressed deep racial pride and his knowledge of the languages and traditions of the enslaved Africans brought to the island; they also *re-sounded* a transnational, Afro-diasporic collective identity while highlighting the contradiction between legal "freedom" and equality and the persistence of racism. Arsenio rootworked[23] the Afro-Cuban musical continuum: pulling on multiple strands of the son/rumba complex while remaining firmly grounded in the African antecedent, he spoke to and of the black people of the barrios, their history and present, their aspirations and experiences. Arsenio's music lyrically and stylistically went far beyond the vogue of Afro-Cubanismo, by repositioning blackness on its own terms and forcefully asserting black pride in the context of deepening racism and disenfranchisement. The musical innovations of Arsenio and his *conjuntos* were adapted by big-band leaders in the forties and fifties and achieved international fame as "mambo."[24] His style and compositions were crucial to the development of salsa in the sixties and seventies.[25]

Arsenio gave the music a "blacker" sound that remembered Africa and the diaspora and revolutionized clave consciousness in three important ways: through his instrumentation, his aesthetic vision and style, and his lyrics. Instrumentally, he developed the conjunto format, expanding the septeto with the addition of tumbadora, piano, campana (cowbell), and a second trumpet. The addition of the second trumpet brought a raucous density to the ensemble; the inclusion of tumbadora contributed to the further "rumbanization" of son and expanded the rhythmic possibilities; in the montuno sections, the bongo player would put down the drums and hammer out the "one" on campana, adding to the rhythmic drive; and the interlocking *guajeos* of the piano and the tres made the music both tighter and more dynamic melodically. Arsenio's band embodied the "heterogeneous sound ideal" (Wilson 1973) so characteristic of the musics of Africa and the diaspora: musically full and richly textured, and insistently locked in clave. Arsenio's music crystallized the clave consciousness and montuno aesthetics that lay at the heart of Afro-Cuban musicking and cultural sensibilities.

Aesthetically, Arsenio's compositional style and his conjuntos' performative approach were rooted in the traditional rural Afro-Cuban idioms and practices he had learned as a youth in Matanzas and Güines, but versioned to capture the modern complexity of urban Havana. His style forcefully re-centered the tumbao (the ostinato pattern resulting from the interlocking rhythms played by the rhythm section), making it heavier and deeper, through the interweaving parts of the ensemble and by consistently emphasizing and accenting the off beats, which corresponded with the movements of the dancers. The tumbadora augmented the rhythmic texture of the music, and the anticipated bass patterns moved between rhythmic and melodic roles, reinforcing the groove. Arsenio's technical virtuosity expanded the harmonic and melodic role of the tres in the music, and he structured the horn arrangements in tight integrated segments. Finally, he put a more pronounced emphasis on the montuno sections, with the campana steadily building the tension/release and aural climax, foregrounding antiphony and highly syncopated breaks, creating an agonizing swing while also providing room for instrumentalists to solo. Arsenio's style was the epitome of montuno aesthetics—the groove was literally relentless. And the whole conjunto moved, they created an infectiously danceable sound that brought clave consciousness to new dimensions. The new musical consciousness resonated with new cultural and political consciousness as Afro-Cubans began to recognize and represent their unique place within the social fabric of Cuban society (recall, Garvey's UNIA had a tremendous following on the island).

Lyrically, while writing about the usual romantic themes of love and country, Arsenio wrote tunes about racial pride and the specific concerns and everyday lives of Afro-Cubans. He wrote and performed a number of guaguancós dedicated to the youth and soul of the barrios ("Juvenad Amaliana," "A Belen Le Toca Ahora," "Los Sitios Aceré," "Juventud de Cayo Hueso," "La Gente del Bronx"), expressing the marginalization and segregation of the black working classes and instilling a pride of place and history by "representing" neighborhoods and communities of the disenfranchised. Songs like "Aquí Como Allá" and "Vaya P'al Monte" demonstrated his commitment to black struggle and his Afro-diasporic consciousness. Others, like "Sandunguera," "El Palo Tiene Curujey," "Dundunbanza," and "Chango Pachanga," alluded to African heritage and Afro-Cuban sacred traditions and folkways, and articulated some of his cultural frames of reference. Arsenio wrote many songs in *bozal* speech, invoking the history and legacy of slavery through the use of *lengua* and "pidgin" Spanish. At the same time, he was reclaiming and resignifying the linguistic traditions of his ancestors that had long been parodied in the *teatros bufos* (the Cuban equivalent of the minstrel show). The song "Bruca Maniguá" (an "afro-son") was the first of Arsenio's songs to be recorded, ironically by a white Cuban band, Casino de la Playa, in 1937. The lyrics are indicative of Arsenio's linguistic resignifications, historicism, poignant critiques, and racial pride: "Yo soy Carabalí / Negro de nación / Sin libertá / No puedo vivir."[26]

From the formation of his first conjunto in 1940 till his death thirty years later, Arsenio Rodriguez consistently rootworked the traditions and innovated the music of Afro-Cuba. He moved to the United States in 1954 and continued to perform and record until his death in Los Angeles in 1970. Interestingly, his releases during his time in the United States never met with much commercial success, despite his seminal role in the development of the modern son montuno and mambo. Ironically, in the years directly before and after his death, many of his compositions became veritable standards for the salsa musicians of the sixties and seventies, and his musical conception and aesthetic vision was in many ways the "sonic ideal" and essence of the típico era (see ch. 4).

The music of Cuba reveals the layers of the transculturative matrix of the circum-Caribbean and historical development of African peoples in the New World. The transformation of ethnicity into race is demonstrated in the development of clave consciousness, both musically and philosophically, and the distinctively Cuban approach to musicking (montuno aesthetics). As the enslaved became freed people and the freed people became citizens, the music chronicled their hardships, victories, and everyday lives, and the dances embodied knowledge of the struggles and the pleasures of making musical meaning through motor-muscle memory. The rhythms and dances carried the history, the melodies the diversity of experiences. The musics of the enslaved of Cuba and their descendants, once maligned and repressed, became a national symbol and international sensation. Their popularity among the peoples of Africa and the diaspora is a testament to the profundity of their grooves. Calypso and jazz, which developed contemporaneously with the son/rumba complex, are the only other musics of the circum-Caribbean that can claim a similarly powerful impact.

In 1951 Arsenio Rodriguez permanently left Cuba and moved to New York City to attempt to have corrective surgery for his blindness. While never able to regain his eyesight, Arsenio contributed heavily to the music scene in Nueva York. He played regularly with his reconfigured conjunto and other artists (including Machito and his Afro-Cubans; see the following chapters) and recorded several albums. In 1957 Arsenio went into the studio to take part in the recording of one of the most storied Afro-Cuban records of all time, Sabu Martinez's *Palo Congo*. This record was remarkable for several reasons: it featured top-notch Cuban musicians, presented traditional ("authentic") Afro-Cuban religious and folkloric music, and offered this rich musical world up to a very different potential audience. Significantly, *Palo Congo* was recorded on Blue Note Records, the iconic jazz label, at the height of the "hard bop" revolution.[27] It is to this "hard bop" revolution that we now turn.

3. Dedicated to the Struggle

The Aural Making and Unmaking of the Third World 1955–1965

But the black musician, he picks up his horn and starts blowing some sounds that he never thought of before. He improvises, he creates, it comes from within. It's his soul, it's that soul music. . . . Well, likewise he can do the same thing if given intellectual independence. . . . He can invent a society, a social system, an economic system, a political system that is different from anything that exists on this earth. He will improvise, he will bring it from within himself. And this is what you and I want.
—Malcolm X

Making Changes

On February 15, 1961, Adlai E. Stevenson Jr., Kennedy's new ambassador to the United Nations, rose to defend the Security Council's handling of the crisis in the Congo, less than 48 hours after the news of Patrice Lumumba's execution had been made public. Since independence in 1960, ethnic strife, neocolonial machinations, and political turmoil had devastated the former Belgian Congo. Lumumba appealed to the UN for help, but the world organization was unable to persuade the Belgian forces to disarm and evacuate. Lumumba then turned to the Soviets for assistance. Rebel forces, with the aid of the Central Intelligence Agency (CIA), captured Lumumba and assassinated him in January 1961 (his death was kept secret until the following month). As Stevenson began his remarks, a group of between fifty and sixty African Americans, clad in all black in testament to the slain leader, stood in the gallery in silent protest. A fight (a "riot," according to the *New York*

Times) ensued as security personnel attempted to suppress the protestors, setting off the most violent demonstration in UN history.

The demonstration at the UN represented a significant shift in black activism from passive nonviolence to a more aggressive militancy, an ideological shift that demonstrated the increasing internationalization of the black liberation movement. As John Henrik Clarke bluntly put it, "Lumumba became Emmett Till" (1961, 285). The composition of the demonstrators—made up of activists, artists, and musicians—also revealed the broadening political front of the black liberation movement of the 1960s. The protestors in the gallery included Daniel Watts (president of the Liberation Committee for Africa), Rosa Guy of the Harlem Writers Guild, writer/poet Maya Angelou, poet LeRoi Jones (Amiri Baraka) percussionist Max Roach, and singer Abbey Lincoln. As James Baldwin put it, "The negroes who rioted in the United Nations are but a very small echo of the black discontent now abroad in the world" (1961).[1] In the early 1960s, the slackening pace of civil rights reform at home and foreign policy failures and misadventures abroad coincided with the spread of anticolonial struggles in Asia, Africa, and Latin America, and marked a decisive shift in black liberation politics. Baldwin continued: "The power of the white world to control [black] identities was crumbling as these young Negroes were born; and by the time they were able to react to the world, Africa was already on the stage of history."

> It was not just a matter of chance that the Negro movement caught fire in America at just that moment when the nations of Africa were gaining their freedom. Nor is it merely incidental that the world should have fastened its attention on events in the United States at a time when the possibility that the nations of the world will divide along color lines seems suddenly not only possible, but even imminent.... It is clear that what happens in America is being taken as a sign of what can, or must, happen in the world at large. The course of world events will be profoundly affected by the success or failure of the Negro American Revolution in seeking the peaceful assimilation of races in the U.S. (from *The Moynihan Report*)

By the early 1950s it was becoming increasingly clear to the US government that images of racial segregation and racial violence in the United States were providing "grist for communist propaganda mills." In 1954 the Supreme Court handed down a unanimous verdict in the *Brown v. Board of*

Education case overturning the legal justification of the "separate but equal" principle and ordering (in May 1955) school boards to draw up desegregation plans "with all deliberate speed." That same May in Bandung, Indonesia, Asian, Middle Eastern, and African leaders, thinkers, and politicians gathered for an Afro-Asian Conference of non-aligned nations. The conference marked the emergence of the Third World[2] as a political force and entity on the global scene. By refusing (at least in theory) to succumb to the Cold War pressures of treaty obligations, the emerging nations (re)created themselves as a "third force" on the political economic scene and revealed some of the possibilities and potentialities of a decolonized world. A new (theoretical) configuration of national liberation struggles and international solidarity was emerging, and Afro-Asian and African American struggles intertwined and intersected in the colored, counter-public sphere of the so-called Third World. As Penny Von Eschen has said: "A new political constellation emerged as anti-colonial issues acquired a new prominence and stood side by side with domestic demands in the political agendas of leading African American protest organizations" (1997, 7).

This was a remarkable time period for African Americans, who were simultaneously looking inward—domestic events like the Montgomery bus boycott and the brutal beating and lynching of fourteen-year old Emmett Till—and at the same time facing outward (toward the East)—the Korean War and nascent decolonization struggles in Africa and the Third World in general. As racial domination increasingly came to be viewed from an international perspective, the colonial question began to intersect with Cold War imperatives, and the growing interrelation between foreign and domestic affairs became increasingly evident to black Americans. However, the heightened awareness of Africa and the ideological import and impact of the geopolitical meanings and resonances of anticolonial (and diasporic) racial identities and solidarities on local struggles in the United States were not entirely new in the contexts of the lives of black people.[3]

Nasser, Nkrumah, Nehru, Sukarno, and Sékou Touré were the new faces of the non-aligned movement and the anticolonial struggle. Malcolm X, Stokely Carmichael, and Martin Luther King Jr. were the faces of the struggle at home. Widely covered in the African American press at the time, the Bandung conference helped extend and expand the register of African American demands and strategies beyond the prism of Cold War politics. The symbolic accomplishments of the Afro-Asian conference (most of the attendees were from nations heavily subsidized and supported by US and foreign aid) and the *Brown* desegregation decision (a ruling that would result in a lot more "deliberation" than "speed"), set the tenor for the next decade of anticolonial struggle, and the two events marked a turning point in the psychological awareness of colonized peoples on a global scale. The decline of formal empire, the intensification of challenges to Western hegemony, the inflexibility of US capital in the conduct of foreign relations, the unflagging racism of American society, and a new sense of international solidarity and vocabulary of political dissent all added fuel to the fires of racial identification and visions of Third World unity.

As images of African Americans being beaten and tortured were circulating worldwide through media outlets, the US State Department sought to counter these negative portrayals with their own Negro "goodwill ambassadors."[4] In 1956 the US government began to take notice of jazz, and realized that its popularity and global influence could be used to "patriotic advantage." The State Department began organizing tours of jazz musicians as "jambassadors" through Africa, Latin America, the Middle East, and the Soviet Union. As jazz was gaining mainstream respectability and beginning to be legitimized in concert halls and on college campuses in the United States, it was also being marketed abroad as a symbol of American democracy and freedom. The music became a multiply contested site of black creative expression, social aspirations, and political protest, as well as government co-optation.

The linking of Africa and Asia was a prominent theme in the diasporic sensibilities of the late 1950s and 1960s, "which was fostered in part by Islam and in part by an anticolonialist perspective that connected the fates of black, brown and yellow people from around the world" (Monson 2000, 145). Ghana became independent in 1957, and the Cuban Revolution brought the Cold War to the Caribbean and Latin America in 1959. Between 1945 and 1960, forty nations achieved independence; seventeen (twelve of them African) won independence in 1960 alone; and the "political as well as epidermal complexion of the UN General Assembly appeared permanently altered" (Plummer 1996, 289). On the home front, discussion regarding the efficacy of the tactics of what had come to be called the Freedom Movement was continuing, particularly in light of the dynamic events abroad.[5] Black nationalist rhetoric and ideas were in increasing circulation among African Americans, as the gradualist and reform approaches of groups like the NAACP and Urban League revealed their pragmatic impotence. Serious debate regarding the tactics and strategy of the civil rights movement coincided, counterpointed and harmonized with decolonization struggles, liberation conversations, and Third World movements. As Houston Baker has said, "The black civil rights struggle, and particularly during the decade from 1955–1965, exemplifies the active working of the imagination of a subaltern, black American counterpublic" (1987, 12). The reconsiderations taking place among the activists in the black liberation movement found intersecting variants within the creative black music of the late fifties and early sixties.

The "Hard Blues"

The musical tradition that has come to be called jazz[6] was created by Africans in a primarily (though not exclusively) US-based context of transforming social and political structures, amid the cyclical developments and underdevelopments of the twentieth-century capitalist economy, the centrifugal pressures of subjection and domination, and the centripetal forces of "indignities and solidarities" that characterize the political economic milieu of black America and the diaspora generally. The developments of this black creative music from the period from 1955 to 1965 shed much light on the geopolitical transformations and exigencies of the post-Bandung period and the civil rights era, as well as, the "practice of diaspora" (Edwards). The music also provides a model for theorizing the Third World as a political and ideological entity, an imagined "nation" apart from the "state."[7]

Black music during this era reveals an intimate and persistent syncretism and symbiosis between musical-aesthetic expression and the communities out of which it was being continually created and gestated, and the larger sociocultural milieu. This is not to reduce the music to a mere epiphenomenon of sociological effects, historical imperatives, economic exigencies, or ideological agendas it (of course) responds to, contains and models all of these; it is rather to locate the music and its development within complex and shifting structures of historical particularity, to understand the stories music tells—the multiplicity of places, spaces, meanings, resonances, and rhythms invoked and evoked in the music.[8] To quote Guthrie Ramsey, "specific post-WWII musical 'texts' as well as the discourses that surround them, do not simply reflect or symbolize the ethnicity process among African Americans; they are important sites within which the very process itself is worked out and negotiated" (2003, 37). We can think of the jazz tradition as an ongoing stream of musical discourse and dialogic expressions, what LeRoi Jones called the "Changing Same." Which is to say that the music is "saying something," speaking to both location and direction.

This chapter attempts to re-present the intricate cultural matrix of black creative music during the era of Third World decolonization and civil rights struggles. Following upon the rootwork and polyrhythms laid down in the previous chapters, I seek to explore the processes of continuous innovation, renovation, and reconstruction in the productions and performances of black culture at the height of anticolonial struggle. The Music can be read/heard as a cartography of re-locations, re-collections, histories, trajectories, and changing configurations, condensed and crystallized in sound, absorbing and articulating cultural frames of reference, shared semiotic focus, and performative orientation in the "core stability" of the Changing Same. Its developments outline an interesting, elaborate, and ongoing conversation among the musicians themselves, the black communities from which they emerge and with whom they speak, and the larger social body; it is necessarily a dialogue of creative visions and historical retentions, of political ideologies and historical aspirations.

The history of the music is often narrated as a neat historical and ideological progression, emerging from the deep recesses of the Delta, pausing briefly to change outfits in New Orleans, and continuing up the Mississippi, to Kansas City, Chicago, and other urban areas, and finally uptown, to Harlem, where it matured ("jes grew") into its "modern" form. Like most myths, this tale contains a grain of truth; however, this causal and facile explanation tends to obscure much more than it reveals. Confusing causes and effects, this evolutionary (and teleological) model serves to reify systems apart from their circumstances, disguising the multivalent and truly polyrhythmic and polyphonic nature of cultural exchange and production, the continuities and retentions endemic to the tradition, as well as the ways in which culture simultaneously anticipates and responds to historical transformations: "In Black culture, the thing (the ritual, the dance, the beat) is 'there for you to pick it up when you come back to get it'" (Snead 1981, 150). The music is rooted in the constant revitalization and critical interrogation of the tradition; figures, forms, rhythms, and ideas are constantly recycled, reexamined, and reconstructed. This continuous musical dialogue plays at the margins where ideological debates, historical vectors, demographic shifts, material conditions, and diaspora overlap, intersect, and come into conflict and temporary resolution.

The music, then, offers us a crucial site of investigation into histories of black struggle placed against the backdrop of American society and institutions, in a global context. As we have seen in the previous chapters, black music and culture have always occupied a curious position of "lure and loathing" within the dominant imaginary, and jazz provides us with a fascinating glimpse into the conflicting and contradictory spaces created for blackness. Few expressive forms in the tradition have generated as much worldwide attention, critical acclaim, ardent devotion, "intellectual" scrutiny, and institutional legitimacy. Jazz is one of the more well-documented spaces in which the glaring paradox of simultaneous exaltation and exploitation of the music becomes readily apparent. Merod suggests that it is the peculiar position of black musical traditions that create a situation of "double reification," one internal and the other external—"cultural warfare" on the one hand, and "commercial (albeit tepid) success" on the other (1995, 13).

Black musicians have quite logically observed and theorized their own political and economic positions as African Americans within the music industry in relation to the larger emancipatory struggles of the community in general, and this knowledge finds its expression in a wide variety of ways and means.[9] The music is a communal collaboration, and it is the "stream of musical discourse" that makes the tradition the Tradition. There is an iconicity between the new music and the social movements of the post–World War II period; the music and the movements were both intra- and international, responding to new desires, political and aesthetic aspirations, changing relations of global forces, geopolitical shifts of capitalist production, and the ideological transformations of anti-racist and anti-imperialist movements in the postwar era: "The Music changed, because the musicians changed" (Baraka 1963, 66).

The period after World War II witnessed the upsurge and development of an increasingly militant black political resistance, which echoed the disillusion and frustrations of black aspirations as well as new senses of expectations and heightened self-awareness. Prior to and during the war, African Americans had moved in large numbers out of the agricultural South and entered the northern industrial labor force and the military in large numbers; increasing numbers also entered colleges and universities. The movement and urbanization of African Americans from the South was paralleled by the immigration of large numbers of people of African descent from the Caribbean.[10] In 1942 A. Phillip Randolph had threatened an organized, massive march on Washington, D.C., for equal opportunity; activists initiated the "Double-V" campaign against fascism and racism at home and abroad. Militant articulations of black anti-racism and self-determination corresponded with increasingly volatile anticolonial dissent and nationalist aspirations in the Third World. The geographic, political, and economic movements of black people in the postwar context are revealed and anticipated in the music that came to be called bebop.[11]

The musicians reacted and responded to the world around them, drawing as freely upon the ideas other musicians, artists, thinkers, activists, and cultural workers as they did upon the music of other genres and groups (Afro-Caribbean, Tin Pan Alley, modern classical music, show tunes, etc.). This multiplicity of sources and eclecticism is central to what Ramsey calls "Afro-modernism" and the idea of Afro-diasporic cosmopolitanism.[12] Ethics and aesthetics have always been intimately linked in black musicking traditions; thus, located in the music *itself* are "an elaborate set of generative themes which pattern the experience of everyday life," and make these experiences meaningful and feelingful. In this sense we can speak of an under-determination from within in black musical practices. As African Americans migrated, moved, and responded to sociopolitical, technological, economic, and cultural changes, the political significance and implications available to and inherent within the music expanded and extended in relation to and in anticipation of cultural struggles. Eric Porter states:

> We might consider modern jazz as an expression of an urban black American "structure of feeling" ... wherein the music and its reception articulated a collective lived and felt experience of expectancy and demand for change. Although this feeling cannot be reduced to any particular ideology or set of material conditions, it was a product of a combination of them.... Rather than a dialectic of class-based ideologies, then, the aesthetics of modern jazz reflected a heteroglot collection of meanings, orientations, and experiences which influenced one another. (1997, 37)

The intricacies and interpenetrations of the music's political location are further complicated by the overdeterminations of mainstream economic imperatives upon the semi-autonomous sphere of black cultural production. As Kofsky put it, for jazz musicians "it has always been the great depression" (1970, 61). During the Bandung era many black jazz musicians, as an overexploited working class, acutely understood the colonial metaphor, or at least the "sharecropping" nature of the economic system, since for black musicians underdevelopment and exploitation have always characterized the market and access to the means of production. The ideological militancy of bop in the late forties in many ways foreshadowed the transformations of the freedom movement in the late fifties and early sixties. While certainly the product of its moment, the aggressive stance taken by the boppers—their insistence on both the seriousness of their music (rather than mere entertainment) and artistic self-determination—predicted and resonated with the changing demands of the struggle to come.

By the onset of WWII, the heyday of the big bands had come to an end, though they would never die out entirely. Financial considerations, transportation costs, and higher taxes on dancehalls all contributed to the emergence of the small combo. The war also affected the music and the music industry in other ways: many musicians enlisted or were drafted; shortages of building materials brought the construction of new venues and clubs to a halt; and shortages of shellac drastically reduced the number of records being produced. It was the small, "hot," soloist-centered combos that were to produce the new revolution in jazz. The small combo gave more room to each of the instruments in both solo and ensemble playing, allowing for more exploration and extension of the harmonic and melodic aspects of the music, as well as freeing up the rhythm section to do more than simply keep time. "What evolved in turn was an aesthetic of speed and displacement—ostentatious virtuosity dedicated to re-orienting perception even as it rocked the house. Every instrument became immediately more mobile, everything *moved*" (Lott 1988, 461).[13]

The new music was inseparable from the black migratory streams of the interwar years. Expectations rose and with them a new generation of musical pioneers, in search of new sounds to express new experiences. Regional styles, generational differences, and aesthetic accents coalesced and colluded in their music; 4/4 midwestern backbeats and northern urban-industrial tempos, southern inflections and uptown harmonics, country rhythms pulsing through sophisticated city blues: the migratory histories and cultural geographies of black America and the diaspora were incorporated formally and structurally into the music. No doubt the shellac shortage and wartime recording ban significantly affected the perception of the musical revolution that was (ostensibly) taking place in and around Minton's Playhouse and Monroe's Uptown, spearheaded by musicians like Charlie Parker, Thelonious Monk, Dizzy Gillespie, Bud Powell, Kenny Clarke, and Max Roach (to name a few). But in the music itself recurring melodic, rhythmic, and technical conventions were recycled, repeated, and reworked again and again, in dizzying combinations. The self-referencing possibilities and inherent historiography of the sonic that characterize black musical conversation meant that the tradition necessarily drew upon what had come and gone before. The stability of frames of cultural reference provided the social backdrop of the musical collective against which creative individuality was defined and differentiated. It is useful to conceptualize the bop trajectory along a cultural and political continuum of black expression, part of the progression of styles in changing contexts; the dialogic of innovation and continuation, oscillation and accumulation, rupture and repetition.

The work of the beboppers developed and expanded musical precedents put forward by the swing big bands. Most of the defining melodic and harmonic devices in the bebop vocabulary—such as chord substitutions, inversions, dissonant voicings, etc.—had been used by the big bands and composers like Billy Strayhorn and Duke Ellington. The dense chromaticism, breakneck-speed fills, and solos had also been employed earlier by horn players. Even the more complex polyrhythmic patterns, triplet/swing style, dropping bombs, and offbeat accents had been utilized by earlier rhythm sections. We can think of bebop as both a mastery and extension of the idiom, which has led at least one writer to quip that bebop was less of a revolution and more of coup d'etat. To which we may add that virtually all the major practitioners of modern jazz received their training in the black powerhouse battalions like those of Count Basie, Chick Webb, Roy Eldridge, Cab Calloway, Duke Ellington, and others. It was in these big bands that the modern players received their first musical instruction, learning fundamentals of composition, arranging, and ensemble playing, and mastered the basic blues vocabulary that they would later expand and expound upon. These musical qualities and frequential values, rooted in folk innovations and urban sophistications, would continue to define the music through to the present day. The bebop period represented an important moment in the codification and dissemination of the new styles and a redefinition of the vocabulary that would influence and (in)form what was to follow, and was itself a product of the historical development of the swing bands.

Bebop's militant stance was an ideological departure (or, at least, a re-innovation). Its rapid tempos, extended improvisations, technical intricacies, and the demands placed upon soloists in the small-ensemble format brought virtuosity and musical proficiency to new heights. Bebop's wide-ranging and eclectic forays into other musics were something *new*: polyrhythmic ideas and harmonic and melodic devices (dissonant and complex chord extensions, alterations, substitutions, inversions—altered and unaltered ninths, elevenths, thirteenths; free use of passing tones, flat fifths, and modulations into unexpected keys); reworkings of thirty-two-bar pop songs to derive different melodies from the originals (e.g., "How High the Moon" becomes "Ornithology"); its re-presentations and re-constructions of twelve-bar blues; and finally, the heightened self- and race-consciousness of the musicians as serious artists rather than entertainers. Taken together, all of these aspects indicated new directions, aspirations, and changing cultural imperatives. Of course, we do not want to romanticize the "non- or a-commercial" aspects of bebop. As Kodat (following DeVeaux) points out: "Bebop was born not out a desire to escape culture industry swing . . . but rather out of a deliberate effort to create new commercial opportunities, within the existing entertainment industry, for black jazz musicians" (2003, 11).[14] Hence the doubleness of the bebop idiom (what Brathwaite calls "double-language"), the conflicting pressures of freedom and commodification, at once a response to market imperatives as well as aesthetic ones.[15] Bebop was both a reaction to the postwar culture industry and consumer society and an artistic movement responding to new sonic ideals.

The bebop movement challenged musical conventions through its form, content, and militant articulation. At the same time, it was part of and deeply implicated within larger political and aesthetic movements of black people in the United States and throughout the diaspora. This spirit of restless creativity, "divine irreverence," adventurousness, and experimentation would also pose a challenge to bebop itself. As the idiom became more codified and confining, the search for new musical ground continued. Interestingly, two of the most imposing formidable musical challenges would come from the Afro-diaspora, and more African modes of musicking. Two of the figures who symbolize this challenge and encounter are Thelonious Monk and Chano Pozo.[16]

The musical "architectonics" and conceptions of Thelonious Monk challenged not only the range and ability of the musicians, but also the musical conventions themselves. Monk introduced "not just new progressions and new chordal structures but also a different relationship between his harmonic and rhythmic foundation and the melody" (Kelley 1999, 16).[17] His use of harmonic and melodic dissonance, clusters, unique chord voicings and intervals, whole-tone explorations, and insistent repetition of the melody, and his reassertion of the lower register by emphasizing the left hand, challenged the music (and musicians) with a polyrhythmic and polyphonic conception that shared many common traits with a variety of African forms: "Though the rhythms [and melodies] are played apart, the music is unified by the way the separate parts fit together into a cross-rhythmic fabric. Only through the combined rhythm does the music emerge, and the only way to hear the music properly, to find the beat ... *is to listen to at least two rhythms at once*" (Chernoff 1979, 108).

Monk's "metaphysics of rhythm" contain some of his most compelling experiments and daring assertions, and would prove to be lasting contributions to the music. The deliberate pressure he exerts on time and the continuity of the pulse; his use of single notes, block chords, and repeated phrases to create "communicative certainty in a context of rhythmic ambiguity"; and the iconicity that inheres between his rhythmic and harmonic displacements all anticipate the numerous musical directions and paths that would be explored by many musicians in the late fifties and sixties. Perhaps most important for our discussion was Monk's profound simplicity, his ability to deconstruct harmony and melody to their most basic foundation as an architectonic principle of his music. Monk's music would play a vital role in inspiring and influencing a whole generation of musicians, writers, and artists, and at the same time informed the "eastern wind" that was about to blow the music into new avenues of expression and theorization.[18]

It is also significant that Monk led some of the quintessential hard bop sessions in the late 1950s. As Rosenthal points out, Monk had been "returning to the roots" in some of his earliest recordings in the 1940s. Consistently rootworking the tradition, he combined gospel, stride, boogie-woogie, and blues in his playing. He began playing organ in church and those sounds moved with him into secular music. After being billed as the "high priest of bebop" in the forties, Monk's music and artistic conception fell out of favor with critics and musicians alike for being too "weird" and too "out." But given his proclivity for roots music, "[i]t seems a natural development that a new appreciation of Monk in the mid-fifties coincided with the rise of hard bop" (Rosenthal 1992, 133). In 1955 Monk's recording contract was purchased by Riverside Records for a nominal fee, and this would lead to his so-called comeback, with epic hard bop sessions like *Brilliant Corners* (1956), *Monk's Music* (1957), and *Misterioso* (1958), to name a few. Monk both anticipated and responded to the new music that would epitomize the Bandung period (Kelley 1999, 187).

Another interesting challenge that confronted the beboppers was the reintroduction of Afro-diasporic rhythms, instruments, and musicians into the music. As we have seen, the circum-Caribbean cultural circuits connecting peoples have always played an important role in the creation of music and expressive cultures. The ongoing transculturation, creolization, and cross-pollination also marks the music of the Bandung era. I find it useful to think of New Orleans as the northernmost port of the

Caribbean archipelago. Afro-Caribbean musics and rhythms have held a central place in the music dating back to (at least) Jelly Roll Morton's crucial "Spanish tinge" (the habanera rhythm), which was also picked up by W. C. Handy in his travels through Cuba and Latin America (what he called the "tangana"); the vital contributions of West Indians to the big bands of the swing era, musicians like Mario Bauzá (see ch. 4), Juan Tizol, and "Tricky Sam" Nanton; and of course, the Latin inflections of Slim Galliard and the "calypso swing" of Louis Jordan. Duke Ellington, in a quotation as fascinating for the historical connections he makes as well as the (romantic?) ambiguity it conveys, brings a number of these transculturative connections to the fore:

> When a guy comes from the West Indies and is asked to play some jazz, he plays what *he* thinks it is, or what comes from applying himself to the idiom. Tricky [Sam Nanton] and his people were deep in the West Indian and the Marcus Garvey movement. A whole strain of West Indian musicians came up who made contributions to the so-called jazz scene, and they were all virtually descended from *the true African scene*. It's the same now with the Muslim movement, and a lot of West Indian people are involved in it. There are many resemblances to the Garvey schemes. *Bop*, I once said, *is the Marcus Garvey extension*. (1973, 108)

The Ellington big band of the late twenties and thirties had a pronounced West Indian character;[19] however, the Dizzy Gillespie big band's 1947 Carnegie Hall concert, with the legendary Afro-Cuban percussionist/singer Chano Pozo, and their continued experimentations perhaps most poignantly symbolize this circum-Caribbean reassertion. The Gillespie-Pozo association marked a departure from previous fusions and experiments, in that they "juxtaposed the most intellectually demanding form that jazz had produced with a purer and more profound Afro-Cuban singing and percussion than the world had ever dreamed of" (Roberts 1999,52). Gillespie's initial introduction to and incorporation of Afro-Cuban and -diasporic idioms is also of note, because it was an important instance of direct linkages between music and politics in the bebop era. His first entrée into African and Afro-Cuban drumming came from a series of concerts that he, Charlie Parker, and Max Roach performed in conjunction with a group of (unnamed) African and Caribbean percussionists to benefit the African Academy of Arts and Research (AAAR).[20]

The AAAR was founded in 1943 by Asadata Dafora (Horton), a singer, dancer, and choreographer from Sierra Leone, and Kingsley Ozoumba Mbadiwe, a Nigerian politician, educator, journalist, and activist; its membership consisted mainly of African scholars and students studying in the United States.[21] Their stated goal was "to promote cultural bonds between Africa and the United States" (anonymous, 1943). Founding members and contributors of the AAAR included Austin Briggs-Hall, Pearl Primus, Katherine Dunham, and Melville Herskovits. It is significant that Gillespie's initial immersion in the rhythms of Africa and the diaspora was to come via an explicitly culturally and politically oriented group of transnational scholars, artists, and activists at the height of the bebop era of American jazz.

Foregrounding the clave sensibility within the extended harmonic and expansive rhythmic vocabulary of the bop idiom, the Gillespie-Pozo association simultaneously interrogated and revealed underlying, feelingful grammars and structures in sound, unifying tonal and timbric resonances "vibrating" throughout the diaspora. Pozo's virtuosity exploded the already vast and dynamic rhythmic lexicon of bebop. His seemingly unending rhythmic permutations elaborated complex syncopations and multimetric values, and articulated profound effects both *in* and *of* time. The overwhelming expressivity of the drum (so intensively mastered and dramatically evidenced in Afro-Cuban traditions, as explored in the previous chapter) and the complexities of Afro-Cuban metric pleasures and meanings were forcefully (re)introduced into and imposed upon African American performance, and would solidly imprint the music through to the present day. Sadly, Pozo was killed in 1948, but Gillespie (and others) would continue remembering the African diaspora throughout his career.

Overall, the (sometimes) successful outcomes of these experiments (both Monk's and Pozo's) reflected larger challenges and issues that were to confront African Americans, not only in creative expression and practice but also in social and political thought and theory. These moments reveal an early awareness of a variety of political, artistic, and coalitional possibilities; their potential for simultaneously expanding aesthetic and political struggle; and the problematics of realizing them "on the ground" (or "on the one," as the case may be). But Monk's "moods," and the Third World challenge symbolized by Pozo, would be addressed and answered in many ways in the following decade, as the music began to remember Africa in diaspora.

"Before the Music Got Separated"

By the mid-fifties, the burgeoning black nationalist "renaissance" and mass movement culture emerging largely out of the church had found eloquent musical expression. Three musical events serve to symbolically mark the beginning of this new period: the 1954 recording of "Walkin'" by Miles Davis; the release of the album *Afro* by Dizzy Gillespie (1954); and the death of Charlie Parker in 1955. Parker was *the* bebop icon, and his passing left a void in the music that will never be filled. *Afro* continued Gillespie's experimentations with the Afro-Cuban and African American musical fusions, well illustrated in tunes like "Con Alma" and the "Manteca Suite," and aided by such Cuban percussive luminaries as Ubaldo Nieto, Candido Cameron, and Ramon "Mongo" Santamaria. Davis's recording's vernacular title anticipated the political culture and strategies of the civil rights movement that literally would take it to the streets in the fifties. The title track's twelve-bar blues structure was both a "return to the source" and revealed the shape of things to come, a revitalization of the core black blues matrix. Bird returned to the ancestors, "Con Alma" metonymically realized and valorized the "roots and routes" of the African diaspora, while "Walkin'" symbolically took the music back to its southern blues heritage via "modern" modal progressions and became a signifier for and an early indication of the musical "family reunion" that was to come to be called hard bop.

Reflecting the struggles of black musicians to vitalize their music and find their own voice, hard bop revealed an attempt to reach out to and reestablish a connection with black audiences who were leaving jazz (most notably for the incredible rhythm and blues revolution spearheaded by Ray Charles and James Brown, among others). Many musicians shared saxophonist Johnny Griffin's belief that jazz had been taken out of the community and put in Carnegie Hall. There was a demand for "blacker" sounds and a music that spoke more forcefully of the blues aesthetic, with stronger rhythmic drive, more pronounced bottom end and bass, and more "roots" (blues and gospel) inflections in the melodic lines. The music's return to the church and the hard blues finds parallels in the politicization of traditional black institutions by the civil rights movement, and in the reclamation and reinscription of public space by militant pacifist black protest. At the same time, it is important to remember that, as Andrew Hill put it, "before the music got separated," many jazz musicians paid their dues in R&B bands. Relying fundamentally on the bebop vocabulary without sacrificing any of the virtuosic heights scaled by the beboppers, the musicians took the music simultaneously backwards and forwards, inwards and outwards, extending it back through blues past and "back to Africa," all the while innovating, experimenting, and refining the craft.

Hard bop was (ahistorical) industry shorthand for a much more complex moment in jazz, in which a bewildering diversity of sounds and styles burst out of the black musical continuum of the late fifties.[22] The desire to "blackenize" the sound and "return the music to the people" reflected economic and social imperatives, and the external challenges to the bebop movement. In the early fifties, as swing began to sound anachronistic and bebop became codified and sterile, in the words of Eric Porter: "the jazz industry as a whole faced economic crisis from post-war recession and competition from other musical forms such as popular vocal music, country and western, urban blues, and R&B" (2002, 81). Many historians and critics cite the beginning of bebop as the end of jazz as a popular form in black communities, at the same time many of those same critics attacked the new music. Rosenthal, however, argues that in fact hard bop was not only popular but in fact maintained the viability of jazz in African American communities: "[t]he years from 1955–1965 represent the last period in which jazz effortlessly attracted the hippest young black musicians.... and hard bop was the dominant jazz style in the neighborhoods where such youngsters live" (1988, 24).

During the late fifties and early sixties hard bop and "soul jazz" reflected the nature of African American tastes in the civil rights era. People wanted funky, danceable music, and the hard bop musicians returned jazz to its musical roots while simultaneously popularizing the music with a new generation of listeners.[23] In a sense, by venturing into R&B and groove-oriented numbers the music was able to "cross back over" into the community. Small nightclubs began to open, which were both economically and aesthetically more practical and provided venues for the experimentations of the new musicians. "For similar reasons, small groups became attractive to the smaller record companies that proliferated after the war" (Ramsey 2003, 118). These labels, while clearly trying to make a profit, brought a different philosophy to the jazz recording industry, what Ramsey calls an "artistic approach." The three independent labels that specialized in hard bop were Prestige, Riverside, and Blue Note (significantly, these independents often used musicians and artists as A&R men to scout new talent). During this period jazz record sales were higher than ever. Easier to sell than jazz LPs and distributed to black radio stations and jukeboxes throughout black communities, the 45rpm single enabled the widespread dissemination of the new, "funky" sounds. The fact that the primary vehicle for hard bop was the 45 indicates that the music was reaching a wider audience. As Clifford Jordan has said, "Yeah, all the jukeboxes, they had jazz, but nobody called it 'jazz' then. It was just music. It was just our music, folk music" (Rosenthal 1992, 69).

Blurring the line between jazz and R&B with vernacular titles like "Dis Here," "Moanin'," and "The Preacher," hard bop became the basic jazz idiom. The (re)turn to "funky" or "soul" jazz was also a practical economic response to the difficulty of making a living as a jazz musician and to the popularity of "cool jazz" (performed mostly, but not entirely, by whites) and its commercial success among the white middle class and on college campuses. The musicians of the fifties were "highly literate both politically and musically," and the responses to African American urgings for "down home" as well as "way out" music were many and varied; the blues/soul/funk stylistic trend was but one tributary in the stream of black musical discourse.

The infusion of the music with new and revitalized political meanings was part of the broadening political awareness of the 1950s, as the musicians drew upon the roots—black history, culture, and consciousness—to create and express new musical meanings in changing contexts, influenced by the civil rights struggle in the United States and anticolonial struggles abroad. By the late fifties and early sixties, at least three overlapping and interpenetrated styles are discernable, along the jazz shades of the continuum: 1) soul and funk marked a return to decidedly black traditional musical proclivities: blues and gospel; 2) the ascendance of the "composers,"[24] and their militant demand and challenge for and to blackness on its own terms—from the outside and "way ahead" to outer space and everything in between; and 3) the pan-African diaspora re-collections, black–Asiatic collaborations, and Third World explorations.[25]

These new musical discourses both anticipated and responded to the cultural needs and exigencies of black sensibilities at this historical juncture and operated in a polyrhythmic unity and contrapuntal relation. It is important to perceive the inter- and inner relationships among these varied expressions, because each defines the other ("the beat is an entity of relation"), and the musical community involved has always been one of sharing, exchange, informal jamming, and studied perfection—again, the dialogues are the keys in which the music is made. In a context of multiple rhythms, polyphony, and multivocality, artists and improvisers distinguish themselves from one another while maintaining dynamic interrelationships; the tradition "comes alive" through the communal examination and expression of syncopated and percussive individuality against the down beat of tradition.[26]

Some purely pragmatic delineations can be made at this point. The hard blues + gospel = soul aggregations are exemplified in various incarnations of Horace Silver and Art Blakey's Jazz Messengers,[27] the Golson-Farmer-Fuller Jazztet(s), and the Gryce-Byrd Jazz Lab. Of the "composers," here we can think of Thelonious Monk, Charles Mingus, Sun Ra, and Ornette Coleman. Lastly, the pan-Afro-diasporic vein found its most consistent elaborations in the works of Yusef Lateef, Ahmed Abdul-Malik, and Randy Weston. This latter group will be the primary focus of the remainder of this chapter. Of course, these delineations are purely heuristic and matters of convenience, as the realities of historical change, musical creation, stylistic innovation, and ideational exchange are decidedly more complex.[28]

Blues to Africa

When Max Roach entered the studio in the fall of 1960 to record *We Insist: Freedom Now Suite*, the nation and the world had witnessed some startling events. The Sharpeville Massacre in South Africa and the gruesome pictures of unarmed children, women, and men being shot down shocked and horrified people the world over. In February, the sit-in movement was officially born in North Carolina, and rapidly spread across the United States. The calm dedication, endurance, and perseverance of the nonviolent protesters moved the nation and the world. The following year, Randy Weston took a big band (twenty-some pieces) into the studio to record a tribute to the newly emerging African nations, *Uhuru Afrika*. These two records graphically reveal the counterpoint and dialogue between musicians themselves, as well as the larger issues confronting black peoples all over the globe, and, I think, emblematize some of the politics and aspirations of the Bandung era.[29] They also effectively demonstrate the call-and-response (so inseparable from African music) between tradition and innovation, among different traditions and generations of musicians, and between the music and black community writ large. Musicians consciously and frequently expressed their experiences as Africans in America and with the American music industry in ways linked to larger social themes of liberation. The music was (and is) a vehicle and the icon for theorizing and articulating visions of black freedom and collectivity.

There is a long, intertwining history of jazz musicians and Islam. The search for new and different musical forms and ideas naturally paralleled the search for new modes and methods of spirituality and alternative values that went beyond what Amiri Baraka called the "stale purity of the missionaries' legacy." To quote Porter again: "Equal to the political critique and often intersecting with it, was the desire to infuse music with a spiritual purpose.... The activist and spiritual strivings coincided with an internationalist perspective, which was evident during the early fifties, but more pronounced in the late fifties and early sixties in the context of anticolonial struggles and the invention of the 'third world'" (Porter, 164). Artists like Dakota Staton, Talib Dawud, Art Blakey, McCoy Tyner, Idrees Sulieman, A. K. Salim, Gigi Gryce, Kenny Clarke, Ahmad Jamal, Shafi Hadi, Sahib Shihab, Max Roach, and Ahmed Abdul-Malik were all converts to orthodox Islam. "Muslim musicians were prominent in several of the musical projects that made links to Africa and the diaspora" (Monson 2007, 147). But few artists revealed such a sustained and passionate spiritual and aesthetic interest in fusing the music of East and West as Yusef Lateef. Born Bill Evans in Chattanooga, Tennessee, in 1920, Lateef (another product of black migration) moved with his family to Detroit as a child. He began playing tenor saxophone professionally in 1946. He played, successively, with the big bands of Lucky Millinder, Hot Lips Page, Roy Eldridge, and Ernie Fields. Significantly, in 1948, the same year he converted to Islam, Lateef joined Dizzy Gillespie's big band, playing with percussionists Chano Pozo and later Luis "Sabu" Martinez (with whom he became close friends). Returning to Detroit in 1950, he settled down to study and form his own combo; Lateef's band had steady work and room for development and advancement, as the house band at Klein's (a downtown club) for five years. According to Lateef, Klein's Show Bar was a place "where a number of musicians and music lovers congregated to hear and discuss the latest developments in politics and culture" (Lateef 2006, 99). This was certainly a fertile venue for creativity and exploring new sounds in the Bandung era.

In the forties and fifties Detroit was a "hotbed of jazz radicalism"; the "Class of '55" included such luminaries as Paul Chambers, Tommy Flanagan, Terry Pollard, Kenny Burrell, Donald Byrd, Doug and Julius Watkins, Louis Hayes, Curtis Fuller, and Barry Harris (who left a little later than his contemporaries). Of course, mention should be made of some of the earlier "graduates" like Sonny Stitt, Billy Mitchell, and Hank, Elvin, and Thad Jones. By the mid-fifties, Yusef Lateef was immersed in a vital milieu of musical creativity and dynamism. In his formative years, he was raised on the hard-driving, R&B shouting, wailing, and honking of (long obscure) players like Wild Bill Moore and T. J. Taylor. Lateef's musical sound and conception was intimately and directly linked with that (oh-so-southern) "wailing"[30] blues sound, a sound that never left his horn. The blues-drenched quality embodied in his tone and the recurrent wail connect Lateef with his own southern roots, his Deep South contemporaries, and in turn inflected all of his later musical experimentation and compositions. "One should remember that the primary task of aesthetics is to explain prevailing concepts" (Lateef 2006, 97). "I've written and performed blues so I'm familiar with the blues form. But jazz, I'm not acquainted with the term, it's an ambiguous term. So if you should ask me something about jazz, I wouldn't really know what you mean" (Lateef, *Into Something*).

Lateef's comments shed much light on his own development (firmly in the blues idiom), his dislike and distrust of music industry nomenclature, and the inability of musical labels to contain, capture, or adequately express his musical vision. By the mid-fifties, Yusef Lateef was immersed in a vital milieu of musical creativity and dynamism. He began to study the music and instruments of other cultures, and began researching the music of Africa, India, Japan, and China. This was the beginning of a long-lasting exploration of "Eastern" sounds and blendings of the blues matrix and melodies and rhythms of the Third World, despite having never been to Asia, Africa, or the Middle East (at least in the 1950s). As Herb Boyd points out: "He was perhaps the first improvising artist to embrace Middle Eastern and Eastern modes, rhythms and instruments to his music" (Boyd in Lateef 2006, ix). He began making his own instruments like double-reed flutes and earthbows, and incorporating into his music obscure Eastern instruments like the *argol* (a Middle Eastern reed flute), the *rabat* (a one-stringed lower-register Arabic instrument), *shinai* (an Indian double-reed flute), and various rattles, scrapers, and percussion instruments. He was intrigued by non-Western scales and intervals like quarter tones and whole tones, and continuously sought to express what he calls that "East Indian-African flavor" in his music. His work from the period in question demonstrated his technical command, full-bodied saxophone playing, and advanced harmonic conception, but also an honest and moving sincerity. "I like to play about thoughts, feelings and images that are close to people. Music, after all, isn't something you separate from the rest of your life. It's an extension of who you are all the time" (Lateef, *Into Something*).

Yusef utilized different time signatures, including 6/8, 5/4, and 3/4, and had an extended engagement with movie themes. He experimented with standards and tunes like "Love Theme from Spartacus," "Sea Breeze" (a tune he completely transforms via Afro-Latin syncopation and 3/4 tango), or the "Love Theme from The Robe." He also brought his Afro-Asiatic aesthetic to bear on bop standards; his "Happyology" is a "free calypso"-Afro-Cuban-clave-soul version of Gillespie's classic "Woody 'n' You," the tune ends with Lateef (literally) scraping out an agonizing groove on the *guiro*. As he said in an interview: "I have no definite set path in front of me, I am trying to see that everything I do is sincere and not for effect" (Lateef 2006). Yusef even played one of his original melodies backward: "Blues in Space" was later recorded "Ecaps."[31] He was one of the leading voices in the blending of African, Asian, and Near Eastern influences. His ensemble remained tight even in their most experimental passages, with a sound rooted in the soil of many continents and many musics: "I want to keep growing and growing, and in each new musical context, I want to learn something else" (Lateef 2006). Throughout his long and continuing career Lateef's deep and abiding faith in Islam informed his musical and aesthetic choices.[32]

A few of the other musical contexts in which Brother Lateef was learning are of note. In 1960–61 he began playing with the ensemble of Nigerian master percussionist Babatunde Olatunji, and can be heard on the latter's record *Zungo* (which features an all-star lineup including George Duvivier, Clark Terry, Montego Joe, Chief Bey, and Rudy Collins); Lateef also plays with Art Blakey's Afro-Drum Ensemble on their 1961 recording *The African Beat* (which also happened to feature, Montego Joe, Chief Bey, and the bassist Ahmed Abdul-Malik); finally, Lateef was part of the big band that entered the studio, that same year, to record Randy Weston's *Uhuru Afrika*. These three albums are extremely significant as they mark important Afro-diasporic interventions and accomplishments, bringing together musicians and singers from throughout the diaspora in unified and (for the most part) successful musical expression. All three were recorded and released the same year (and on the heels of Roach's *We Insist*), and attest to the cultural and political ideas and possibilities that were imagined and in evidence at the time. Again, the music comes to not simply "symbolize" but also embody and anticipate its own historicity.

Ahmed Abdul-Malik was born and raised in Brooklyn and claimed to be of Sudanese descent. However, recent research by Robin D. G. Kelley shows he was actually of West Indian descent (2012).[33] As a youth he studied violin, bass, piano, and tuba, and attended the High School of the Performing Arts in New York City. In the 1940s he entered the professional music scene, and played with Art Blakey, Fess Williams, and Don Byas. He later went on to play in a variety of settings with Coleman Hawkins, Sam (the Man) Taylor, Randy Weston (recording with him in 1956–57), Odetta, and the Middle Eastern groups of Mohammed el Bakkar and Djamal Aslan. In 1957 Abdul-Malik accepted "Monk's challenge" and handled the low-end requirements in Monk's quartet through 1958. The fusion of Eastern and Western musics always intrigued Abdul-Malik (reinforced by his Sudanese parentage and a State Department–sponsored trip to Africa in 1960); he firmly believed that Eastern and Arabic music exerted a stronger "pre-jazz influence" than had been acknowledged. "He notes that many different cultures—not just the usually cited Congo and West African—were represented in the initial African contribution to American music" (*East Meets West* liner notes, 1959).

In 1958 he released his first album as a leader, *Jazz Sahara*, a recording of traditional Middle Eastern and North African music and rhythms played on traditional instruments (with the interesting addition of Johnny Griffin on saxophone, also from Monk's quartet of the time). His subsequent recordings present a more dynamic fusion of his musical interests. His second recording, appropriately titled *East Meets West*, brought together jazz musicians—Johnny Griffin, Benny Golson, Lee Morgan, Curtis Fuller, and Al Harewood (all alumni of the Jazz Messengers, the Jazztet, or both)—with Middle Eastern musicians Ahmed Yetman (who plays *kanoon*, an obscure seventy-two-stringed Arabic instrument), Naim Karacand on violin, and his close friend and musical associate Bilal Abdurahman on percussion. Ahmed doubles on bass and *oud* (an Arabic ancestor to the lute). The album presents a beautiful blend of blues-based improvisation over quarter-tone and eighth-tone intervals produced by the Eastern instruments playing traditional Arabic religious and secular melodies. Ahmed exploits the full ensemble context to explore the colors and expressive range of pan-Arabism, bedrock blues, and Afro-diasporic hybridity.

Ahmed's next two recordings, for the New Jazz/Prestige label, merit close attention. The first, *The Music of Ahmed Abdul-Malik*, is exceptional for many reasons—first, the instrumentation: Ahmed again doubling on bass and oud, Bilal on clarinet and percussion, Tommy Turrentine on trumpet, Eric Dixon on tenor, a very young and fiery Andrew Cyrille on drums, and the brilliant cello playing of Calo Scott. Second, the music itself travels widely and engagingly through a number of traditions and cultures. "Nights on Saturn" is a space-age vamp that provides a forum for Bilal's soloing on "an ancient Korean instrument so obscure that neither he [Bilal] or Ahmed are sure of its name" (liner notes). The album includes "La Ibkey," a traditional Arabic melody, wherein the drums play in 7/4 while the soloists alternate between 3/4 and 4/4 and multiples thereof; and "Oud Blues," a straight-ahead twelve-bar blues on which Ahmed plays the oud (with Calo walking the bass line on cello). The album also contains two calypso-highlife (re)fusions, "The Hustlers" and "Hannibal's Carnivals" (Ahmed had also played with the calypsonian MacBeth in the forties and fifties). Interestingly, the musical structure of the latter is a sixteen-bar AABA form with two bridges, one a fairly standard calypso turnaround and the second one belonging to Monk's "Epistrophy."[34]

Ahmed's next work in 1962, aptly entitled *Sounds of Africa*, continued his musical and spiritual explorations into the heart of African sounds. The record features Blakey's Afro-Drum Ensemble veterans Montego Joe, Chief Bey, and Rudy Collins, along with Calo and Bilal. The album opens with "Wakida Hena," a straightforward highlife tune the melody of which Ahmed learned in Ghana. Next it moves into "African Bossa Nova" a song that is precisely what the name implies: Brazilian bossa nova rhythms mixed with Gold Coast melody and horn arrangements reminiscent of New Orleans brass bands. The entire second side is take up by two extended pieces, "Communication" and "Suffering," both polyrhythmic and expressive meditations, open-ended forms that allow the soloists and percussionists to explore multiple meters and open harmonics in a modal context, the first piece being in clave and deeply rhythmic, the second piece in the 7/4 and 9/8 Middle Eastern vein.

Ahmed's musical career continued to expand upon his early explorations into the musics of the Third World. In 1963 he played bass for Nigerian guitarist Solomon Ilori on his Blue Note date *High Life*, and that same year he played in a "Latin bag" on the album *Jazz Committee on Latin American Affairs*. He later released an album of movie tunes, *Spellbound*, which featured Hamza El Din, the famed Sudanese oud player, with whom he would later perform a duet on the latter's *Music of Nubia*. Abdul-Malik constantly sought to develop new ideas, study different cultural expressions, explore syncretic possibilities and continually relate and return them to the common Afro-diasporic tradition, organizing and communicating an aesthetic context for community action.

Throughout the late fifties and sixties, musicians and artists strove to realize the artistic potential and creative possibilities that were emerging in tandem with the idea of the Third World and the politicization of the civil rights struggle. The desire for freedom in the political context of decolonization paralleled searches for spiritual and aesthetic freedom in the music. Both movements challenged musical and political conventions to visualize and theorize the conditions of possibility of unity and post-colonial liberation. Musicians drew upon the rich resources of the black musical matrix (particularly as it was manifest in the bebop period), inflecting the skills and aesthetics of the tradition with contemporary meanings and new and different forms and syncopating the music with contemporary situations, to continually re-create vital, lasting, and feelingful music.

In 1960 Max Roach began to record a portion of a work in progress co-written with singer-lyricist Oscar Brown Jr. The results of this collaboration were the record *We Insist! Freedom Now Suite*. The album brought together a diverse group of musicians and performers; "it occupies a space somewhere between mainstream jazz modernism and the New Thing" (Monson 2007, 176). Brown was known for his compositions (he wrote "Strong Man" for Abbey Lincoln in 1957) and his work as a soulful pop vocalist with socially conscious lyrics (as demonstrated on his albums *Sin and Soul* and *Between Heaven and Hell*, on Columbia). As a young vocalist, Abbey Lincoln already had three albums to her credit, for the most part in the straight-ahead jazz idiom (with the exception of her version of Cuban percussionist Mongo Santamaria's "Afro Blue").[35] On saxophone was the "old master," Coleman Hawkins. Quite literally the first star of the tenor saxophone, and a defining force in the music since the twenties. Hawkins's tenor sound influenced to some degree virtually every player that was to follow in modern jazz. According to Orrin Keepnews, Hawkins was "one of the few to change effectively with changing jazz times. Hawkins joined with and encouraged modern jazz in the mid-1940's." Roach was accompanied on percussion by Afro-Cubans Ray Mantillo and Tomas DuVall, and Babatunde Olatunji. Also on the date were Booker Little (trumpet), Julian Priester (trombone), Walter Benton (tenor), and James Schenck (bass).

Roach's previous LP, *Deeds Not Words*, in name evoked the civil rights struggle, though the content of the album itself is more or less standard hard bop fare. However, *We Insist* was something altogether different. The first side of the LP reviews some of the significant points and periods in black American history, musically tracing the long road from slavery to freedom, and setting the stage for the contemporary struggle. Opening with the haunting "Driva' Man," an intensely expressive evocation of forced labor, brutality, physical abuse, slave catching, and rape: "Only two things on my mind / Driva' man and quittin' time." Lincoln's voice weaves fluidly and accents the steady fall of the rhythmic hammer, evoked by her tambourine. "Freedom Day" recalls the great day of Emancipation, the rumors of "freedom" and the disbelief of the enslaved. The side ends with "Triptych: Prayer, Peace, Protest," an extended dialogue between Roach and Lincoln, in which the latter sings vocables while Roach freely improvises behind her, each pushing, answering, and supporting the other in musical rapport. "I feel this," Lincoln explained of the recording. As the movement enters the "Protest" section, Lincoln wails while Roach rolls all around the drum kit; the drive of the protest finds resolution in "Peace." As Max explained to Abbey before the take: "["Peace"] is the feeling of relaxed exhaustion after you've done everything you can to assert yourself. You can rest now because you've worked to be free. It's a realistic feeling of peacefulness. You know what you've been through" (liner notes).

The second side turns its attention towards Africa and the sweeping changes taking place on the continent and graphically reveals musical and political concerns of the Bandung era, and the perceived connections—real and imagined—between the civil rights movement and Third World liberation. In "All Africa," Lincoln sings the names of tribes from all over the continent, and Olatunji, playing *apesi* drums, answers her calls in his native Yoruba. Finally, "Tears for Johannesburg" recalls the Sharpeville massacre, which occurred less than a year before the recording. The song evokes the incident and the continuing and ongoing struggle as well as the ghastly nature of the oppressors. The rhythmic conversation between Roach, DuVall, Mantillo, and Olatunji speak to the polyrhythmic unity of the diaspora. All in all, the mood of the album is one of righteous indignation and revolutionary change, is in direct communication with the battles of the emerging Third World at home and abroad, and presents a musical portrait of the past, present, and future of black liberation.

Randy Weston's *Uhuru Afrika*, recorded in 1960 and released in 1961, was in part a realization and culmination of his long-standing interest in and engagement with the musics of Africa and the diaspora. His salute to "New Africa" signified the changing face of a decolonizing world—new nations in the UN, Castro up in Harlem. It is also significant that Weston pulled together an Afro-diasporic "powerhouse battalion," a truly big band with players from all over the United States and the diaspora.[36]

> This particular record is kind of hard to describe. First of all, the purpose of the record was to show that all the Black people of African descent are related to one another. So we deliberately got musicians from

Africa, Cuba and the U.S. We got people from different fields of music and entertainment. We had Brock Peters and Martha Flowers, who is a concert singer, to show that there was a connection between us. The connection was the African rhythms. Langston Hughes wrote the lyrics for a composition of mine called "African Lady". Melba Liston wrote the arrangements and conducted. We also used Swahili to show the beauty of an African language and how the African language is also part of the African rhythms. It came out during a time when we could see things going down ... we could feel it happening. We wanted this to be a symbolic gesture by Afro-Americans, to show our pride that some of the countries in African were getting their freedom. So the album was called *Uhuru Afrika*. *Uhuru* means "freedom" in Swahili. (Randy Weston, qtd. in Taylor 1993, 23)

Weston's music and philosophy strove to reveal the interchange and interrelation, not simply the debt, of modern music to Africa, but also the wealth of ideas and inspiration to be gathered from the diversity of the continent's expressive forms and rich history. "I've always stressed in interviews whenever I've spoken in public my whole life I have been reading about and immersing myself in Africa. I have been forever fascinated by and deeply interested in the history of Africa, the current problems of Africa, the triumphs of African people, the political situation in Africa. ... I've always seen the similarities in people of African descent, not the differences" (Weston 2010, 82).

The album is a suite composed of four movements: "Uhuru Kwanza," freedom first and self-determination; "African Lady," a tribute to the strength and perseverance of black women everywhere; "Bantu," a call for and recognition of black unity; and "Kucheza Blues," "for the glorious moment when Africa would gain its full independence and black people all over the world would have a tremendous global party to celebrate" (Weston 2010, 93). The album is a richly multi-layered, multi-part, and polyrhythmic evocation and tribute to the black past and an expectant future. Liston's arrangements (she and Randy had a long and fruitful history of collaboration)—her use of sonorous harmonies, and crafted unison passages—vividly capture Weston's lush orchestral vision and the spirited intricacies of his musical ideas, and provide an excellent platform for the soloists. Langston Hughes's lyrics find eloquent expression in the voices of Brock Peters and Martha Flowers.

The final movement of the piece is a 3/4 African blues-ballad, as Hughes describes in the liner notes: "Had I been in charge of naming these sequences, I would have called the final movement *The Birmingham-Bamako Blues*, for in this section there are overtones of both Alabama and Africa, Dixie and the Negro Motherland. The final sequence is called *Kucheza Blues* meaning, in Kiswahili, the *Swinging Blues*" (liner notes).[37] The cohesive sound of the ensemble on the final movement is a testament to Weston's compositional, percussive, and physical piano style and (Monk-inspired) two-handed technique, and links him to the centuries of African drummers long separated by the black Atlantic. The way the track came about in the studio is indicative of black cultural practices and processes, as Hughes explains in the liner notes:

> The *Kucheza Blues* was performed before the recording mikes in true improvisatory style—without a score. Preceding the recording of this blues there was only a brief run through with Randy Weston playing the melodies and by way of 'arrangement' Melba Liston suggesting *this* here or *that* there—largely by gestures, hummings and osmosis. But every Afro-American worth his salt has the blues in his bones, feels the blues and no matter how 'contemporary' he may be, loves the blues.... To the African drumbeat have been added the Birmingham breaks, Harlem riffs and Birdland trimmings. The basic beat of jazz, which began in Africa, thence transplanted to the new world, has now come back home...

However, this epic musical endeavor was not without problems. Roulette Records' initial enthusiasm soon cooled due to disagreements over proprietary rights and artistic control. "They wanted to make some sort of deal where I would be giving them power over my music. They promised to do a big promotion on me, but I have learned one lesson: Never sell a tune! I refused, and therefore the album got buried. There was no publicity put behind it. So because of that and the message on the record, it was very hard to find" (Weston in Taylor 1993, 23). The age-old contradictions of black artistic freedom within capitalist structures of production arose again. The militant vision of a "Free Africa" and her free (musically and politically) descendants came crashing into the barriers of external economic forces that shape, condition, contain, and control its dissemination. *Uhuru Afrika*, in its successes and failures, was a vital and telling moment in Weston's career.

"I saw *Uhuru Afrika* as the most important music I had written" (Weston 2010, 93). His visions of black unity were sustained and stimulated by his personal background, growth, and development as well as the changing political, social, and artistic contexts of the times. The threads and fabrics from which he creates his intercultural weave are cut from the cloth of history, experience, education, and profound feeling. As he says, "Oh but its African. . . . It's all African."

Randy Weston was born on April 6, 1926, and raised, as he puts it, "in an African village in Brooklyn." His parentage sheds some light on his early inspirations. As Weston says: "I've always been interested in history. I've always been interested in the history of myself and my people, wherever they may be. I guess maybe it's because I'm sort of a half-breed in the black community. My father was from Panama and my mother came from Virginia. . . . But I always noticed there was a similarity between them, that there were certain basic things which were very much alike. So I discovered it was Africa" (Weston in Taylor 1993, 24). His father was a Garveyite who stressed the importance of racial pride and knowledge of Africa. "He talked to me about Africa from the time I was 3 years old. He let me know that I had a very rich heritage and that one day I should go back to Africa" (Palmer 1973, 23). His father's diverse Caribbean roots and routes and strong avowal of African pride began an early diasporic education for Weston. His mother's spirituality and influence shaped his appreciation for the profundity of black religious expression. He was also exposed to a variety of sounds: "[his father] had all kinds of music in the house—Basie, Andy Kirk, Duke, calypso. 'My mother took me to the A.M.E. Church, where I fell in love with the Black music of the church. Of course, there were always the West Indian street carnivals and all these different Black people out in Brooklyn, allowing me to stick my ears into all kinds of things'" (Crouch 1983, 6).

Brooklyn was an attractive destination for southern and West Indian migrants and had a long-standing and diverse black community. Brooklyn also had a vibrant musical scene. In the 1930s and 1940s, the borough boasted more bars and clubs than Manhattan (Weston 2010, 11). Immersed in a rich musical environment, Weston grew up with players such as Cecil Payne, Al Harewood, Ray Copeland, Ernie Henry, Duke Jordan, Eddie Heywood ("who lived across the street"), Max Roach, and Ahmed Abdul-Malik. "The individual homes of the musicians were also places of culture, places to learn; like Max Roach, Ray Abrams, or Duke Jordan's homes. We younger guys were welcomed into their houses all the time. I met Dizzy Gillespie, Miles Davis, Leo Parker at Max's house; George Russell was living at Max's house when he composed 'Cubana Be, Cubana Bop' for Dizzy Gillespie's Afro-Cuban Orchestra" (Weston 2010, 27). However, Monk was to exert one of the strongest and most lasting influences on Weston's music.

After returning from serving in Okinawa and the Philippines during WWII, Weston slowly entered the professional music scene. He was first exposed to Monk's playing in the late forties, when he was playing with Coleman Hawkins (Randy's first musical hero) on 52nd St. As Weston recalls: "I didn't think Monk was playing at all at the time. But, I had such respect for Hawk that I said, 'This guy must be saying something or Hawk wouldn't have hired him', and I found myself going back.... I went back, listening harder and then it came to me that this was the way to play modern piano, it had everything in it ... no time or style barriers" (qtd. in Gitler 1964, 16). Weston introduced himself to the "high priest": "I went to Monk's house, asked if I could come by and visit. He said 'Yes'. I went to see him, spent nine hours at his home. He didn't speak at all, just sent vibrations like the great Sufi masters. And he refused to answer any of my questions." Monk would give purely musical instruction, communicating through the oral/aural tradition of African and Afro-diasporic expressive traditions. Weston was most taken with and impressed by Monk's "simplicity and unique sense of rhythm."

Monk's strong, percussive left hand, his decidedly funky rhythmic conception, and "harmolodic" inventiveness left a lasting imprint in Weston's playing. Monk's extensions of the bebop vocabulary would find further development and elaboration in Weston's writing and artistic conceptions, and within Monk's "mysteries" lay deeper lessons.[38] Weston learned from Monk an "ethnic connection with self-expression. You're taught to play a piano a certain way and if you don't play it that way, it's not the correct way. Without saying a word, Monk taught me, 'Play what you feel although it may not be the way it's supposed to be'" (qtd. in Gitler 1964, 16). Weston's relationship with Monk enabled him to develop his own style, percussively expressive as well as highly melodic and harmonically innovative.[39]

As young musicians on the scene working with local bands, Weston and Abdul-Malik were to an extent challenging their peers to go beyond simply running bop changes, but to hear things another way. "The power of Duke Ellington and Thelonious Monk, who were both composers who more or less played their own material, was a heavy influence on me. I admired that kind of self-sufficiency and wanted to emulate them" (Weston 2010, 58). Studying with Monk helped him dig into mental and emotional depths in his music, and actualize it at all costs. As Randy Weston said in an interview: "And what I learned most of all from those experiences was to be *myself* on the piano, not to hold back. You see, when I was a youngster in Brooklyn, playing informally at sessions, I used to be doing some things that were considered rather far-out. Because some of the other young musicians didn't quite get what I was doing, I lost some of my confidence and came to hold back in my playing. Monk's message—*the message in his music*—was freedom. I learned to play what *I* felt and thought" (qtd. in Hentoff 1964, 34).

Weston spent every summer from 1950 to 1960 in the Berkshires, working as a cook in a resort not far from Music Inn. Music Inn was a "cultural center" and resort that, due largely to the work of Marshall Stearns, was becoming a site for showcasing "folk arts" and artists were celebrated and anointed with high art legitimacy. Stearns had a "pan-African concept" and instituted a jazz program consisting of musicians and speakers. Eventually, Weston began playing piano for the history of jazz series and would work in collaboration with Stearns on presentations and lectures. Beginning 1958 Stearns and Weston began to present a history of jazz series in public schools and universities around the country. They would trace the history of the music from its West African roots, through Caribbean styles, early jazz and blues, big band swing and modern jazz. At Music Inn, Weston was not only able to study and refine his technique and compositions but was also exposed to musicians and artists like the dancer-choreographer Geoffrey Holder, writer Langston Hughes, Willie "the Lion" Smith, percussionists Olatunji and Candido, and the calypsonian Macbeth. It was from Macbeth that Weston learned to swing waltzes and began to compose in 3/4 and 6/8 time and began experimenting with calypso-inspired melodies.

In 1954 Weston became the first modern jazz artist to record on Riverside Records, a solo piano recording of Cole Porter standards. He also went to work for the label in the shipping department. He released a second 10" on Riverside, *Trio and Solo*, which contained an initial version of "Pam's Waltz." However, not until his third LP do we really see the directions that Weston was headed. *Get Happy*, released in 1956, revealed a strong gospel influence, Monk-inspired melodic phrasings, and his percussive attack. His version of the traditional West Indian tune "Fire Down Below" signaled some of the motions on his musical horizon and reflected his Brooklyn past and present. He would record several calypsos during this time period. On *Jazz Bohemia* he records the classic calypso "Hold 'Em Joe"; on *Modern Art of Jazz* he does a version of "Run Joe" (the highlights of which include the beautifully melodic trumpet solo of Ray Copeland).

In 1957 Weston met Melba Liston, who became an essential collaborator in his work. Randy Weston teamed up with Melba Liston in 1959 to create the album *Little Niles*, dedicated to his two children Niles and Pamela. All of the selections on the album are in 3/4 time and arranged by Liston, who also plays trombone on the record. Liston, originally from Kansas City, made a name for herself early on the West Coast, working with and arranging for the big bands of Gillespie and Quincy Jones. As saxophonist Vi Redd put it, "Melba didn't write easy," and her skill with her pen and her instrument challenged the homosocial domain of the jazz world, and achieved her a begrudging acceptance and eventual respect from her male counterparts as a "triple threat"—writer, arranger, and player.[40] So when, Melba and Randy entered the studio that spring, it was a meeting of minds and a convergence of diverse influences, histories, and experiences, in waltz time.

Randy states that the musical influences for *Little Niles* were "American, African and Asian," and the rich, textural colors, incisive and insightful melodies, performed by a standard septet structure (Copeland and Idrees Sulieman on trumpets, Johnny Griffin on saxophone, Liston on trombone, George Joyner and Charlie Persip on bass and drums, respectively), reveal that there is more to imagining Africa than just changing instrumentation. Langston Hughes describes this music in the liner notes: "Modern tone poems, impressionistic pictures, cool tantalizers of the imagination are the lyrically lovely compositions in sound by Randy Weston." These are more than just songs; they operate on a much higher plane. This is a music very much alive, vital, and enmeshed in the ecology of the wider world and the lives of the listeners.[41]

After recording *Uhuru Afrika* in 1961, Weston went on a tour of Africa sponsored by the State Department and the American Society of African Culture.[42] Weston went as part of a delegation that included Langston Hughes, Geoffrey Holder, Al Minns, Nina Simone, Booker Ervin, and Clarence "Scoby" Stroman. At this juncture in Cold War politics the State Department was utilizing black American emissaries as a propagandistic means of diffusing socialist and/or Soviet influence. Jazz, as part of mainstream American popular culture, was a symbol of freedom, and by extension free trade and free enterprise. At the same time that the music and musicians and their music were being appropriated by the federal government to symbolically influence the directions of decolonization, it was also allowing and enabling musicians, writers, thinkers, and artists the chance to travel and gain firsthand knowledge of Africa and her peoples. The same political and economic forces shaping the conditions of neocolonialism were fostering Third World solidarity. Having grown up in the rich musical environment of Brooklyn as a child of the African diaspora, imbibing the music and culture of Afro-America and the Afro-Caribbean from his parents and surroundings, for Weston his first trip to Africa bridged the black diaspora and Africa on both a musical and personal level. While in Nigeria he played with and saw musicians like Fela Kuti and Bobby Benson, and was able to experience and record some of the rich varieties of indigenous African music, and the wealth of material that these forms presented to jazz musicians. He went to Africa again in 1963 and when he returned he recorded *Highlife: Music from the New African Nations*, for Colpix Records.

Highlife contained different styles of African music ranging down the western coast to the Congo, and four inspired originals based on African rhythms and melodies both folk and popular. With arrangements by Liston, and wonderful horn work by Ervin and Copeland, *Highlife* is a return trip for listeners and reveals the circles and circuits of Afro-diasporic cultural exchange, as the music returns again across the middle passage "stamped by Melba Liston's unifying vision." As one reviewer put it: "He perceived how highlife imposes churchy, three-chord harmony onto the stately motion of African choral music. Weston likes to point out that jazz, blues, gospel, highlife and calypso are different manifestations of the same musical force; each piece highlighted a different Afro-centric rhythm" (Gitler 1961, 91).

> In composing these songs, I have been very aware of drawing upon my own heritage, an invaluable part of which is the uniqueness, variety and beauty of indigenous African music. These compositions express my conviction that there is a living and vital relation between the blues-based music of America and authentic African music. I am also paying tribute to the not-always-recognized fact that African music has been the source of inspiration to and an important influence on many other kinds of musicians and composers throughout the world. (Weston 1961, liner notes)

Weston's music and philosophy strive to reveal the interchange and interrelation, not simply the debt of modern music to Africa but also the wealth of ideas and inspiration to be generated from the diversity of the continent's expressive forms and rich history. "I've always stressed in interviews whenever I've spoken in public my whole life I have reading about and immersing myself in Africa. I have been forever fascinated by and deeply interested in the history of Africa, the current problems of Africa, the triumphs of African people, the political situation in Africa.... I've always seen the similarities in people of African descent, not the differences" (Weston 2010, 82).⁴³

The music and movement of the hard bop era was a complex conversation of idioms, ideas, experiences, and expressions. What tends to be elided in the standard narratives of jazz history are the social and material conditions of production, and the cultural content that makes the music meaningful and feelingful: the notes and tones mean something, they're *sayin' somethin'*. This something cannot be understood apart from or outside of the lives of the blues people who create, sustain, and continually revitalize the music. To understand this we must return to Amiri Baraka: "It is the question that cannot be adequately answered without understanding the necessity of asking it" (Baraka 1963, 10). The long politics of decolonization, at home and abroad, and the will to be totally expressive in black sound necessarily affected the shape and direction of the music in the late 1950s. The music was and has always been a means of evoking and invoking the shape of history, memory, experience; of interpreting experience and envisioning beyond the given, of speaking to the past, present, and future. "The form and content are both mutually expressive of the whole ... both identify place and direction" (Baraka 1963, 185). In the hard bop moment the music became a means of constructing and envisioning post-colonial black identities in sound, in diaspora: echo-locating sound, sentiment, and memory. It expressed "the meeting of the tones, of the moods of the knowledge, of different musics, and the emergence of the new music, the really new music, the all-inclusive whole" (Baraka 1963, 192).

The life, times, and music of Lateef, Abdul-Malik, Roach, and Weston help clarify some of the intersections of aesthetics, politics, biography, history, and expression. Through an examination of the places, spaces, and resonances of black musical culture, we can perhaps come to a more comprehensive understanding of the stories music tells. The confluence of Cold War geopolitical and domestic developments—decolonization, the invention of the Third World, and civil rights militancy coupled with a black (inter)nationalist renaissance—was counterpointed and elaborated in black cultural practices and creative expressions. This period of musical creativity made audible (and visible) oppositional aesthetic collectivities, articulated a critical musical vocabulary of resistance, and embodied an "alternative archive" of the historiography of decolonization (at home and abroad) in sonic iconicities and allegorical forms. The musicians' immersion in diverse cultural and political matrices enabled their visions to musically and ideologically encompass, express, and echo-locate African American and Third World political aspirations and community formations at a critical historical juncture, and to create and shape sophisticated aesthetics, profound rhythmic philosophies, and poignant political visions all rooted firmly in the blues tradition. The black musical dialogue of decolonization engaged with Africa, the diaspora, the Third World, and the musics and musicians of these areas, in polyrhythmic and multi-vocal discourse. The so-called hard bop moment was an expression of unities in difference, and a vision of freedom and solidarity worked out, in and through sound. The music of the period is simultaneously the product of its historical situatedness and the result of the long-standing and ongoing musical and creative conversations, transformations, and (re)innovations of the changing same. "What we are attempting to do now is based on a dream for the future. Whether we succeed or not, we are planting a seed. If we are able to accomplish great things, this is beautiful. If we don't, we have started something for others" (Weston 2010).

By 1965 the vision of a Bandung/Third World challenge was beginning to unravel. In the United States the ghettos were erupting in rebellion, the largest and most infamous being the Watts Rebellion of 1965.[44] At the same time, US imperialist and anti-communist aggression against Vietnam was no longer a simply a "police action." In 1966 Nkrumah, the first black leader of the Ghana, first independent nation in sub-Saharan Africa, and one of the founding fathers of pan-Africanism, was deposed by a CIA-backed coup. In neighboring Nigeria the political rivalries and machinations that would lead to the disastrous Biafran war were beginning. In the mid-sixties the gains of the civil rights movement began to unravel and Black Power began its ascendancy. The "dreams of the future" would take on interesting musical dimensions in the coming years, signaled eloquently by the rise of tipico salsa (*salsa dura*) among the Nuyorican community, to which our next chapter turns. The anticolonial project of the Bandung era, as an attempt to envision a broader connected history and a wider politics, was vanishing. The "young bloods" would have to move differently. As Arif Dirlik has quipped, "after the post-colonial comes the neo-colonial."

4. "Cosa Nuestra"

Salsa "Folklórico y Experimental" 1965–1975[1]

Culture is all that we say and do. It is the way we move our hands when we speak, whether delicately outlining the pattern of our thoughts or roughly molding our passions. Culture is the reason we say "negro" to those we love, it is the warm, moist, almost liquid tropicalness of the Latin dancehall. . . . It is our walk and our talk, our highs and our sighs, it is all that we are and all that we can be.
—Felipe Luciano

Oye Borinquén

On April 15, 1966, the Palladium Ballroom on 53rd and Broadway in New York City shut its doors. The legendary venue had been the hub for "Latin" music in Manhattan; its central location attracted musicians, dancers, and music lovers from throughout the surrounding boroughs and the tri-state area. In the 1950s the Palladium was one of the most important Latin dance clubs in the New York City, known for its high-caliber music acts, dancing, and stage shows. This was at the height of the mambo craze in the United States, when Cuba (in the period before the revolution) was still effectively US a colony. The Palladium was the Latin music mecca, and the popularity of the club played an important role in disseminating and popularizing the music, dance, and the "Latin sound." In addition to booking all the top acts and dancers of the day, there were ongoing musical battles between the "big three" Latin bands in New York: Tito Puente, Tito Rodriguez, and Machito's Afro-Cubans. The Palladium played an important institutional role in the creation, innovation, production, and reception of Latin music and dance for a multiracial, multi-ethnic population in New York City.[2]

The closing of the Palladium was not only the loss of an important cultural institution to market forces and competition, but its closing also symbolized both the end of an era and an important musical and political shift that was taking place among the youth of El Barrio, the South Bronx and Brooklyn. Just as the political landscape was undergoing significant transformations in response to the civil rights struggle, the musical landscape of Latin New York was being transformed as well. The triumph of the revolution in Cuba and the subsequent cessation of relations in 1962 made New York City the Latin music capital of the world. The riots of the 1960s that marked the migration of the "racial problem" to the North and would sweep the nation in the following years began in Harlem and Bedford-Stuyvesant in 1964. That same year the Gulf of Tonkin Resolution was passed and the United States officially entered its imperial war on Vietnam. The escalating violence against the people of Vietnam would parallel the escalating racial violence at home.

The heyday of the big mambo bands was over; smaller conjuntos and charangas were dominating the scene, while the youth were listening to the sounds of doo-wop, Latin soul, and R&B and calling their new music boogaloo. By the time the Palladium closed in 1966 there was a "new breed" on the scene, a new generation of both musicians and political activists. As the ideological and organizational philosophy of the civil rights struggle was shifting to Black, Brown, and Red Power, the roots music of Latin New York was coming to be called salsa.

The term *salsa* came into popularity in the late 1960s due largely to the marketing efforts of Fania Records.[3] It was essentially industry shorthand for a range of styles and genres being performed and recorded by young, predominantly Nuyorican bands in the 1960s and 1970s. Not unlike the terms hard bop or rock 'n' roll, salsa was a marketing label to brand and promote what was being called the "new sound." In this sense, salsa was not a musical genre per se but rather a set of diverse ensembles and styles grouped under a common commercial rubric. At the same time, it was marketed as something new, the "New York Sound," a faster, rougher sound whose style and lyrics spoke more to the mean streets of the city than to the tropical Caribbean. Salsa was to become a marker of Latino identity in general and Nuyorican identity in particular. As such, salsa was more of a sound and a sentiment, an attitude reflecting the changing cadences and rhythms of urban life.

The first documented allusion to "salsa" was in "Échale Salsita," a song written by the Afro-Cuban bandleader of Septeto Nacional, Ignacio Piñero in 1933. Later, on Cachao's 1961(?) recording of the song "La Luz," after a particularly riveting round of solos from the percussion section, Cuban *bongocero* Yeyo Iglesias can be heard to shout, "*Más salsa que pescao.*" In 1962 the Joe Cuba Sextet released a song "Salsa Y Bembe" on their Seeco LP *Steppin' Out*, featuring vocalist Cheo Feliciano. In 1963 Charlie Palmieri's charanga orquestra La Duboney recorded the LP *Salsa Na' Ma'* for Alegre Records. In the liner notes, producer (and owner of the label) Al Santiago wrote (tellingly): "'La Duboney' is a musical aggregation that functions as an individual unit and possesses that all important 'sauce' necessary for satisfying the most demanding of musical tastes" (the title track was written by Johnny Pacheco). The use of salsa was further popularized in 1964 by Cal Tjader on an album recorded for the Verve label called *Soul Sauce*; the title track was an updated version of his older hit "Wachi Wara" (itself based on a Chano Pozo composition "Guarachi Guaro"). By the late sixties salsa was being used interchangeably and in tandem with words like "azucar," "sabor," and "filin" to describe the groove of Latin music, and by the seventies it emerged in popular parlance and numerous song lyrics as a generic title for the new music of Latin New York: *Nuestra Cosa Latina.*

Like the term jazz, as a musical descriptor salsa has been contested since its coinage. For many Cubans the term was a thinly veiled (if not deliberately misleading) attempt to obscure the Afro-Cuban base in the son/rumba complex of the so-called "new" music and a way for record companies in the United States to monopolize the profits generated by Cuban music under the politics of the Cold War. To many musicians and listeners it was simply Cuban music in "Boricua drag." Viewed as the bastardization or outright plagarization of a variety of distinct Afro-Cuban songs, rhythms, and genres, salsa, according to this view, was deemed to be the music of a young generation untrained in the intricacies of *auténtico* (real) Cuban music—a perspective shared by many older Puerto Rican musicians who at the time were being displaced in the market by new, younger groups, as well as by some young musicians more wedded to Cuban musical orthodoxy.[4]

Others argued that while salsa as a genre did have a Cuban foundation, the long-standing musical and cultural linkages between Cuban and Puerto Rican musicians, especially in New York City, had effectively "indigenized" Afro-Cuban music and the new generation of musicians reinterpreted and resignified the music of the Afro-Cuban working classes for Puerto Ricans on the island and in New York (Glasser 1995, 24). The music that came to be called salsa had long been played by Cuban and Puerto Rican musicians alike—each influencing the other—and thus by the late sixties it was transformed into "Latin" music, not simply watered-down Cuban rhythms. Further, Afro-Cuban styles had long been a musical lingua franca throughout the circum-Caribbean region, as evidenced by its influence on a variety of distinct styles: jazz, calypso, and meringue, among others. In the context of Caribbean New York, with migrants from all the islands, the music that came to be called salsa naturally incorporated a wide variety of styles and rhythms from throughout the Caribbean and beyond, and is thus related to but distinct from its Afro-Cuban roots.

The complexities of situating salsa and the controversies around the status of the genre point to music's abiding role in the construction and expression of identity, as well as to the "audible entanglements" that inhere between music, race, ethnicity, gender, class, and nationalism in a global capitalist context. Following Aparicio, we have to examine the term salsa from its multiple and contested sites. There is a "semantic polyvalence contingent on the cultural context in which it is listened to, produced, and performed" (Aparicio 1998, 66). Many Cubans were rightly concerned that "their" music was being co-opted and their history obscured by unscrupulous US recording companies, viewing the term as both imperialist and homogenizing. However, we want to situate salsa historically, socio-musicologically, and philosophically: first, as the label of the "New York Sound" from 1965 to 1975; second, as the sound and symbol of a young generation of Latinos (largely Nuyorican) who resignified and recombined a variety Afro-Cuban and Afro-Caribbean musics within their urban context; and, third, as an approach to music-making, a way of doing and being. Salsa is both cultural translation and transculturative practice, a relational reconfiguration and resignification of meaning and feeling in a changed socio-historical context. As Willie Colón has said, "salsa is not a rhythm, it's a concept." Again, polyrhythm and rootwork are key here.

Salsa literally means "sauce" and reveals the iconicity of style that inheres in circum-Caribbean expressive forms (as evidenced in the kaiso, son/rumba complex, and jazz). Music, dance, feeling, and flavor are interpenetrated cultural processes, mutually reinforcing practices and concepts that give semantic meaning to musical feeling. "Salsa," like "soul food," is reflective of what Raul Hernandez calls the "gustatory imperative," at once indexing the groove and pointing to the working-class origins of the music. The term initially referred to ways of playing and feeling the music: to play *con salsa* meant you were "grooving" or "cooking" ("cocinando") or playing *con filin* ("with feeling"). Like "swing" in jazz parlance, the term was initially used as adjective to describe intangible yet moving qualities in the music—to indicate particularly feelingful arrangements or solos, "tasty" licks, or precise rhythmic placement—and became a noun for the commercial packaging of the genre.[5] Like soul, its African American contemporary, salsa refers to both the music itself and its affecting presence, both style and approach. Washburne, following Raymond Williams, argues that "groove," "swing," and "feel" are the constitutive elements that create the "structure of feeling" for playing *con salsa*: "the feel encompasses what notes are chosen, how they are played, and where they are placed by the musician. The groove refers to the overall effect of those choices and their interaction. Swing is achieved when a balanced tension and resolution between the feels of the musicians create momentum within the music" (1998, 161).

Salsa, like virtually all African and Afro-diasporic musics, is inextricably tied with dance, language, and cultural manifestations of style. The musical form itself—with its call-and-response, dancer/drummer/audience dialogisms, polyrhythmic character, and the priority placed upon improvisation—demands engagement: the groove becomes feelingful and acquires meaning through active participation (dancing, singing, listening, jamming) and coming together and communing through the music. As Steven Feld concisely put it, "it feels good to know how to feel good" (1990), and it is with this notion that we can come to understand how salsa as a cultural expression of Latino and Nuyorican youth served to articulate and reinforce individual and group orientation toward shared histories, experiences, and remembrances. We must look to the cultural matrices and conditions from which these bodies of practices and peoples emerge to understand the pleasures and meanings that were made.

The foundation of salsa, like most Afro-diasporic musics, is clave. As seen in chapter 2, clave is the rhythmic organizing principle (or "cell") that not only unites the musicians and audience in musical experience, but also unites the musics of the circum-Caribbean region as a whole. As Roberta Singer has said: "The importance of *clave* lies not only in its centrality to the music but also in its importance as an identity marker. As an objective feature it marks off Afro-Caribbean music from other musics.... The historical dimension is also crucial to this issue. *Clave* is seen as one of the primary features of the music that has been constant over time. Most of the performers recognize the principle of a rhythmic organizing pattern as traditional in African and African-derived musics" (Singer 1983, 189–90). Clave structurally forms the root(s) of the salsa, while as the metarhythm of the

African diaspora it also serves both to link the musics of the circum-Caribbean to one another and the African continent and, at the same time, to remind participants and performers of both history and the present. "As the pattern is repeated, an alteration from one polarity to the other takes place creating pulse and rhythmic drive" (Amiri and Cornelius 1992, 15–16). This complementarity in contradiction moves the music simultaneously forward and backward in space and time: driving the music in the (phenomenologically) present spaces of performance and reception while continually repeating, reconnecting, and rearticulating its own historicity. Clave grounds the changing same of Afro-diasporic music in the simultaneity of its presence and absence. It is the clave that anchors our notion of polyrhythm.

Exploring polyrhythm and rootwork, both musically and conceptually, as metonyms of history and clave as a grounding principle, we can hear in salsa the complex articulations of cultural identity and expression the sound historiographies that are at once incommensurate, paradoxical, overlapping, and interpenetrated. Clave can also serve as a metaphor for the transnational dialectics of identification for Puerto Ricans on the island and in the diaspora. Like the two measures of the clave, the island and the diaspora are defined in relation to one another. Although the term salsa did not come into widespread use until the early seventies, I want to use the notions of polyrhythm and rootwork to situate salsa—the concept and the practice—in a particular historical moment and locus. Most of the generation of musicians associated with the music began performing and recording in the early sixties what would later be called salsa. As will be discussed below, we can say that—as a style and an approach, rather than merely an industry label—salsa begins around 1964 (the same year Fania Records was formed), although, as we will see, all of the elements were in place much earlier. Also, many of the record releases by artists of the boogaloo period (the style most commonly associated with Puerto Ricans and Latinos in New York in the mid-sixties) contained songs and rhythms that would be described as salsa a few years later. The production of salsa must be located in the historical context of New York in the 1960s and early 1970s, and we must understand that salsa—as praxis and process—was "pan-Latino" and Afro-Caribbean, but decidedly Nuyorican.

The histories and cultural politics of these urbanized and racialized, working- and underclass "Diasporicans" are sounded on a different level, a deeper rhythm and a lower register, told and retold through memory, desire, aspirations, and the necessary ideology of survivalism that articulates the structural position, emotional/affective predispositions, and historical conditions of a "nation on the move," coming of age in the era of late capitalism. Listening to salsa has much to tell us about the "tropicalization" of the global city that was/is Nueva York—the northernmost city of the Caribbean—with its crossed (*cruzao*), fractal patterns of circular migration and urban displacement, and the vibrant cauldron of so much Afro-diasporic production; the lived cultural identities and struggles of Nuyoricans to forge and sustain cultural community and national identity in the face of rampant discrimination, grinding economic inequality, and a unique neocolonial predicament; and finally, the socio-historical context for the production and reception of the music, its rhythms, re-presentations, articulations, and *inspiraciones* re-sounding off the backdrop of the changing same of cultural identity and political struggle.

Mi Tierra

With the US invasion and occupation of Puerto Rico in 1898, the question of its territorial status—from Spanish colony to US protectorate—has been central to political and cultural discourses on the island and in the Puerto Rican diaspora. Until the nineteenth century, Puerto Rico had remained a largely undeveloped colony, eclipsed in the empire initially by Central and South America, and later by the larger and more profitable islands of Cuba and Spanish Santo Domingo. Like Cuba, Puerto Rico experienced a sizeable increase in sugar production and cultivation in the first half of the nineteenth century, but only for a brief period. Unlike Cuba, and most of the rest of the region, the scale of the plantation economy and, hence, the demographic effects of slavery and were less pronounced in Puerto Rico. The island was somewhat exceptional in the Caribbean in that, throughout the history of slavery on the island, not only did whites outnumber people of color, but free people of color always outnumbered the enslaved, and "free" labor was predominant during the plantation regime (Williams 1971, 291; Mintz 1974, 126).

The ecology of the island also dictated the modes and relations of production; like Cuba there was a counterpoint between economy and geography. The transformation of the island from a subsistence-based to an export-based economy created two distinct spheres of production. The highlands (*altura*) were populated by small, independent farmers (*journaleros*), peasants (*jibaros* and *peones*), and sharecroppers (*agregados*) who grew coffee, tobacco, and other subsistence crops. The lowlands (*bajura*) and coastal areas were given over to sugar cultivation and the plantation complex. The general predominance of Afro-Puerto Ricans along the coastal lowlands followed the geographic distribution of the plantation system and its production and distribution needs (Mintz 1974). In the highlands, *jibaro* culture developed on the haciendas with their semi-feudal relations of production; in the lowlands, the plantation system ensured that enslaved Africans formed the backbone of the rural proletariat.

The counterpoint between commodities, geography, and relations of production was also reflected musically—"crops and *canciones*," as Glasser puts it. "The contrast between rugged interior and coastal plain, coffee hacienda and sugar plantation, peasantry and proletariat, was carried over to the sphere of folk music in Puerto Rico" (Duany 1992 [1984], 74). The dominant folk form of the *jibaros* was the *seis*, a Spanish-derived form sung in *decimas* (ten-line stanzas), in which the singers improvise over the stanzic form. The seis is generally accompanied by guitar, *cuatro* (a small eight-stringed guitar, related to the Cuban *tres* but indigenous to Puerto Rico), maracas, and *guiro* (a scraped gourd). Another important musical form of the jibaro was the *aguinaldo*. While related to the seis and retaining the decima structure, aguinaldos are traditionally sung around Christmas time.

The African-derived *bomba* evolved in the coastal towns and around the sugarmills. The rhythms of bomba demonstrate the transcultural complexity that characterizes the musics of the African diaspora. Bomba began with the arrival of Haitian slaves and masters fleeing the revolution in the early nineteenth century. Bomba played an integrative role in the slave barracks, bringing Africans of different ethnicities and the enslaved from different islands together in a shared Afro-Puerto Rican culture. Bomba is a drum dance, played on three drums (*requinto, seguidora,* and *cua*) and sung in call and response, in which dancers engage with drummers in a polyrhythmic dialogue. The requinto improvises and responds to the movements and steps of the dancers.[6]

After the cessation of the slave trade, the planter classes in Puerto Rico turned to legalized coerced labor to meet shortfalls in the labor supply. Vagrancy laws were passed in the early nineteenth century and the *agregados*, whose "crime" was being landless, were forced onto the plantations and haciendas. As coffee haciendas expropriated the small farmers, particularly after 1850, the rural peasantry, while nominally free, was tied to *hacendados* through a system of debt peonage. Sugar production on the island had always relied on a combination of slave and free labor, and from the earliest days of slavery the uneven and irregular economic development of Puerto

Rico made it cheaper for slaves to purchase their freedom than to remain in bondage. When slavery was finally abolished in 1873, slaves made up less than 7 percent of the population of the island. The rural proletariat in Puerto Rico was mixed race, while the exploitative modes of production differed only in degree from slavery. These racial and class relationships had important implications for national identity and the making of the Puerto Rican working class.

After Puerto Rico's long and unsuccessful struggle for independence from Spain, US annexation in 1898 brought "colonialism unrelieved" (E. Williams 1984). With Puerto Rico as an unincorporated territory of the United States, capital penetration, aided by tariff protection, expanded rapidly. Investment was directed almost exclusively toward the sugar sector, leading to the massive concentration of land ownership in a few corporate hands and a sharp decline in coffee and tobacco farming. Thousands migrated from the rural highlands to the cities and coastal towns in search of employment, as sugar became the major industry on the island. Workers of all hues found themselves "doing battle" (*bregando*) with the cane (Mintz 1974, 16).

After emancipation, the freed people had also begun to move around the island and around the Caribbean region as a whole. Inter-island migration came to be a defining feature of the Caribbean in the late nineteenth century. Puerto Rico received a large group of immigrants from the Anglophone Caribbean, *los ingleses*, particularly from St. Kitts, Nevis, Barbados, and Jamaica (Flores 1993, 63). The immigrants moved to the southern coastal towns, particularly Ponce, where the huge capitalist plantations dominated and where Afro-Puerto Ricans were concentrated. It was in Ponce and the coastal towns the musical form *plena* was born: "Porque la plena viene de Ponce / Viene del barrio de San Antón."

It was the coming together of rural peasantry, ex-slaves, and *los ingleses* in the coastal towns that created the plena. The development of plena is directly tied to the growth and maturation of the Puerto Rican working class in the late nineteenth and early twentieth centuries; it became Puerto Rico's first truly national music. As Juan Flores explains: "The first two decades of this century when *plena* was evolving ... saw the gravitation of all sectors of the Puerto Rican working population—former slaves, peasants, artisans—towards conditions of wage labor, primarily in large-scale agricultural production set up along capitalist lines" (1993, 64).

Plena is often described as a mulatto/a genre, a fusion of the Afro-Puerto Rican bomba, the seis of the jibaro, and the imported styles of *los ingleses*.

Plena, like the Trinidad calypso, was urban folklore, the "poor man's newspaper." A street music played on *panderetas* (handheld frame drums), the lyrics spoke to current events, politics, strikes and working conditions, gender relations, and daily experiences. The increasing urbanization and socioeconomic homogenization of a racially and ethnically heterogeneous workforce, the deepening underdevelopment of the island's economy by US capital, and the everyday lives of working-class peoples found expression in plena. The hybrid development of the music reveals the intra- and inter-island aesthetics and cross-fertilizations that are at the root of so many "national" popular culture expressions and the entanglements of class, region, and race in the construction of Puerto Rican national identity.[7] And it was this semi-rural and recently urbanized, multiracial working class that swelled the ranks of the Puerto Ricans migrants to the United States in the twentieth century.

En Clave

The Puerto Rican community in New York City dates back to the nineteenth century. Scattered throughout downtown Brooklyn and Manhattan were concentrations (*colonias*) of Puerto Ricans and other Spanish-speaking groups from the Caribbean (Sánchez-Korrol 1994, 52–55). By the turn of the "American Century," the dramatic effects of the infusion of foreign capital were being felt acutely on the island. The Depression resulted in a crisis in the sugar industry and the effects reverberated throughout the island economy. Mass migration from the interior highlands resulted in falling wages, deteriorating standards of living, and widespread unemployment and underemployment. The socioeconomic crisis on the island, the potential employment opportunities, and the close proximity to New York helped fuel emigration. Having been granted citizenship in 1917, the Puerto Rican diaspora community in New York began to grow steadily.

After World War II, the United States undertook rapid industrialization of the island, a program dubbed Operation Bootstrap (*Manos a la Obra*), offering tax incentives, low-interest loans, tariff protection, and cheap labor to expand Puerto Rico's industrial sector. As a result, the entire economy of the island shifted from agriculture to manufacturing and tourism. With the demise of agricultural production, overpopulation became an issue in the cities and coastal towns, and the government began actively encouraging the unemployed and underemployed to leave for the United States. While the earlier waves of immigrants had been largely from the professional and skilled and semi-skilled working classes, the new wave of postwar immigrants was overwhelmingly poor, unemployed, and underemployed, many lacking skills and education. "This avalanche of newly arriving families, a significant part of the country's displaced agricultural proletariat, drastically changed the character of the Puerto Rican immigrant community..." (Flores 1993, 147).

Migration during this period corresponded with the postwar economic boom, and structural transformation of the labor force in New York City facilitated the absorption of large numbers of immigrants into manufacturing and the low-wage service sector. With the growth of the postwar economy the need for white-collar workers grew; the government set up special programs that promoted upward social mobility for whites, while government subsidies to corporations and small businesses, federal housing programs, and special education programs like the G.I. Bill enabled whites to flee deteriorating urban environments and stimulated the growth of the suburbs (Lipsitz 1998). The pre-existing kinship and community networks, socioeconomic locations, variations in phenotype, and linguistic barriers, led to the overwhelming majority of the Puerto Rican migrants settling in the ethnic enclaves in El Barrio, the South Bronx and Brooklyn. The Puerto Rican migrants found themselves forced to make do with the already substandard housing and living conditions in the slums of New York, undergoing a simultaneous process of urbanization and ghettoization, living next to the remaining white ethnics (Jews, Italians, Russians, and Irish), and recently arrived African Americans from the rural and semi-rural South and the West Indies.

These demographic changes fundamentally altered the composition of the city, and New York was effectively becoming "tropicalized" by the waves of migrants from the global South. For the Puerto Ricans, proximity to the island, the continual influx of new arrivals and the patterns of circular migration sustained a process of re-territorialization.[8] New York City became the site for the emergence of Nuyorican communities and the negotiation of transnational Boricua identities, linked to the island and the circum-Caribbean through the rhythms of memory, culture, migration, and, of course, music. In the barrios and ghettos of New York, Puerto Ricans formed a transnational community, reflecting and engendering a cultural nationalism[9] that served to decouple the nation and the state through the embodiment and interpolation of overlapping and syncopated discourses of *la Tierra* (Escobar 2002). Music played a critical role in forging this transnational Boricua identity in diaspora, sonically re-presenting and re-membering *la nación en vaivén*, and keeping the community *en clave*.

The people brought with them the sounds of the island: the jibaro forms (aguinaldo and seis), bomba y plena, and the Afro-Cuban styles that, after close cultural contact, had long ago been integrated, creating distinctly pan-Latino practices. The sounds of home were transformed in new contexts and helped articulate the collective consciousness of shared history, culture, and language in a hostile climate of racial and ethnic discrimination, job insecurity and unemployment, diminishing living conditions, and chronic hardship. At the same time, Puerto Ricans entering the New York after WWII were entering a vibrant space of musical and artistic creativity. In the late 1940s, the beboppers were taking small ensemble jazz to new levels and the foundations "Cu-Bop" were being laid, after Mario Bauzá convinced Dizzy Gillespie to hire an Afro-Cuban percussionist named Chano Pozo. Around the same time, Bauzá with Machito and his Afro-Cubans were "integrating" the Palladium, and the popularity of Latin dancehalls grew with the increasing migrations.[10]

As noted in the preceding chapter, Mario Bauzá and Machito y Sus Afro-Cubans were to have a profound influence on the musical scene in New York City and beyond. Paul Austerlitz elaborates: "The vital black renaissance that Bauzá and Machito witnessed in Harlem inspired them to re-examine their identities as black Cubans and forge their own brand of musical pan-Africanism. Their music combined Harlem jazz with the supremely dance-based aesthetic of Afro-Cuban popular music, thus connecting two centers of the African diaspora" (2005, 43). The "latin tinge" in US popular music was wedded to the jazz tinge in Latin music. Bauzá's sonic ideal was not simply to superimpose jazz changes onto Cuban rhythms, but rather to use jazz elements that were structurally and rhythmically consonant with the deep structures of Afro-Cuban music. Machito's band was innovative and experimental in ways few bands could match. With Bauzá's cutting-edge arrangements, Harlem-style swing, and foregrounding of unrelenting Afro-Cuban grooves, Machito was the "king of uptown." As Austerlitz says, their music was "gut-bucket and sophisticated," quintessentially Afro-cosmopolitan. Machito and Bauzá were heavily influenced by the innovations of Arsenio Rodriguez, and brought the conga drum and clave to the fore in their compositions. In addition, their regular gig at the Palladium ballroom brought them into contact with African American dancers and listeners, and many of the dance steps worked their way into black popular music. The Palladium was across the street from Birdland (the famous jazz club); the geography of the city invited cross-fertilization. The revolutions in jazz and Afro-Cuban music fed into one another.

It is also important to remember that two of the "Big Three" bands playing Afro-Cuban popular music in the city were run by Puerto Rican bandleaders (Tito Puente and Tito Rodriguez). At the same time, a series of Latin dance crazes began to sweep the nation in the mid-fifties, providing commercial opportunities for Latino musicians to record and perform for Latino and non-Latino audiences alike, spreading island sounds through the global city. Puerto Rican musicians had been the primary performers of Cuban music in New York City since the 1930s. With the increase in popular commercial appeal of Latin music, combined with the swelling numbers of musicians and migrants from Puerto Rico and the Caribbean (and from Cuba after 1959), the well-known Afro-Cuban styles and their subsequent innovations and reinterpretations played a critical role in the creation of a transnational Latin identity rooted in the Puerto Rican community but crucially tied to a broader circum-Caribbean aesthetic (Quintero Rivera 1998). At the same time, the tremendous popularity of Cortijo Y Su Combo, and their dynamic lead vocalist Ismael Rivera, brought a revitalized bomba y plena style and sound to audiences and dancers on the island and in diaspora.[11] During the 1950s the major styles—mambo, cha cha, *charanga*—continued to emanate from Cuba; however, the stylistic elaborations and other musical influences reflected a sonic difference that spoke to new cultural exchanges, networks, and aesthetics and reflected changed circumstances and contexts.[12]

Puerto Rican and African American youth came together (*"en clave"*) in the barrios of New York City in the mid-1960s, fusing Afro-Caribbean rhythms with African American R&B, to create a distinctly Nuyorican sound, *bugalú* (boogaloo). In the late fifties the sounds of doo-wop, R&B, and rock 'n' roll had commanded the lion's share of the youth market. Boogaloo was a response to the rise of mass popular culture aimed at the new adolescent demographic.[13] The music was also the expression of the Boricua community; combining the various musical sounds of the city and put to a Latin beat, boogaloo was the musical product of the first generation of New York Puerto Ricans. Though the Afro-Cuban styles that formed the musical roots of boogaloo were intact in the early sixties, it was not until 1966 that the "new" sound was given an industry label and stylistic codification.[14] The word itself was the name of a popular dance, and there were a string of R&B hits in the early sixties with the same name. It was taken over by the Puerto Ricans to describe a highly danceable style that combined the straight 2/4 and 4/4 backbeat of R&B with the Latin tinge of Caribbean music and instrumentation. The lyrics were usually in English, with Spanish phrases thrown in, and were generally either nonsensical or fairly insipid; it was essentially party music—not protest music.

While the lyrics themselves were not overtly political, the boogaloo moment was a testament to the Puerto Rican identification with black culture and politics, part of a dynamic, diasporic dialogue between African Americans and Afro-Caribbeans. Juan Flores argues that Puerto Ricans came to a deeper appreciation and understanding of the African cultural heritage of the island upon migrating to New York. "Crowded into ghettos that invariably border on black neighborhoods, exposed to the pervasiveness and intensity of anti-black racism, and profoundly alienated by the injustices that they themselves suffer from North American white supremacy, Puerto Ricans become more aware of the multi-racial of their people and more affirmative of their African roots" (Lipsitz 1994, 78). Emerging against the backdrop of the civil rights struggle and its attendant politicizations and mass mobilizations, boogaloo represented a mass movement of its own: a cultural dialogue, cross-fertilization, and a series of "lateral appropriations" between black and Latino youth locked into the decaying infrastructure of the modern city. It was an expression of their shared location at the bottom of the social ladder, an evocation of their shared "colonial" histories, and a hopeful, coalitional anticipation and response emerging with the rising expectations generated and invigorated by renewed political struggle. "The rise of the Civil Rights Movement in the U.S.A. . . . provided a language of upward mobility and advancement without deracination, seeking the rewards of inclusion into American society without deracination, seeking the rewards of inclusion into American society but not the cultural erasure that seemed to presume" (Lipsitz 1994, 79).

In 1965 the Joe Cuba Sextet, one of the premier bands of the boogaloo period, recorded a song called "El Pito," a raucous number anchored by a repeated ostinato figure on the piano, hand-clapping, and a lyrical refrain repeating "I'll never go back to Georgia, I'll never go back." Dizzy Gillespie first spoke the line on his famous recording of the song "Manteca" featuring Chano Pozo and the Machito orchestra, perhaps the archetypal song of Latin/Afro-Cuban jazz. Dizzy Gillespie and Mario Bauzá were early pioneers of the fusion of Afro-Cuban and African American musics to create CuBop or Afro-Cuban jazz in the late 1940s and early 1950s (see chapter 3).

In an early version of sampling, Jimmy Sabater, the vocalist for the Joe Cuba Sextet, took the line and made it the choral refrain, repeating it throughout the song. By recontextualizing an explicitly African American historical and cultural reference from an Afro-Cuban jazz standard, in a crossover musical style that fused African American R&B with Latin rhythms, the young musicians were simultaneously invoking a history of musical collaborations, racial discrimination, and professional musical aspirations, while resignifying the complexities of race, class, and culture for a generation of multiracial Nuyoricans, the majority of whom had never been to Georgia, at a time when the civil rights movement was being widely covered in the national and international press.

The Joe Cuba Sextet would continue their fusion experiments with African American and Latino culture on their next (and biggest) hit in 1966, "Bang Bang." The song was probably the biggest single of the boogaloo fad, reaching #63 on the *Billboard* pop charts and #26 on the R&B charts. The whole atmosphere of the recording is a party, beginning with a simple piano lick (borrowed, apparently, from a Richie Ray tune from the previous year, "Lookie Lookie"); the song builds to a *montuno* break with the vocalists singing "Cornbread, hog maws and chitterlings," and interspersed with shouts of "comienda cuchifrito" and "lechon," referencing the "gustatory imperative" through allusions to African American and Puerto Rican cuisine. The bilingualism and cultural references express a distinctly Nuyorican perspective, the party vibe of the recording aimed solidly to appeal to the youthful audience of dancers and listeners—it is classic boogaloo.[15] It seems somewhat natural that the music of the youth of contiguous and overlapping communities, united by slavery, colonialism, and continued racial and economic oppression, would fuse at this particular historical moment that, while short-lived, "forged a common space of joint African American and Latino musical expression" (Flores 2000, 112).[16]

The musicians playing boogaloo initially were ridiculed by the older musicians, who on the one hand, viewed the music as amateurish and not particularly musically accomplished (which in many cases was true),[17] and, on the other hand, resented that the popularity of the new phenomenon and the top-billing accorded to boogaloo stars was eclipsing their own careers (financial concerns were tied with professional jealousy). Significantly, virtually every older musician who decried the new music capitulated to market pressures at some point in the sixties and recorded at least one album featuring boogaloos (Charlie and Eddie Palmieri, Kako, Tito Puente, El Gran Combo, among others). It is also important to remember that—although the music emerged as a semi-spontaneous creation from the interaction of blacks, Puerto Ricans, and others as well as musicians and audience/dancers, conjoining R&B and Latin musicking traditions—once established the form was rapidly commodified by the burgeoning local record industry and local radio. It was viewed by many in the industry as Latin music's greatest opportunity to make a foray into the lucrative teen market. The label Cotique began as almost exclusively a promoter of boogaloo acts. The music became yet another youth trend to be capitalized on, due to the perception of its tremendous crossover potential.[18] There had been mambo, rumba, and cha-cha crazes in the fifties, but none of them had ever achieved the kind of mass-market and mass-audience appeal of boogaloo. However, like most pop fads, boogaloo was destined to planned obsolescence on the market.[19] This was due in part to the music itself (the style became formulaic) but also in part to the changing tastes of consumers, as well as the changing political and cultural climate of the United States, particularly after 1968.

Típico

In the late 1960s, salsa became *the* vehicle for the cultural expressions of community, aesthetics, values, and identity for Puerto Ricans, Nuyoricans, and other Latinos in New York City and the circum-Caribbean. With the Cuban revolution, the subsequent recording ban of 1961, and the embargo of 1962, New York City became the center of Latin music. After the brief but interesting boogaloo explosion, the music was transformed again, reflecting the cultural matrix and changing conditions of its production and reception. To quote Peter Manuel: "The heyday of Salsa witnessed a dramatic and unprecedented valorization of Nuyorican identity . . . salsa emerged as the voice of the barrio youth with all their restless, alienated energy and exuberant optimism" (1995, 43). The beginnings of what came to be called *salsa tipica*[20] coincided with the radical politicization of youth and students in response to the lagging civil rights movement, unrealized Puerto Rican independence, the rise of the counterculture and the heightening opposition to the war in Vietnam, as well as, the more assertive, insistent, and militant modes of ethnic identification and affiliations emerging in the late sixties. If boogaloo can be seen as an anticipation of and response to the civil rights movement, salsa was Black Power.

The success of the U.S. Civil Rights Movement in the 1960s in challenging white supremacy made African American politics and culture an important source of inspiration and information for other aggrieved communities of color. . . . As the Civil Rights Movement evolved into a Black Power Movement dedicated to securing resources and self-determination for Black communities rather than merely an end to legal segregation, nationalism emerged as a powerful tool for political and cultural mobilization. (Lipsitz 1994, 79)

In the spring and summer months of every year between 1964 and 1968 in almost every major urban area in the Northeast, the Midwest, and California, massive black rebellions literally set fire to US politics, creating both a crisis of governability as well as marking an in important "left turn" in contemporary politics. Particularly after the assassination of Malcolm X in 1965 (which had a profound impact on the shared Puerto Rican and African American space in the city), Black Power became the slogan and self-determination (variously defined) the ideology for a new generation of community-based and militant activists. The emphasis was on roots, a reassertion of identification with the revolutions in Africa, Latin America, and the Third world, as well as, a reassertion of soul, of the critical role of the "black aesthetic" and cultural expression in black political struggle. The Young Lords Party was founded originally in Chicago by radical Puerto Rican youth, closely modeled on (and frequently working together with in coalitions and political mobilizations) the Black Panther Party; the organization spread to Spanish Harlem and the other barrios of New York in 1969. Under the ideology of "serving the people," the Young Lords organized free breakfast and health care programs, political education classes, a day care center, and cultural events, emphasizing that people had to take control of the politics of their communities through garbage strikes, hospital takeovers, and local community initiatives (Lao 1995; Torres and Velasquez 1998; Melendez 2005).

In tandem with the political shift, there was a surge of creativity in the visual arts, theater, music, dance, poetry, and literature, with an explicit emphasis on political art by and for the community and an engaged aesthetic that spoke to the people's history and present. In conversation with and responding to Black Power and the Black Arts movement was an intertwined Nuyorican political and cultural renaissance. The Original Last Poets, two African Americans and one Puerto Rican (Gaylan Klain, David Nelson, and Felipe Luciano, an important activist, community leader, and Young Lords member) are a prime example of the interweaving of African American and Puerto Rican music, arts, and politics. On the 1968 LP *Right On* and in the film of the same name, backed by rumba rhythms played on congas, the Poets recited poems about the streets of New York, the everyday struggles of the people of el barrio, and the politics of economic racism juxtaposed with poems dedicated to James Brown, jazz, and Puerto Rican rhythms.[21] The radicalization of popular politics, the internationalization of political struggles, the assertions of "roots" and "soul" resonated with and reverberated through Nuyorican musical and artistic productions. "The efflorescence of Nuyorican creativity during the 1960s and early 1970s centered around self-generated projects in the arts and media, bringing people in the community their own radio, theater, art, television, and publications for the first time on a large scale" (Yglesias 2005, 10).

Salsa, like its African American counterpart soul, became an important signifier of Nuyorican identity in the late sixties and early seventies. Although the rhetorical emphasis was on típico (roots), the music that fell under the heading salsa was varied and diverse. As Chico Alvarez has said: "In my opinion, there is no such thing as salsa music or a salsa band. Salsa is that undeniable something extra, that certain ingredient that individual musicians put into their work. *It is a feeling*" (1974, emphasis added). By the early 1970s salsa had become the label for Puerto Rican music in New York, and a potent symbol of cultural nationalist identification. In many ways salsa was less a return to Afro-Cuban and Puerto Rican traditions eclipsed by boogaloo and more a reemphasis reflecting transformed political consciousness, social contexts and sonic awareness. Salsa was necessarily pan-Latino due to its musical origins in Afro-Cuba and development in New York City and spoke to the marginalization, aspirations, memories, and experiences of the new generation. As Pablo Guzman put it in the epigraph above, "This was *our* Latin thing. Not our parents."

While remaining rooted in the son/guaracha/rumba complex, salsa musicians combined their multiple musical influences (Afro-Antillean rhythms, R&B, jazz, rock) with advanced recording techniques and sophisticated production to create a distinctly New York sound. While típico or salsa dura became the dominant vein (see below), the period was filled with exploration and experimentation. The roots of salsa dug deep into the soil of Puerto Rican reworkings of Afro-Cuban traditions; however, the music itself blossomed during the boogaloo period. New York City, birthplace of the mambo and the home of boogaloo, was strategically placed to take the lead in new developments in the music. Many "classic" boogaloo recordings contained traditional rhythms and older styles as well as novel hybrids. A good example of the transition from boogaloo to salsa (the "break and the bridge") is Sonny Bravo's 1968 recording of the song "Tighten Up." The song had been a dance craze and a #1 hit the previous year for the R&B group Archie Bell and the Drells. The first half of Sonny Bravo's version is a basic cover with English lyrics, swinging brass, and the standard 4/4 backbeat. The second half of the tune the song changes completely into a slow montuno in 3-2 clave anchored by cowbell (*campana*), over a rolling piano vamp, the chorus sings in Spanish: "*apretando, se baila asi, apretando.*" The musical and linguistic changes in the song "harmonized" with the changing political and cultural awareness, a symbolic return to the polyrhythm in the heart of the barrio.

The music of Latin New York has for the most part always been independently produced and distributed, with local radio and small labels playing the leading role in recording and disseminating new music and styles; R&B and rock 'n' roll had similarly humble beginnings. But despite the various Latin dance crazes of the fifties and sixties, major labels took only fleeting interest in boogaloo and salsa, concentrating instead on the proven mass appeal of other sectors. Most of the major labels had special "ethnic" and "Spanish" music series (residual categories from the old "race" records catalogs), and some labels, notably RCA and Decca, were influential in recording and promoting Latin and Afro-Cuban music (primarily before 1959). However, with few exceptions, little effort was made on the part of the major labels to engage in any serious fashion with the new music coming out of New York in the late sixties and seventies.[22] While several independent record labels dedicated to Latin music had been around since the 1940s (Tico, Alegre, SMC, Seeco, Ansonia, Gema, and Panart—whose influential *Cuban Jam Sessions* Volumes 1–5 were to play a seminal role in the new music), the sixties witnessed the emergence of many new labels, open to and willing to take risks with younger, non-established musicians and indulge musical experimentation in the studio, signaling a shift in both the market and the times.

The Tico and Alegre labels retained a strong foothold, as established purveyors of "quality" Latin music; having recorded the biggest names of the fifties and sixties, they had also been signing and recording many of the future salsa stars in the early 1960s.[23] In addition to the older companies there emerged a new crop of labels (Cotique, Mericana, Mañana, Rico, MIO, Salsa, Mary Lou, and WestSide) that began tapping into the new sounds and new movements. Like the locally generated and community-oriented political movements of the time, the newer labels responded quickly and decisively to the call to "serve the people" (albeit for profit) and sought to capture and market the new rhythms, musical innovations, and cultural sensibilities. Although most of these companies would not survive the decade (as is common for small record labels), the creation and development of independent labels, dedicated to the recording and promotion of Nuyorican music, "salsa," for a local and transnational market was an important political move supporting and sustaining a marginalized music at the precise moment the major record labels were consolidating their dominance over various youth demographics and all things deemed popular.[24]

The population of the Nuyorican communities in the sixties was overwhelmingly young, poor, and urban, and if boogaloo spoke to the streets in tones of playful soul, the new New York sound got down into serious Afro-Cuban funk, psychedelic jazz, Latin blues, and of course, típico grooves. The music coming out of New York had a rougher, rawer sound, at once "down home" and "down these mean streets." The new music had *fuerza*, a sound that spoke to the material conditions and social circumstances of its production, its sonic qualities echoing the spatial economy of the city and the multiple cultural influences and transnational imaginary of a new breed of Latin youth. Far removed from the relaxed rhythm of the *son oriental*, the propulsive insistence (*pa'lante*) of salsa bands turned clave into a weapon of the contemporary racial and class struggles. Combining hard-driving, jazzed-up horn arrangements (with several of the most important bands foregrounding the trombone, little used in the Afro-Cuban conjunto format), solid percussion, and strong *tumbaos* with lyrics both topical and dance-oriented, this new breed succeeded in creating a powerful, working-class ("pueblo pueblo") expression in sound. "This New York sound—shaped by racial, gender, social, cultural, economic, migratory, and political ideologies and processes, with distinct instrumentation, phrasing, and arrangements—highlights local agency in reconstructing innovative techniques within and across musical traditions" (Escobar 2002, 165).

The most important record label in the history and development of salsa was Fania Records. The label was founded in 1964 by Jerry Masucci, a lawyer, and the talented Dominican multi-instrumentalist and producer Johnny Pacheco, and went on to create the "now" sound for the new generation of Latinos and Nuyoricans. They began on a shoestring budget, selling records out of Pacheco's trunk, and rapidly ascended to become *the* label of the period. Due to their ability to recruit top-notch musicians and market dominance, they were often known as the "Fania Mafia." In many ways, salsa was the product of the success of Fania (the name itself was taken from an Afro-Cuban song of the same name). Combining a deep and diverse musical roster, innovative production, and a slick look and sound, and with relatively low overhead, Fania effectively created and cornered the salsa market. The label had numerous subsidiaries (International, Vaya, Inca, Ghetto, and others), which enabled them to both attract established bands and experiment with new acts, and also to diversify their musical output (they went on to buy the distribution rights for Tico and Alegre, their main competitors). The label also had close ties to local radio, ensuring heavy rotation and strong promotion of new records and live performances. If Motown was the "sound of young America" (as Berry Gordy put it), Fania was the soul of the barrio.

As a musician, producer, and A&R man, Johnny Pacheco was one of the chief architects of salsa and the return to típico. In the early sixties he had one of the most important charanga ensembles in New York City (closely modeled musically and stylistically on that of Cuban flautist Jose Fajardo). With the founding of Fania, he switched from a charanga to a two-trumpet conjunto format and began to release a string of hits based on (and sometimes note-for-note renditions of) classic Afro-Cuban compositions. Virtually every song on his 1964 album *At the World's Fair* blurs the line between re-signification and outright appropriation. His following album, appropriately titled *Sabor Típico* (with a drawing of a black guajiro playing bongos on the cover) continues in much the same vein. Rondón (1980) has (somewhat ungenerously) called the musical movement and sound Pacheco initiated a *mantecerización* of the music, after the famous band Sonora Mantecera who were considered to have a whiter and slighter sound than some of their Afro-Cuban counterparts. While the típico style did come to predominate, the music known as salsa was a heterogeneous complex of styles and rhythms, and Fania Records was in the vanguard of its production.

In 1967 the label began an ongoing string of hit records exploring a wide variety of styles and approaches that would set the tone and stage for what was to come. The label signed a young trombone player named Willie Colón, who with his singer-collaborator, Hector Lavoe, would become one of the biggest stars of salsa.[25] His first record *El Malo* was a hit; with its jazzy breaks, boogaloo riffs, and jibaro seasonings it solidified his place in salsa with his *guapo* image as urban outlaw: "No hay problema en el barrio / De quien se llama El Malo / Si dicen que no soy yo / Le doy un puño." Although often ridiculed by more accomplished musicians for their amateurish sound and for not keeping clave, Colón and Lavoe would continue to release a number of hit records for the label. The brassy, out-of-tuneness of the wailing trombones, the free rhythmic interplay and combinations of jazz, R&B, and Afro-Cuban styles, and the unique vocal sound of Hector Lavoe, combined with the streetwise lyrics and gangster posturing to make them one of the most popular bands of the time. They spoke musically and lyrically to the marginalized youth of the barrios, and captured the New York sound.[26]

In 1967 Fania also signed Ray Barretto, the accomplished jazz and Latin conguero. His first release on the label, *Acid* (an obvious counterculture reference) uses the traditional conjunto format and moves through a variety of styles and rhythms: heavy son montuno ("Sola Te Dejare"), boogaloo ("Deeper Shade of Soul"), and progressive Latin-jazz fusion ("Espiritu Libre"). The album demonstrated the versatility and creative capacity of his ensemble (most of these musicians would later quit to form Tipica '73) as well as the range of styles that came under the heading of salsa. Joe Bataan (an "Afro-filipino") and Larry Harlow ("el judio maravilloso") were two other important acts on the roster. Bataan consistently combined soul music and Latin rhythms; his first record, "Gypsy Woman," a cover of the 1961 hit song by the Impressions, was a crossover success in the R&B market, and his popularity increased with subsequent releases. Using electric bass and guitar with a standard Latin rhythm section, he created a unique sound that moved easily between Afro-Antillean grooves and soulful ballads.

Pianist Larry Harlow's output was equally eclectic. His first record *Heavy Smokin'* combined psychedelic boogaloo with conjunto standards (his early recordings were driven by the trumpet playing of Alfredo "Chocolate" Armenteros), and he persistently experimented with fusions of traditional Afro-Cuban music and jazz- and rock-inspired sounds. He recorded a tribute album to Arsenio Rodriguez after the composer's death in 1970, and premiered a Nuyorican "salsa opera," *Hommy*, on stage in 1973.

By the early seventies, Fania had virtually turned salsa into its own brand, and accompanying the new sound and ideology was a new iconography responding to and in conversation with the Nuyorican arts movement and the political developments.[27] The success of Fania was due not only to their market saturation and commercial dominance, but also their innovative marketing and the aesthetics of their album covers. They created a visual analogue to the music and the scene. Most of the early work was done by WE-2 graphics, an independent graphics company composed of Izzy Sanabria and Walter Velez. Sanabria had been designing covers since the late fifties for labels like Panart and Alegre, and was the mastermind behind most and (certainly the most memorable) album covers on the label. Blending pop art, psychedelia, drawings, and photography, referencing street life, urban decay, drug culture, and jíbaro nostalgia, the new album covers combined urban surrealism, ghetto realism, and tropical fantasy to create a truly Nuyorican style of representation (Yglesias 2005). The grooves on the record were the soundtrack and the LP cover became a canvas for the sonic and iconographic expression of Nuyorican identity and reality.[28]

Within this maelstrom of Nuyorican creativity, the típico sound became both a marker of identity and a marketing strategy. Not simply a reversion to the Afro-Cuban styles, típico was rootwork and re-signification, a dialectic of tradition and experimentation. The clave was reemphasized and many of the musicians went back to the strict 2/3 and 3/2 syncopation—but this clave was harder: the tumbaos were deeper and more ominous, the drive of the timbales, the voicings for the horn arrangements were more complex harmonically and played with frenetic intensity. The whole effect was to re-sound everyday life in the city: it was *popular* music. Salsa became, as Rondón put it, the music of the urban Caribbean, musical diasporas and circular migrations in sound. The old Afro-Cuban records of the classic conjuntos were archives and study guides; the songs and styles of the "old school" became the raw materials for the "new breed." In the charged context of the 1960s and in the wake of the wake of Third World revolutions, the return to older Afro-Cuban forms was itself a political act, "an identification with and an allegiance to the notion of historical continuity that is a basic ideological precept of Third World movements for self-determination" (Singer 1983, 185).

Musicians and dancers kept the son/guaracha/rumba/complex alive and thriving from the forties on; thus, típico was a continuation and an extension. Though solidly based on the sound of earlier conjuntos, the Afro-Cuban antecedent was rootworked through subtle sonic and structural alterations; and the new social context transformed the cultural significance of the genres into deep signifiers of Boricua identity. Whole tunes were studied, "rican-structed," and "versioned."[29] The music of the legendary conjuntos of the fifties was revitalized and revalorized in the service of Nuyorican aesthetics and the context of political struggle. Significantly, Arsenio Rodriguez was one of the most important composers for the musicians of the típico period, not only in terms of the sheer quantity of his compositions that were recorded and re-recorded; more importantly, his son montuno style prefigured and embodied the típico sound, and many young composers emulated his ideas. "[T]he son montuno's defining features of contratiempo, sonic power and density, and climatic energy, as well as its allotment for solos in its arrangement scheme endure as core aesthetic values ... of salsa dura" (García 2006, 124). The innovations Arsenio introduced decades earlier became defining features of the New York salsa sound, and at the same time his emphasis on African roots lyrically and musically resonated with the political landscape.[30]

Eddie Palmieri stated that the key to the music was "the rhythmic phrasings of the instruments." He went on: "I can use the same phrasings as the groups use [Arsenio, Chappotin, et al.], and I could extend it and build master structures around it—make such high-tension chords that everybody would blow their minds—but the phrasing would not disrupt the rhythmic patterns. Rhythm is your foundation." This is a clear and succinct description of the music of the típico era: old tunes were recycled and "sampled" either as whole songs or fragments; new compositions were inspired by older techniques; songs were arranged with more complex chord voicings and progressive harmonies; the funky, bass-heavy tumbao (pioneered by Arsenio) was given center stage and driven by the rhythm of the clave. However, típico was not overdetermined by Afro-Cuban influences; although fifties Afro-Cuban conjunto sound predominated, it was not a monolithic moment. It was a heterogeneous sound, drawing on a wider body of musics, motions, and conversations that were all simultaneously being articulated as Nuyorican identity. Groups like La Conspiracion, La Conquistadora, La Tentacion, La Uñica, La Flamboyan, La Protesta, Sonora Poncena, and Roberto Roena Y Su Apollo Sound all innovated the Afro-Caribbean/Cuban styles and were equally fluent in the Puerto Rican "national" styles of bomba and plena.[31]

To understand the rich complexity of the típico moment, a closer examination of two groups is in order. In the early sixties pianist Eddie Palmieri founded an incredible band aptly dubbed La Perfecta. This band, fronted by vocalist Ismael Quintana, institutionalized the trombone frontline sound (which would later be adapted by Willie Colón). La Perfecta was one of those "apocalyptic" units in music history, highly skilled, wildly popular, and swinging. Palmieri was one of the most innovative and experimental piano players on the Latin scene,[32] and the band was on fire, playing some of the hottest music of the típico period. They recorded epic albums for Alegre and Tico before disbanding in 1969. That year Palmieri put out an album that was more experimental. *Justicia* (the title itself an index of Eddie's concern with social change and racial justice; he studied sociology at the New School) was an eclectic and bewildering blend of styles and influences, ranging from traditional guaguanco "Lindo Yambu" to the moody, modal extended jazz improvisations of "My Spiritual Indian," and a version of "Somewhere" from *West Side Story*. The record was a hint of what was to come.

In 1970 Palmieri released two heavyweight LPs, *Superimposition* (on Tico) and *Harlem River Drive* (on Roulette, the label that bought Tico in the mid-sixties). *Superimposition*, as the title implies, brought together Eddie's two strongest influences: "classical" Afro-Cuban styles and "classical" African American styles (jazz). The first side consists of three típico classics: "La Malanga," Guillermo Rodriguez's "Bilongo," and Arsenio Rodriguez's "Pa Huele." The second side features extended improvisatory Latin-jazz jams, which "set modal phrases against—or even into—montuno patterns," and augmented Afro-Cuban derived guajeos with harmonically advanced chord voicings, substitutions, and alterations.

His other LP of that year, *Harlem River Drive*, was really something else. Palmieri hooked up with an African American funk band, the Harlem River Drive Singers, and brought together Latin and jazz players (including Victor Venegas, Andy Gonzalez, Nicky Marrero, and Ronnie Cuber) with funk all-stars like Jerry Jemmott and Bernard Purdie.[33] The results of the experiment are a deeply funky and socially conscious album, addressing issues of poverty, unemployment, and general conditions of ghetto living. At the same time, the grooves themselves serve to mediate the tensions of the working-class profile, and the band itself reflects the shared histories, performative locations, and potential political possibilities for positive social change. *Harlem River Drive* was a stunning artistic and creative experiment, made all the more fascinating by the political and musical context of the Típico Era. The following year the band would record live at Sing Sing penitentiary (two volumes, with Felipe Luciano as poet and master of ceremonies).

Another interesting formation of the period was the band Ocho. The ensemble began in the late sixties, founded by pianist/vibist Chico Mendoza (real name Ira Roberts, who essentially "converted" to Latino because "it was easier to get gigs"). Mendoza had been working and playing on the scene since the Palladium days, experimenting with various combinations of Afro-Cuban rhythms and jazz. They signed in 1972 as an instrumental unit with United Artists, who was expanding their "Latino Series" and around the same time buying up the publishing rights and catalogs of defunct Latin labels like Seeco and Tropical, so the musicians on the label had legal access to a wide body of sources. The band featured an all-saxophone horn section, which combined with the solid tumbao of the rhythm section to give the conjunto a James Brown–inspired funk feel; the traditional-style singing of guest vocalist Manny Roman was added at the insistence of the producers and label executives. Ranging between Latin styles, funk, and jazz, the band was solidly típico. The band's first release, the self-titled *Ocho*, was a diverse blend of old and new. The record opens with a version of Silvestre Mendez's 1950s recording "Oriza" and moves through a blend of standards and originals, with heavily jazz-drenched melodic lines over the smooth drive of the piano/vibe feel. They also included a Latin soul number, "Undress My Mind," a sort of Delfonics-inspired Latin blues with tremendous crossover appeal, but the band never got much backing from the label.

Their second release, *Ocho II*, in 1973 continued their forays into jazz- and soul-inspired, yet thoroughly típico music. The straight-ahead "El Guayabero" is juxtaposed with a Latin-jazz version of "Last Tango In Paris"; and "Guaguanco En Tropical" appears side by side with the heavy funk of "Fool 'Ja." Their third album in 1974, *Tres*, continued the musical explorations, including típico standards and a James Brown–inspired "Hot Pants Road." Despite their experimental approach, Ocho was one of the bands from the típico period most in line with Arsenio's musical vision in their compositions, arrangements, breaks, rhythms, and executions, even down to the sonics of their recordings (listen to their "Oriza" back to back with Arsenio's "No Ha Viste Caridad"). Ocho's aesthetic choices updated and re-vamped Arsenio's *sound ideal* ("musical metaphysics"), infusing jazz and funk into a Nuyorican típico style; and, to reflect the funkiness and particularity of the historical moment, the members of Ocho were all African Americans.

The cultural moment that was típico was a fertile and diverse time of musical and community formation and expression—a fascinating cultural conjunction in which Latinos (mainly Puerto Ricans, Dominicans, and some Cubans) and some African Americans, emerging from the cross-fertilizations and exchanges of the boogaloo moment and the civil rights struggle, into the Black Power context, began to make new motions in the music. By symbolically and musically returning to the roots, mainly Afro-Cuban, re-signifying and re-creating them through musical and ideological operations, Nuyoricans produced a powerful music that not only captured the contemporary situation and community but also provided a vehicle for pan-Latino and Afro-diasporic identification. While a product of New York ghettos, salsa became the music of the "urban Caribbean." The renewed liberation struggles emanating from the milieu of black, brown, and Third World militancy provided further syncopation to típico's forceful assertions of Boricua identity. It was the sound of Nuyorican youth, the voice of the people, marginalized, superexploited, politically disenfranchised, and consistently oppressed who, in the midst of New York City hardship, were still able to find and create "moments of freedom" that would resonate throughout the circum-Caribbean and the African diaspora.

Conclusion

What is *funky* is history, what comes goes.
—Amiri Baraka

The popular musics of the circum-Caribbean present us with a rich mosaic of the expressions and experiences of the people of the African diaspora. The music articulates history, memory, myth, and contemporary reality; its feelingfulness derives from its ability to simultaneously re-present the past and the present, and through rootwork and polyrhythm, the continuous innovation of the tradition. The music remembers Africa in diaspora, and listening to black music informs us of the dialectics of history and cultural memory, as well as the interpenetrations of sound, sentiment, movement, and pleasure: the politics of participation. "Because participation models style, reinforces the feel of the groove, strengthens the naturalness of it, keeps it from the realm of abstraction and keeps it in practice" (Keil and Feld 1994, 171).

The preceding chapters have demonstrated Afro-diasporic musics' distinct yet interconnected geographies and temporal transformations. The music is a window onto the histories of the diaspora as well as a vehicle for re-articulating the voices of the people of the region. The musical history of African *arrivants* in the Americas enables us to focus on the dialectics of resistance and accommodation, tradition and innovation, through an examination of overlapping styles of musical transformation and exchange. "It is style and form, but it is the continuum of the content, the ideas, the feelings' articulation that is critical as well as the how of the form. Yet the form and the content are expressions of each other (Baraka 2009, 23). The development of calypso demonstrated the interpenetrations of word, sound, and power (or lack thereof) for the working classes of Trinidad in the late nineteenth and early twentieth centuries: the poetics of rebellion and resistance in a colonial context. The music of Cuba in the first half of the twentieth century highlighted the legacies of slavery and sugar, the ambivalent identifications with blackness on the island, as well as the relationships between nationalism and empire, race and nation. In the Bandung era, black musicians used music to embody and communicate a vision of Third World solidarity and Afro-diasporic unity in the midst of anticolonial revolt abroad and the deepening civil rights struggle at home. In the late 1960s and early 1970s, Nuyoricans and others rootworked Afro-Cuban and Afro-Puerto Rican traditions to create salsa as the voice of the barrio, empowered and invigorated by the renewed militancy of the freedom struggle. Throughout, all of these musics (as processes and products) served as means of identification, modes of sociality, and expressions of politics and aesthetics on a "lower register," as well as refracting the complications and complexities of the "work" of art in the age of capitalist commodification and cooptation. The interference patterns created through the examination of Afro-diasporic musics in different times and spaces reveal the polyrhythmic nature of their interrelatedness and generate an image of the sonic unity of the black aesthetic (echo-location).

There is chronologically based relay between the musics under examination, and each style is a vanguard fusion of music and politics in the twentieth century. Each musical mode provides a dynamic center, wherein the music creatively and constructively engages the social and political forces of the time periods in question. Shared cultural codes map the territory in which sound waves meet sound-ways, and people create life-ways out of no-ways. The feelingfulness that music makes ever available is learned and shared through the cultural over-toning, inflecting, and "coherent deformation" of the Afro-diasporic musical tradition. The "rightness" of sound, the "suchness" of form and feel, being in time and in tune, are affective phenomena, the products of history and experience. The affecting presence of the music abides in the iconic presentation of cultural wholeness, a "flowing architectonics" of style, vibrating through the bodies and experiences of its creators and audiences. The music moves and is moving. It is the audible sign of the collectivity: thinking, feeling, and dancing together, projecting and reflecting the inner form of this unity. Its affect operates through its immediacy, it is what it is, but this "being" is highly charged socioculturally (as well as metaphysically).

Black music's feelingful presence articulates in time a central body of cultural experience. The emotional placement and effect of rhythm, instrumentation, and sound, the sheer weight of tonality, and its will to expression, give power to the music: "we are moved and directed by our total response to the possibility of all effects" (Baraka 1963, 181). But, again, this experience is somehow more than the pitch bends, hollers, buzzing, slurred notes, muddy tones, antiphony, polyrhythms, multiple meters, flatted thirds and fifths that make it musicologically intelligible. There's a soul force behind the bewildering diversity of black Atlantic musical traditions; the groove, the entire way of "doing the do," expresses an ontology and a metaphysics, a common core of shared conceptual approaches to the Afro-diasporic processes of making music. There's a shared spirit at the affecting roots of the music, a blackness perhaps imagined but no less real. A blackness that is not tied to phenotype, but a cosmopolitan style rooted in the tradition: a certain field of force.

Physicists sometimes speak of dark matter when discussing the shape of the universe. Visible matter makes up only about 5 to 10 percent of the matter in the universe; this mass is not enough to account for the observed gravitational force. Dark matter is all the matter in the universe that cannot be apprehended directly; its gravitational force is felt, but it cannot be detected from the light it emits. We simply cannot "see" what keeps the universe from flying apart. Dark matter reveals that there is much more to the universe than just the "luminous stuff." In accordance with the laws of its own being, that deep feeling behind black music illuminates the dark matter of the changing same. This dark matter of the black musical universe is the vast fund of emotion, ideas, sounds and symbols, histories and memories, traditions and transformations that stylistically give form to the collective ethos, and at the same time make meaningful and feelingful a people's experience: a projection in consciousness of consciousness, reorganizing thought and perception as it realizes it.

As James Snead has said: "In black culture, the thing (ritual, the dance, the beat) is there for you to pick up on when you come back to get it" (Snead 1981, 150). The groove of black music, its magic with mood and memory, makes sense out of sound, syncopating black history and black identity through the groove of aesthetic participation. "The creation of musical affect always takes place within a historical context. Musical forms have meaning only as they can be interpreted by knowing subjects" (Lipsitz 1990, 169). Black music sounds a shared consciousness proceeding from the whole historical experiences of the people of the African diaspora, not as some primitive unanimity nor merely reducible to the indignities of racial oppression, the social formations of slavery or the relations of production of colonialism (Robinson 2000). In the coalescence of African styles and New World experiential sites, black music reveals a "continuous though constantly evolving social philosophy" that gives insight into the shape of time and history as well as making meanings and pleasures (continuously) available, through participation, affirmation, articulation, and re-creation of identities and identification in sound. "So the dialectic between sound and the social is the rationalizing of what it means to be *of* this place" (Keil and Feld 1994, 179).

The music indexes and references black ontology and being, and the goals of artistic expression are dialogically (re)created through the deep identification of the performers, dancers, participants, the people, and their social experiences. The "doubly social" operation of music—conjuring and re-presenting a people to themselves—reveals the music's role as cultural repository, resource, and temporal art. Rhythm is the core of black music; and that "hard black core is African" (Baraka 1969). Black music, through its rhythmic density, layered breaks and accents, percussive contrasts, and "heterogeneous sound ideals" (Wilson 1973), generates a reciprocity of grooves and an iconicity of styles and feelingful vibrations, "embodied, formed and performed, through form, performed into feelings that are enacted" (Keil and Feld 1994, 166).

Through the comparative examination of the calypso, son/rumba, jazz, and salsa, we can glimpse some of the intricate ties that bind these diverse genres together. Using rootwork and polyrhythm as structuring principles allows us to examine the ways in which history is encoded in the music and the ways in which the music is embedded in history. Black music continuously mediates individual participation and collectivity, mobilizing traditions and traditions of mobilization. The musics of the black universe are held together by the dark matter at the core of their being, the groove, creating sonic holograms and musical visions of Afro-diasporic unity: Chocolate Surrealism.

A student of music, if he goes back far enough, will find that the main source of our music is Africa. The music of the western hemisphere (not just our music)—the music of Cuba, the music of Brazil, the music of the West Indies . . . is primarily of African origin. The people of the calypso, the rhumba, the samba, and the rhythms of Hayti all have something in common from the mother of their music. Rhythm. The basic rhythm, because Mama Rhythm is Africa. Africa's children in the western hemisphere used different means of expressing their closeness to Mama. The Brazilian Africans created samba, the West Indians created the calypso, the Cubans created the rhumba and various other rhythms, and my own is blues, spirituals. All of them were different and showed different characteristics. Yet they're together. . . .
—Dizzy Gillespie

Notes

Introduction

1. The title *Chocolate Surrealism* is taken from a 1992 recording by the Bay Area–based band the Broun Fellinis. Following some of the aural clues in their music and their representations of blackness, I am attempting to use the notion of surrealism in an extremely capacious (if slightly unorthodox) sense. My use of the term is less to reference the early-twentieth-century art movement, though it is clearly related, and more to denote both a method of exposition and analysis that attempts to both evoke and invoke the musical unconscious through strategies of heterogeneous juxtaposition, rhythmic counterpoint, multiple cultural modalities, spontaneity, and disjunctive, creative approaches to the analysis of black expressive culture. The surrealist strategies have always characterized the cultural productions of the African diaspora. From Cachao to Claude McKay, from Romare Bearden to steel drums, from Jayne Cortez to Jimi Hendrix, Pixiguinha to double-dutch, Sun Ra to bacalao, the musical, philosophical, literary, visual, and everyday representations of "chocolate surrealism" abound.

2. It is useful to think of "keeping time" in a dual sense, as both performative/rhythmic consciousness and as an act of critical (re)appropriation situated at the material level. Music generates functional structures of collective consciousness within the historical dimension, and at the same time realizes inherent potentialities and latent tendencies unconsciously and implicitly willed to expression by "the shared sense of obligation to preserve the collective being, the ontological totality" (Robinson 2000, 171).

3. "To music is to take part, in any capacity, in a musical performance, whether by performing, by listening, by rehearsing or practicing, by providing material for performance (what is called composing), or by dancing" (Small 1998).

4. Musical organization presupposes social organization, just as musical expression presupposes that the members of any given society have arrived at the point where they "have something to say to each other" (Engels 1972, 173). As we shall see, in the musical contexts of the African diaspora, sayin' something is of the utmost importance.

5. Affecting presence is a notion, borrowed from Armstrong (1971), that I think eloquently speaks to the evanescent and immanent nature of the phenomenology of

musical experience itself. As Armstrong says, suggestively if somewhat cryptically, "the affecting presence exists and persists in the being language of its *what-ness*" (75; emphasis added). Music is sound realized in its own demise—time is the medium and its affectivity is its groove—"pure passing" (Zuckerkandl), the essence of temporal and spatial being or, following Whorf, "durating" (1956).

6. Leonard Meyer's distinction between "referential" (i.e., external) and "embodied" (i.e., internal) aspects of meaning in music is useful here (1956, 1–4). However, I think he establishes it in a dichotomous fashion that mistakes the fluidity of both. Music's essence lies in its transcendence of both the material and the ideational.

7. "The significant feature of musical communication is not that it is untranslatable and irreducible to the verbal mode but that its generality and multiplicity of possible messages and interpretations brings out a special kind of 'feelingful' activity and engagement on the part of the listener, a form of pleasure that unites the material and mental dimensions of musical experience as fully embodied. It is in this sense that we might speak of music as a metaphoric process, a special way of experiencing, knowing and feeling value, identity and coherence. If our interpretations of musical sounds are general, floating frames and boundaries that exist simultaneously and instantaneously, it is because we momentarily apprehend value, identity, and coherence through the 'thisness of that or the thatness of this' . . . through the simultaneous recognition of relationship and difference" (Keil and Feld 1994, 91).

8. Following Moten (2003): "[B]lackness, in its irreducible relation to the structuring force of radicalism and the graphic, montagic configurings of tradition, and, perhaps most importantly, in its very manifestation as the inscriptional events of a set of performances, requires another thinking of identity and essence" (255).

9. This notion is evident, as Nketia says, "in the musical cultures of the African diaspora which, torn from their African roots, have nevertheless created music that reflects not only their new cultural environment and its pressures and challenges, but also certain aspects of musical procedure characteristic of the African musical tradition" (1974, 157).

10. E. P. Thompson's oft-quoted preface and remarks on class take on interesting interpretive and explanatory dimensions when thinking about black culture and consciousness in the African diaspora: "Class-consciousness is the way in which these experiences are handled in cultural terms: embodied in traditions, value-systems, ideas and institutional forms. . . . Consciousness of class arises in the same way in different times and places, but never in just the same way. . . . [W]e cannot understand class unless we see it as a social and cultural formation, arising from processes which can only be studied as they work themselves out over a considerable historical period. . . . because class is a cultural as much as an economic formation . . ." (1966, 10–12).

11. As Feld (1990) puts it: "it feels good to know how to feel good." Again, it is precisely the multiplicity of registers of meaning that music makes available that provides it with its richness as an expressive mode and ritual of history, memory, and sociality. The centrifugal tensions of music's connotative and emotive density are mediated by the collective nature of its performance and reception. The groove (metaphorically and

materially) carries the collectivity to its maximum possible consciousness, expressing its structural coherence precisely through its performative character, its production and consumption, its unfolding dynamism and openness of form (of content).

12. For a wealth of invaluable historiographic and anthropological studies examining these processes of ethnic identification and formation, as well as cultural retention and reinvention in the African diaspora, see Herskovits (1990); Bastide (1978); Freyre (1986); Midlo Hall (1992); Warner-Lewis (1991; 2003); Sidbury (1997); Reis (1993); Fick (1990); Lovejoy et al. (2000); Alleyne (1988); and Thornton (1992), to name a few.

13. These regional and cultural areas can be delineated as follows: Senegambia; Sierra Leone region; the "Gold Coast"; the Bight of Benin; the Bight of Biafra; and West Central Africa. See Gomez (1998, 27–37).

14. I am drawing on the suggestive work of Hayden White (1973) and his "tropological" investigations, as well as the more recent theorizations of historicity and historiography by Michel-Rolph Trouillot (1995). I am, however, a little uneasy with White's (structuralist) analogy of historiography as grammar (1973, 29–31). I am attempting to argue that musical processes and forms ("musicking") provide a better model for historiography, since they exhibit all of the "lexical, grammatical, and syntactical" features of language without being reducible to them. Further, the fluidity and dynamism of the musical model provides an interpretive poetics that evades some of the characteristic determinisms of linguistic "meaning," while illuminating the elasticity of its social, symbolic, and communicative aspects. For useful socio-linguistic and cultural analytical comparisons see Voloshivov (1986); Benveniste (1971); Sapir (1966); Whorf (1956); Saussure (1986); Piaget (1970); Hymes (1977); Keil and Feld (1994).

In a later work, White comes closer to a musical conception when he notes that, "even if we cannot achieve a properly scientific knowledge of human nature, we can achieve another kind of knowledge about it, a kind of knowledge which literature and art in general give us in easily recognizable examples" (1978, 23).

15. The notion of the "Changing Same" actually belongs to Baraka's 1965 essay of the same name. However, the concept is initially explored and explicated in *Blues People* (1963).

16. It is useful to quote Robinson here: "For those African men and women whose lives were interrupted by enslavement and transportation, it was reasonable to expect that they would attempt, and in some ways realize, the recreation of their lives.... it was the ability to conserve their native consciousness of the world from alien intrusion, the ability to imaginatively re-create a precedent metaphysic while being subjected to enslavement, racial domination, and repression.... [I]t was the materials constructed from a shared philosophy developed in the African past and transmitted as culture, from which revolutionary consciousness was realized and the ideology of struggle formed..." (2000, 309).

17. As has been said: "history is black people." Or as Kojève (paraphrasing Hegel) put it: "History is the history of the working slave" (1980, 20).

Chapter 1

1. There are varying ideas about the origins of the word *kaiso*, but it is generally accepted that the word was a widely used early name for the calypso musical complex. According to the calypsonian Atilla the Hun: "the first word which I heard used to describe this song and dance form was kaiso. Kaiso was used to describe the song when sung as well as a means of expressing ecstatic satisfaction over what was in the opinion of the audience a particularly excellent kaiso.... Through the years I have heard the words kaiso, caliso, rouso, wouso and finally calypso in that order" (Quevedo 1983, 4). Crowley cites the Trinidadian performer Edric Connor, who said kaiso was an "African word meaning 'Bravo'" (May 1959, 59). Warner-Lewis seems to be in agreement, suggesting the word to be an Igbo expression for "good, continue," "bravo," or "well done" (1991). Errol Hill provides an alternate explanation, stating that the word kaiso is derived from the Hausa word kaito or kaitcho which could be pronounced either as "kaitso" or "kaicho"; the word is "an exclamation expressing great feeling on hearing distressing news. 'Alas! What a pity! Ba ka da kaito, 'You will get no sympathy'; 'you deserve no pity; it serves you right.'" Hill goes on to propose two alternate theories of its linguistic development. On one hand the word could have passed through various stages of folk etymology, from kaiso to cariso, to ruso or wuso, to caliso, and eventually becoming calipso or calypso (1972, 361, 364). On the other hand, he suggests that the term may have been retained in the song lyric and its musical function could have translated in the creole *sans humanité*, a conventional ending of calypso song lyrics (more on that later). Warner (1985) offers four additional etymological possibilities: 1) the Carib word *carieto*, which evolved into cariso; 2) the Afro-French creolization of the old French *carrousseaux* (an archaic form meaning to carouse), which was corrupted into *cailisseaux*; 3) the Spanish-Venezuelan topical song *caliso*; and 4) *careso*, a topical song genre from the Virgin Islands. Regardless of the word's actual origin, the multiple possibilities point to the complex cultural mixture of the region and the cross-cultural poetics and oral/aural entanglements that characterize the "subterranean convergences" of the circum-Caribbean. The words kaiso, caliso, and cariso (except in its specifically nineteenth-century female mode, discussed later) are all used interchangeably in early accounts of calypso (Crowley 1959; Cowley 1996). Throughout, I will be using kaiso and calypso interchangeably (in deference to Atilla's insistence).

2. Even in the late nineteenth century, the Afro-French character of Trinidadian culture was still pronounced. As late as 1881, the former head of the police, L. M. Fraser, stated, "in an island which never belonged to France for even a single day the French element . . . largely predominates" (in Pearse 1956, 181).

3. Liverpool (2001) points out that, given the cultural areas from which many of the enslaved Africans were taken, most of the slaves would have been familiar with the numerous and varied masquerading traditions of West and West Central Africa. This would have profound effects on carnival celebrations in the New World (62–69).

4. The planter classes established the connection between music and rebellion early on, and in the French Antilles, a series of ordinances prohibiting these assemblies were passed in 1654, 1685, and updated in 1758 and 1772 (Rohlehr 1990).

5. Also spelled calinda, kallendar, callendar, etc. The kalinda complex appears to derive from the Congo (although this is uncertain because Africa, Asia, and Europe all have stickfighting traditions) and in its stick-play and martial arts aspects seems related to the makulele and capoeira of Brazil and the makuta of Cuba (Warner-Lewis 1991, 190). Accounts of wrestling and stickfighting to drum rhythms are found throughout the circum-Caribbean area, and it remained a central feature in Haitian folk life well into the twentieth century. Early accounts of kalinda are given by Labat (1724); Moreau de St. Mery (1796); Descourtilz (ca. 1803); Pinchard (1816); Alexander (1833); Day (1852); Kingsley (1876); Hearn (1890); Puckett (1926) (see Elder 1966; Emery 1988; Warner-Lewis 2003; S. Johnson 2005).

6. "Chantwell" (rendered in creole orthography as "shàtwèl" and also spelled shantwell, chantrel, or chantuelle) may have been creolized from the French *chanter* or *chanterelle* (?).

7. Raymond Quevedo (1892–1962), better known as Atilla the Hun, was a legendary kaisonian from the earliest days of the form (the "Old Brigade"). Renown for his razor-sharp wit, highly political lyrics, and progressive consciousness, after a successful calypso career spanning nearly five decades, Atilla went into politics and became a tireless worker for the poor, oppressed, and aggrieved and a fighter for social change. He served on the Port of Spain city council and as president general of the Trinidad Labor Party. His book, *Atilla's Kaiso: Short History of Trinidad Calypso*, is an invaluable firsthand account of the music and the men and women who made it, from the eyes and ears of one of its finest practitioners. His chosen sobriquet, Atilla, with its alternative spelling, is an interesting example of Caribbean linguistic creolization, or better, "Calibanization."

8. Gayap in Trinidad is clearly and directly related to the Dahomean *dokpwe*, the Haitian *combite*, and the Brazilian *troca dia* or "exchange of a day's (work)" and, of course, exhibits features and aspects of communality found throughout the diaspora (Herskovits 1937, 290).

9. These post-emancipation immigrants added to the Afro-diasporic heterogeneity already in existence on the island. Mention here should be made of two early-nineteenth-century groups of black immigrants. First, Africans (largely Mandingo and Malinke speakers) from the West Indian Regiment disbanded in 1815, who had served with the British forces, were settled in villages around Manzanilla. Second, black veterans of the War of 1812 who had fought in the Corps of Colonial Marines against their former masters were sent to Trinidad and settled in seven villages organized according to their companies. Interestingly, it was the Americans (as they were called) who introduced the "shouting" style of Afro-Christian worship to Trinidad, with their southern-born emotional and ecstatic Baptist traditions.

10. There are interesting parallels and similarities between the Canboulay in Trinidad and John Canoe in Jamaica; and, as has been thoroughly documented, there was a bewildering array masking practices on the African continent (see Brathwaite 1971; Wynter 1970; Warner-Lewis 2003; Drewal 1974; Bascom 1973; R. Thompson 1974, 1993).

11. "In much the same way the abominable conditions of mid-20th century Kingston were to throw up form after form of the antecedents to reggae and reggae itself"

(Warner-Lewis 2003, 143). To which we may add, in much the same way that the urban blight and deterioration of post-industrial New York and Los Angeles were to create the conditions of possibility for the cultural complex that came to be known as hip-hop.

12. Interestingly, the cultural divisions between the French and British upper classes were also reflected in the divisions among the freed people, with the territories of rival stickbands in Port of Spain divided between the "French Streets" in the east and the "English Streets" in the west.

13. There are interesting parallels with the traditions of the Mardi Gras Indians in New Orleans.

14. "The bragging and defiant songs ... affirm that no woman holds sway over the singer, or he may explain in a kalenda song, 'I sell me soul, give the devil'. He may boast that he is known everywhere in the island, that he is a bongo terror, that he is a Congo lion, that he has been charged 'for murde', or announce himself as 'Lucife', he the son of the man that never surrender" (Herskovits 1937, 281).

15. Here we can see the numerous parallels between the kalinda complex and numerous other Afro-diasporic practices like capoeira, "knocking and kicking," early breakdancing, etc. The music is the meta-archipelago.

16. The female carisos resonate with African and Afro-diasporic song functions and have parallels in West Indian forms like the "parables" of the Grenadines, *pillard* in Martinique, Bel Air in Dominica, etc.

17. Robinson (2000) captures this well: "Thus the ideologic and phatic ingredients of the radical tradition of the slaves were preserved by the African creoles (who were augmented by the liberated Africans) in their culture: their language, the patois 'not understood by most policemen, magistrates and officials'; their profane festivals, such as Canboulay and the Jamet Carnival where thinly veiled disregard for Anglican and Catholic moralities abound; in their syncretic religious sects [Shango, the Shouters, etc.] and noisy wakes; in their music and dance. These evoke hostility and disgust among the Anglicized creole classes, shocked the upper classes and inspired discomfort in official Trinidad. In 1868 obeah was outlawed; in 1883 drum dances (Calenda, Belaire, Bongo) were prohibited as 'immoral'; in 1884 and 1895 the festivals or aspects of them (band stickfighting, the wearing of masks) were suppressed" (246).

18. Hosein (Hosay or Tadjah) was a particularly important Muslim religious festival in Trinidad with processions, dancing, drumming, and the creation of elaborate paper mosques (tadjahs). Like the Afro-Trinidadian carnival, Hosein came under increasing scrutiny and oppression in the late nineteenth and early twentieth centuries.

19. Amon Saba Saakana (2005) provides a brilliant and intriguing explanation for the derivation of sans humanité that is worth quoting at length: "there has been widespread acceptance that the phonology and the word are French. However, closer inspection of the word's phonology, which is pronounced santimanitay, reveals a contextually far more likely origin.... A more pertinent and logical explanation is the Asante call, asantemma ntie: 'children of Asante, listen.' Comparing the two phrases santi manite (santimanitay) and asantemma ntie, shows a simple evolution. The /A/ is dropped and the two words are contracted. The Asante term, furthermore, corresponds to the fact that the use of

'listen' and 'hear' is predominant in both African and African new world popular music" (84–85). Saakana suggests that the French translation of "without humanity" makes no sense in its lyrical context; however, if we recall Erroll Hill's suggestion of the Hausa derivation of "kaiso," the context loses some of its inexplicability. Either way the ambiguity is intriguing, and highlights the continuities and reworkings of African languages in the New World.

20. Atilla's comments must be taken with caution. Although most calypsonians were unable to make their living as full-time entertainers and had day jobs in between carnival seasons, at the same time as musicians they occupied a particular class niche that differed significantly from other members of the working class.

21. As Eric Eustace Williams points out, the unrest and upheavals were pan-Caribbean and regionwide: "The road to revolution had been marked out. The revolution broke out in the years 1935-1938. Consider the chronology of these fateful years. A sugar strike in St. Kitts, 1935; a revolt against an increase of customs duties in St. Vincent, 1935; a coal strike in St. Lucia, 1935; labor disputes on the sugar plantations of British Guiana, 1935; a labor strike which became a general strike in Trinidad, 1937; a sympathetic strike in Barbados, 1937; a sugar strike in St. Lucia, 1937; sugar troubles in Jamaica, 1937; a dockers' strike in Jamaica, 1938" (1971, 473)—to which we may add the 1937 nationalist uprising in Puerto Rico led by Albizu Campos. Throughout the region trade unionism, racial oppression, and underdevelopment were fueling class actions and nascent nationalism.

22. Gerald Clark's band backed almost all the New York recording sessions of the Trinidadian calypsonians, as well as performing throughout the New York metropolitan area (by 1940 they were playing regularly at the Village Vanguard and the Apollo Theater); he also served as an agent for Decca, and was thus at the center of the calypso boom of the thirties and forties. Clark's band fused traditional calypso melodies with strings and horn section reminiscent of early New Orleans brass music (again the circum-Caribbean flavor), and afro-Latin rhythms. The popularity of his band (among blacks and whites) in New York City had a dynamic effect on the New York City music scene.

It is significant for theorizing music and transculturation in the Caribbean to note that Gerald Clark's longtime musical collaborators and colleagues were Victor Pacheco, a violinist from Cuba, and Gregory Felix, a clarinetist from Puerto Rico. These circum-Caribbean roots/routes of the kaiso would be revisited in 1979 when the Growling Tiger entered the studio to re-record some of his classic calypsos from the twenties and thirties, backed by a band that included Daphne Weeks (piano, Trinidad), Alfredo "Chocolate" Armenteros (trumpet, Cuba), Yomo Toro (cuatro, Puerto Rico), Mauricio Smith (clarinet, Panama), and Candido Cameron (conga, Cuba).

23. Although beyond the scope of this project but complementary, Eldridge (2002) offers an excellent discussion of the calypso boom of the thirties and forties in the United States and brilliantly reads the "masked" and conflicted nature of some of the calypsos recorded during this period, as well as offering an insightful analysis of the role of the culture industry, the changing nature of the kaiso once recorded and internationally broadcast, the intricacies of race and class in popular culture, and the calypsonians

themselves as both professional entertainers and transnational islanders in the global city that was/is New York.

24. In interesting counterpoint, the calypsonians recording in the "Golden Age" were exclusively male, and their witty, political, and scandalous songs faced harsh censorship and record bans in Trinidad. During this same time period, in the United States domestic "race" records markets, the top-selling records were recorded almost entirely by women, the "classic blues" singers. This was the era of the Blues Queens (women like Ma Rainey and Bessie and Mamie Smith, to name a few), whose lyrics were far more racy, less overtly political, and whose double and triple-entendres were far more suggestive than the "scandalizing practices" of the calypsonians. Interestingly, these women, while selling millions of 78s, were being recorded by the same companies (Decca, RCA/Victor-Bluebird, Columbia, etc.) as the kaiso singers (Murray 1976; Harrison 1988; Davis 1998).

25. Sam Manning was one of the first West Indians to record kaiso and Caribbean folksong in the United States. A brief look at his biography, as an early New York–based calypsonian and entertainment entrepreneur, sheds valuable light on some of the Afro-diasporic crossings, interconnections, and "audible entanglements" in music and society. Although he did not pay his dues in the tents of Trinidad, he was still a gifted singer and performer. Interestingly, he credits the British West Indian Regiment with the spread of Caribbean popular songs (members of the BWIR were also critically involved in the racial and labor unrest in the Caribbean and the spread of seditious ideas and publications during the interwar period). Having served in the BWIR, Manning recalled pan-Caribbean development of island sounds: "the songs were carried to other islands. Men from the Regiment, garrisoned throughout the Caribbean, sang and played them. They were picked up locally, changed slightly to suit local tastes and included among the local songs. . . . By now, these songs have at one time or another reached every part of the islands, where they remain in varied versions" (from the liner notes to *West Indian Folksongs*, Decca, 1941).

Manning had both a sense of the diasporic nature of musical movement, and also the important migratory paths and crossings that gave calypso its circum-Caribbean and pan-African vitality. He was an early pan-Africanist, and an early recording (1924) was a Garveyite tribute entitled (fittingly, for our purposes) "Africa Blues." According to an article in *Melody Maker* (1936), Manning claimed to have introduced traditional African music to the American stage "when he staged and produced an African review called 'Kunykinor' [sic] ("Witch Doctor") which ran for a year on Broadway" (qtd. in Cowley 1985, 84). This is most likely a reference to Asadata Dafora's production *Kyunkor*, the highly successful first exhibition of traditional African music on Broadway, which premiered in 1933. Manning's possible involvement would not be surprising given his local popularity as both a performer and manager in the New York City music and nightclub scene, as well as his strong pan-Africanist interests. By the mid-thirties he had relocated to the UK, and in 1935 became secretary of propaganda for International African Friends of Abyssinia, an organization founded in London by fellow Trinidadians George Padmore and C. L. R. James in protest of the Italian invasion of Ethiopia. The group went on to become the International African Service Bureau, and published the periodical International African Opinion. Other significant members were Amy Ashwood Garvey, Jomo Kenyatta, Ras Makonnen and, later, Kwame Nkrumah. By the 1940s, Manning was back in the United States and, significantly, utilizing his musical/commercial connections, arranged the first recording session for country-blues singer Brownie McGhee with Savoy Records in 1944. In 1947 Manning helped produce a calypso revue on Broadway, featuring Pearl Primus and Katherine Dunham. Perhaps he met them through his early work with Dafora on *Kyunkor* (?); both women were members of African Academy of Arts and Research (AAAR), founded by Dafora and K. O. Mbadiwe in 1943 (see chapter 3).

26. The broadened popularity base also led to the rise of topical songs specifically for an American mainstream audience. These songs were clearly produced for that burgeoning market and had little or no reference or relevance to Trinidad or calypso's carnival origins.

27. Again we see the intricate linkages between culture and empire: "That calypso underwent its first vogue in the U.S. at just the moment Roosevelt was scheming to take over Britain's possessions in the Caribbean is a complicating irony that didn't escape the calypsonians' notice..." (Eldridge 2002, 632).

28. The 1935 recording of "Congo Bara" by the Keskidee Trio (Atilla the Hun, Lord Beginner, and Growling Tiger) is an excellent case in point. Sung entirely in French Creole, the song intersperses fragments from an old lavway, a kalinda of laments by a Congo prisoner, with improvised verses from the three calypsonians. Blending old and new lyrics with a jazz-styled accompaniment, "Congo Bara" demonstrates the creative recycling and re-innovation of the artists, as well as their improvisatory prowess.

29. This is the period when calypso began to enter the American mainstream. As mentioned, Rudy Vallee and Bing Crosby were so impressed with the performers they had them broadcast on national radio. Calypsos would later be covered and incorporated into the music of African American artists like Louis Jordan and Ella Fitzgerald. The kaiso also had tremendous impact on the music of Anglophone West Africa, where calypsos sold briskly (see chapter 5).

Chapter 2

1. The "affecting presence" of Cuban popular music in West and West Central Africa in particular has been well documented and deserves more than passing mention. With the launching of the Gramophone Company series of classic Cuban recordings in 1933 (*Grabation Victor* in Spanish, or "G.V.," as they were known in West Africa), the son/rumba complex returned "home" and proceeded to have a profound effect on popular musical styles throughout the continent through a sort of "long distance self-recognition." See Stewart (2000) and B. White (2002).

2. Amira and Cornelius employ an architectural metaphor to convey the clave concept, describing clave as "the keystone, the wedge shaped stone placed at the top of an arch which locks all the other stones in place" (1992, 15).

3. "The most important fact about asymmetric time-line patterns is that their mathematical structures are cultural invariables, i.e., their mathematics cannot be changed by cultural determinants. They are immune to all social, cultural, or environmental influences. One can change a time-line pattern's instrumentation, accentuation, speed, starting point, and the mnemonic syllables used to teach it, but not its mathematical structure. Any attempt to change that dissolves the pattern. For this reason time-line patterns are formidable diagnostic markers for detecting historical connections between certain New World African diaspora musical styles and those of distinctive language zones on the African continent" (Kubik, 56).

4. The circumstances, sequence, outcomes, and impact of the Haitian revolution have been amply researched: James ([1938], 1980); Ott (1973); Genovese (1979); Scott (1986); Hunt (1988); Geggus (1982, 2001, 2002); Fick (1990); Du Bois (2004, 2006), to name a few (in English).

5. Knight (1970) gives figures slightly different from those of Pérez; according to his reading of the census records, in 1774 there were 38,879 enslaved, and by 1841 he calculates 436,495 slaves, almost half of the island's population (23). Regardless, the demographic, cultural, and economic transformation was clearly rapid and profound.

6. Ivor Miller (2000) has a very meticulous essay on the history and role of Abakuá in Cuba. See also Cabrera (1954) and Ortiz (1995).

7. The contributions of other ethnic groups to Cuban culture are better documented, so it is worthwhile to list a few instances in which Abakuá cultural forms found their way into Cuban culture. As Miller points out, although Kongo and Lukumí cultures had deeper impact on Cuban culture, "only the Abakuá are endemic to Cuba" (2000, 168). The artists and intellectuals who formed the AfroCubanismo movement in the twentieth century turned to Abakuá as a symbol of Cuban national identity. In classical concert halls, poetry, the visual arts, and popular music, Abakuá symbolism, music, and sayings worked their way into Cuban popular culture. Several composers like "Juanillo" Febles, Enrique Peña, and Miguel Faílde used ñáñigo titles for their compositions. Obdulio Morales, who combined numerous Afro-Cuban cultural influences in his works, wrote several Abakuá-themed pieces; one entitled "La Culebra" draws heavily on Abakuá melodies and language: the chorus "Ven, pa'ca, cuidado con la culebra que muerde los pies" is a direct reference to a ritual chant (interestingly, this song was covered by the seminal típico band Orquesta Conspiracion in 1972—see chapter 4). Sexteto Habanero recorded a song in 1928 entitled "Criollo Carabalí," using Abakuá ritual language and rhythms; the song referred to the "nationalizing" of Abakuá as the society began to accept members from other ethnic groups and later non-blacks. In a 1948 live recording of "Manteca" with Dizzy Gillespie, conguero Chano Pozo (who was an initiate) can be heard to shout "Ua," Efik for "Listen!" Alfredo Zayas and his Grupo Afro-Cubano perform several ritual chants and rhythms on their 1958 recording *Afro-Frenetic*. Carlos "Patato" Valdez and Eugenio "Totico" Arango perform a traditional enkame (song recounting the founding of Abakuá) entitled "Rezo Abacua" on their epic 1967 recording *Patato Y Totico* (discussed in chapter 4).

8. The Arará in Cuba received some cultural reinforcement in the early nineteenth century as white planters fled the Haitian revolutionaries with their black slaves. The Haitian refugees settled in Oriente around Santiago de Cuba. The enslaved Africans brought with them their tumba francesa, adding an Afro-French cinquillo onto the transcultural matrix of Oriente. This early-nineteenth-century Haitian diaspora would have important cultural implications for the musics of the circum-Caribbean, as Haitians migrated not only to Cuba but to Puerto Rico and New Orleans as well. See S. Johnson (2005).

9. Because of their profound cultural impact in Cuba (and Brazil), their rich history, aesthetic practices, and the continued contemporary popularity of their religious practices (santeria and candomble), the Yoruba are one of the most studied ethnic groups of the African diaspora. A number of excellent researchers have detailed the syncretic complexities of their belief systems and religious rituals and rhythms in the New World, including Bascom (1973); Mason (1985, 1992); R. Thompson (1983); Murphy (1988); Amira and Cornelius (1992); Brandon (1993); Hernández (1998); Gregory (1999). What few authors have investigated is the fascinating analogue between the way in which their religion was syncretized in the western hemisphere and its connection to the New World labor regime. On the African continent the numerous gods of the pantheon each represented different locales and, while all were venerated, specific deities were central to specific ethnic groups. In the context of New World slavery, "all the gods came under one house (ile)," a curious parallelism with the production requirements of the factory system in the huge centrales. The "collapse of the spiritual geography of Yorubaland" (Sublette) was mirrored in the slaves' confinement to the space of the plantation.

10. Though I use "Congo" and "Kongo" interchangeably, it is more useful to think of "Kongo" as more of a geographical "cultural zone," not necessarily coterminous with a specific political formation (Smallwood 1975; Warner-Lewis 1991). Following Thompson, "Traditional Kongo civilization encompasses the modern Bas-Zaïre and neighboring territories in modern Cabinda, Congo-Brazzaville, Gabon and Northern Angola" (1983, 103).

11. Warner-Lewis (2003) exhaustively catalogs and analyzes the linguistic, cultural, political, and social contributions and retentions of Bantu-speaking peoples from West Central Africa to Afro-diasporic cultures of the New World and demonstrates the central importance of the Kongo in the making of the modern world.

12. The intricacies of the slave emancipation, the Cuban revolution(s), and the immediate postwar period are beyond the scope of this chapter but have been well analyzed by Foner (1972); Pérez (1983, 1988); Helg (1995); Ferrer (1999).

13. Pérez (1986) gives an excellent account of the complexities and events of this "race war" and its relationship to insurrectionary politics, peasant wars, and race- and class-based rebellion in early-twentieth-century Cuba.

14. One prominent figure in the early debates about the "degeneracy" of black cultural practices was none other than Fernando Ortiz, who began his career adapting the criminological ideas of Cesare Lombroso to the African-derived populations of Cuba. See Ortiz (1917).

15. "Rumba" has a broad meaning, referring to the music, the dances, and the general social context of performance. With the spread of sheet music, radio, and recording, the term was applied to virtually any Cuban-derived rhythm. Many songs, particularly sones, were mistakenly and/or purposefully labeled as rumbas (or "rhumbas," to use the North American misspelling). In commodified popular cultural parlance, "rumba" became a signifier for all things exotic and Afro-Cuban, with little regard for actual rhythms, styles, or genres.

16. "Music and dance are so closely bound together in the thinking of many west Africans that it is difficult to separate song from movement or playing the drum from speech. These various media blend into one another as when the drummer might say of a dancer, 'The dance she spoke.' It is in fact, difficult to find a word in any of the Western African languages that is equivalent to the Western idea of 'music'" (Stone, 15).

17. The instrumental configuration reflects its derivation from both the Congolese yuka, whose three-drum ensemble consisted of the caja, mula, and cachimbo, and the Lukumí batá drums iyá, itótetele, and okónkolo. Interestingly, in rumba the register was inverted: whereas in many African musics the lowest-pitched drum "talks" or "calls," the reverse is the case in Afro-Cuban secular styles.

18. Another way to say it is that as a down home stylistic sensibility the groove feels so right because it accomplishes the social idea or goal of maximized participation. Each voice in a stream of collaboration is at once self-referenced "hardness," an attested skill, and competence—a presence that is rewarding and revealing. Simultaneously, each voice is socially ratified as a cooperative agent, linked and immersed in a myriad of human relations that continually activate the pleasures of identity. What feels good is the familiarity of the local ethos. Simply put, "it feels good to know how to feel good" (Keil and Feld 1994, 146–47).

19. Montuno (Spanish for mountain) refers to the mountainous areas of Oriente, the eastern provinces of Cuba. Musically, it refers to the call-and-response section of the song (also called estribillo). I employ the notion of montuno aesthetics to highlight both the musical and historical orientations of Afro-Cuban musicking. The call and response between dancers and drummers, music and audiences, past and present are all captured in the concept.

20. It is significant that son arose in Oriente, the heart of Cuban revolutionary insurgencies; this added ideological significance to its musical pleasures.

21. The foundations of Septeto Nacional were actually the Sexteto Oriente, a group created by María Teresa Vera in 1926 (according to Sublette) at the urging of Columbia Records due to their competition with Victor. More interestingly, it was Vera who taught Piñeiro how to play the bass, which became his primary instrument. The history of women in what became essentially male-dominated musics in Afro-Cuba is not adequately documented or analyzed.

22. The song "Echale Salsita" is often acknowledged as the first use of the term "salsa," which would come to prominence to describe Afro-Cuban derived (so-called Latin music) in the sixties and seventies.

23. Stuart Hall expresses this concept well: "The active work on existing traditions and activities, their active reworking so that they come out a different way: they appear to 'persist'—yet from one period to another, they come to stand in a different relation to the ways working people live and the ways they define their relations to each other, to 'the others' and to the conditions of life" (qtd. in Lipsitz 1990, 11).

24. There is some contention and controversy around who actually created the mambo, with various scholars and musicians debating whether it was Perez Prado, Arsenio Rodriguez, Orestes "Cachao" Lopez, or Machito as the inventor of the rhythm. However, mambo would seem to be more a product of the circum-Caribbean musical environment in the 1940s rather than the creation of a single musician.

25. David García (2006) gives an excellent and meticulously detailed study of the life and music of Arsenio Rodriguez and the "transnational flows" Afro-Cuban music. He gives a detailed biography, recording and performance history, and enlightening musical and lyrical analyses of the sounds and symbols in Arsenio's music.

26. This song became extremely popular, and was a hit for Ray Barretto in 1972 on his important album *Que Viva la Musica*. The lyrics take on added resonance in the context of the decolonization movements, Black and Brown Power, and COINTELPRO.

27. This was the only recording of this kind put out by Blue Note during this period. While Art Blakey and others put out various fusions of Afro-Cuban and diasporic music (see chapter 3), this was the only "authentic" recording of traditional Afro-Cuban sacred and secular music released by the label. The label did release a recording of African highlife music by Solomon Illori in 1963, but these types of ventures were exceedingly rare, and therefore this recording was quite unique and significant for a label devoted to jazz in general, and hard bop in particular (see chapter 3).

Chapter 3

1. John Henrik Clarke came to much the same conclusion: "The plight of the Africans still fighting to throw off the yoke of colonialism and the plight of the Afro-Americans, still waiting for a rich, strong and boastful nation to redeem the promise of freedom and citizenship became one and the same" (1961, 285).

2. Although the term "Third World" remains a contested one, I believe it can maintain a heuristic valence in the interrogation of the post-Bandung era as long as it is viewed as constituted in process and the specificities of multiple anti- and post-colonialisms are acknowledged. As San Juan has said, "whenever there is imperial domination in any form or disguise in our 'postcolonial' transculturalized planet, there will always be a 'Third World' protagonist fighting for national popular liberation" (2000, 81). Indeed, as Shohat (1992) notes: "'Third World' usefully evokes structural commonalities of struggles. The invocation of the 'Third World' implies a belief that the shared history of neo-colonialism and internal racism form sufficient common ground for alliances among ... diverse peoples. If one does not believe or envision such commonalities, then indeed

the term 'Third World' should be discarded" (111). See also Pierre Chaliand (1989); Aijaz Ahmad (1995); Arif Dirlik (1997).

3. The history, conditions, and survival strategies of the Africans in this hemisphere (Vesey's revolt, David Walker's Appeal, Garvey's UNIA, the invasion of Ethiopia, etc.) provide ample evidence that diasporic and internationalist consciousness has a long, complex history and has made lasting and significant impacts upon black sociopolitical organization, and reveals itself as a recurrent strain of black nationalist theory. See C. L. R. James (1995); Wilson (1973); Gomez (1998); W. James (1999).

4. See Von Eschen (2004) for an excellent explication of this period. Monson (2007) provides an extensive examination of the music of this period and the connection between the civil rights movement and the politics of musicianship. This chapter is informed by her analysis.

5. The literature on the freedom movement is voluminous, and there have been numerous recent studies rethinking and retheorizing the civil rights struggle "from below." See Sugrue (2008); Singh (1994); Kelley (2004); Dudziak (2000); Payne (1995); Horne (1988), to name a few.

6. Many musicians and scholars find the word "jazz" to be a misleading, catch-all term for complex configurations of widely different yet stylistically interrelated creative expressions of musicians, dancers, and artists in the twentieth century—a term that often carries vague and/or pejorative connotations. As such, I will use "jazz" interchangeably with "improvisational music," "the music," and "black creative expression" throughout. For different views on the use and misuse of the word jazz, see LeRoi Jones (1966); Dizzy Gillespie (1979); Art Taylor (1993); Valerie Wilmer (1980); George Russell (1996); and especially Peretti (1992). Yusef Lateef prefers the term "audiophysiopsychic" music (2005).

7. See Blaut (1987); B. Anderson (1984); Jalee (1968).

8. "The power of great music, of a compelling tradition ... is the power of concentrating and pre-empting, organizing, orchestrating and distilling the significance that serves us in our ordinary apprehension of reality" (Wagner 1986, 27).

9. The discourse of black liberation has historically been a masculinist one, and jazz musicians were not exempt from this endeavor. Though not the subject of this paper, in order to (re)assess the interconnections between music and politics we must resituate gender (which gets consistently erased in discussions of the music) amidst the political economic imperatives and social factors that shape and inform the modes and meanings of the music. We must read the absence of a female presence in many of the discourses and narratives around the music not only as a sign of the devaluation and gendered bias of musicians and scholars alike, but also as a work of historical revisionism that privileges certain figures and narratives, and loses sight of the larger conversation in the exaltation of "heroic" figures. This hagiographic tradition of jazz history writing has led to numerous "intellectual" engagements with the "Great Men" of the music ("we know more about the priests than their parishioners") that conspicuously lose sight of the larger conversation between musicians, themselves, and the worlds in which they live.

For black women involved in the industry, the matrix of domination is decidedly more complex. The jazz world is predominantly (overdominantly) masculine and homosocial, and the all-too-easy conflation of black liberation, black creativity, and black manhood served to triply marginalize the crucial contributions of women as artists, participants, and supporters in the music. Despite crucial contributions by women as dancers, writers, arrangers, players, organizers, vocalists, etc., their centrality to the larger story of jazz is often overlooked. The absence of women in conventional jazz history is symptomatic of inadequately theorized notions of the nature of cultural production and reproduction. Again, the larger dialogues from which the music actually emerges get erased in the writing of history. As trumpeter/trombonist Clifford Thorton has said: "As far as Black women are concerned, I think we're all waiting for some kind of exposition detailing the role and function of women in music. And not only as musicians but as grandmothers, mothers, sisters, wives, managers, pillars of strength and encouragement—whatever! Women have been important to the preservation and furtherance of this culture. We know there have been many" (qtd. in Wilmer 1977, 191).

10. The "Great Migration" of African Americans from South to North during the first half of the twentieth century has been thoroughly documented in the historical literature. Between 1910 and 1930, some 1.4 million blacks left the rural South for the industrial North, settling in large numbers in cities like Chicago, Philadelphia, and of course, New York City (whose black population quadrupled in size during this period). Between 1900 and 1930 approximately 40,000 immigrants from the Caribbean (mainly Anglophone colonies) moved to New York City. By 1920 they constituted one quarter of the black population, and by 1930 one fifth (Kasinitz 1992; Watkins-Owens 1996).

11. The history of bebop has been well documented elsewhere. See Spellman (1966) and DeVeaux (1997) in particular.

12. "The interplay of historical circumstances, of intra-group memories, of instrumental and lyrical gestures, and of personal agency and style created a powerful Afro-modernism at midcentury and a cultural scene of lasting consequence in the American consciousness" (Ramsey 2003, 130). This idea intersects nicely with what Feld (2012) has termed "jazz cosmopolitanism" and what Monson (2007) has dubbed "alternative modernism."

13. Floyd (1995) captures quite well the spirit of the matter, to quote at length: "Inspired by the possibilities inherent in the new harmonic, rhythmic, and timbral resources, and by the 'carving' exploits of their predecessors, the young lions of the movement created a music, that in spite of its revolutionary intent and qualities, was based squarely in the tradition of the ring. The blues was its bedrock and propelling force, but in expressing the emerging values of a new age, these experimentalists (1) evolved a new harmonic conception, using extended chord structures that led to unprecedented harmonic and melodic variety; (2) developed an even more highly syncopated, linear rhythmic complexity and a melodic angularity in which the blue note of the fifth degree was established as an important melodic-harmonic device; (3) reestablished the blues as the music's primary organizing and functional principle; (4) returned the percussive sounds of ring culture to their original place of importance; and (5) expanded on the

prevailing extension of improvisation from paraphrase to melodic invention by adding to it harmonic elaborations they described as 'running changes,' the perfection and proper use of which produced prodigious improvisers" (138).

14. As DeVeaux, in a critique of LeRoi Jones, puts it: "Jones sees bop as a conscious gesture of separatism, ignoring the fact that the creators of the style were seeking, whatever their musical intentions—and they were the least political of men—a fresh form of entertainment which would allow them their fair share of the entertainment market, which had been dominated by whites during the swing era" (1997, 252). While the point is well taken regarding the economic imperatives of music-making, DeVeaux seems to have a rather narrow definition of "politics."

15. Adorno's critique of the "Culture Industry" (1967) is salient here.

16. A third and perhaps much more profound and trenchant challenge to bebop was provided by men like Ray Charles and James Brown, whose innovations and immense success in the late fifties are indications of their respective genius, as well as crucially tied to larger developments within black America and transformations within the music and the music industry. As R&B took over entirely the less prestigious popular functions of the music, jazz came to be venerated by the establishment, and, to some extent by the musicians themselves, as a "cerebral" art form of contemplation. See Harlambros (1974); George (1988).

17. Kelley's (2009) seminal biography of Thelonious Monk meticulously lays out Monk's story and captures his life, times, and truly profound contribution to the music with force and eloquence.

18. It is worth mentioning the seminal influence that Monk had on two representative figures of the music of the Bandung era: John Coltrane and Randy Weston. Both men attribute a fundamental shift in their musical conceptions to working and studying with Monk; see Simpkins (1975); Brown et al. (2010); Weston personal communication (2003). To quote Weston: "What people don't realize, despite the fact that we left the continent of Africa hundreds of years ago, is that we approach life and music just as our ancestors did; Africa never left us. When I heard Thelonious Monk play the piano he opened the door, showed me the direction for our music, *where we maintain all the traditions of African music and we create from there* . . ." (2010, 61–62; emphasis added).

19. It is also significant that Duke Ellington had a profound influence on Monk's music. According to Randy Weston, Ellington was Monk's "biggest influence" (2010, 62).

20. As Gillespie says in his autobiography: "Charlie Parker and I played benefits for the African students in New York and the African Academy of Arts and Research. . . . Just me, Bird and Max Roach, with African drummers and Cuban drummers; no bass, nothing else. . . . Those concerts for the African Academy of Arts and Research turned out to be tremendous. *Through that experience, Charlie Parker and I found the connections between Afro-Cuban and African music and discovered the identity of our music with theirs*" (1979, 290; emphasis added).

21. Asadata Dafora (Horton) was the "father" of African dance in the United States and was the first African dancer to present music and dances of Africa on the concert stage in the United States. He was an instrumental figure in the introduction and

popularization of African and African diasporic performers and dance troops beginning in the 1930s. K. O. Mbadiwe, a former student of Nnamdi Azikiwe, an important anticolonial writer and activist, was also one of the founding members of the Association of African Students, the membership of which consisted mainly of African and African American scholars and students. After independence, significantly, he became the ambassador of Biafra.

22. "Hard bop" itself was a contested term among musicians, many of whom viewed it as an industry ploy. Cecil Taylor was once quoted as saying, "the term 'hard bop' was created by white critics to make it easier for Stan Getz to get by" (Russell 1964b, 6).

23. As Yusef Lateef points out: "The musical trend was termed *hard bop* and such groups as the *Jazz Messengers* led by drummer Art Blakey, typified this new style, which to a large degree was nothing more than an extension of the music associated with Charlie Parker and Dizzy Gillespie of the previous generation.

"What actually became very popular in the sixties was already in development in the early fifties and for many of the musicians there was never a real sharp line of demarcation from one style to another during this phase" (2006, 81).

24. A point of clarification is in order here. The aim is not to rewrite jazz history as the march of the Great Men of History, or as individualist "adventure stories", in the manner of (bourgeois) historiography; but rather to highlight some of those voices that emerge from the conversation, that crystallize and exemplify in a particularly heightened and un-self-conscious way the total aesthetic and emotional placement and pattern of the tradition. "Works of rare genius in the arts are 'parts' of culture, culture made out of culture, that miniaturizes it, underdetermines the whole sense and purpose of the culture so acutely that future generations are themselves imitations of the style in which they do so . . ." (Wagner 2001, 171). The "composers," then, are significant in that while they themselves relied heavily (and inevitably) on the bebop vocabulary, they made significant expansions and extensions of the idiom, in such a way as to "underdetermine" the entirety of the musical "soundway" and distill it into new configurations. "The work of the genius consists in bringing his mind through years of practice, so into harmony with things that things can express their laws through him. . . . Every great musical thought is, in its way rather a discovery than an invention" (Zuckerkandl 1969, 223). Their works in this period were to reshape all the jazz that was to follow and introduced whole new conceptual grammars into the music. The rise of the "composers" is certainly also tied to the advent of the 12-inch long-playing record, in 1954–55, which enabled extended compositions by lengthening recording time.

25. The very styles themselves can serve as metaphors for black aspirations and reveal symbolic nodes on the continuum: the soul movement as the drive for integrative excellence; the great composers as both prophets and "bad men" manifest in their outlaw indifference; and the pan-Africanists reflecting the nationalist/separatist outright rejection of western structures and values. . . . The metaphors expand exponentially: discipline, freedom, chastisement, etc.

26. The music must be conceived as a continuous dialogue, revolving around central semiotic foci and musical/cultural sensibilities. "No one plays the main beat in West

African drumming; it finds its limit or absolute demarcation among the other beats, propels the core of an invisible music" (Wagner 2001, 166).

27. See Ingrid Monson's extended and extensive work on Art Blakey (1994; 2000; 2007). Suffice it to say, Art Blakey's attempts at musical expositions of black unity date back to 1947, when he took his first trip to Africa, and are worthy of extended treatment. Along with leading one of the seminal hard bop/funk units in the history of the music, Blakey was an early pioneer in attempting to fuse the music of the diaspora. His 1957–58 output (beyond his classic Blue Note sides with the Jazz Messengers, like *At the Café Bohemia* and the apocalyptic LP *Moanin'*) was diverse both rhythmically and musically. His catalogue includes records like *Drum Suite, Cu-Bop, Ritual, Holiday for Skins Vols. 1 and 2*, and *Orgy in Rhythm Vols. 1 and 2*. All these records utilized master musicians from the Afro-diaspora: Sabu, Candido, "Chihuahua" Martinez, etc. The *Skins* and *Orgy* sessions at times sound strained, but they call forth the symbols of pan-African unity even if they do not necessarily provide a "viable" artistic/aesthetic basis for its realization.

The African Beat, released in 1961, is an interesting outing, particularly the highlife track "Ayiko Ayiko." That this tune is in the highlife idiom is significant in itself, as highlife music symbolically and metaphorically marks the slaves' return home. The music form arose on the western coast of Africa (primarily in Ghana and Nigeria) after WWII, as the sounds of Cuban rumba and its all-important clave, and Afro-Latin syncopation of Trinidadian calypso (both popular fads in Europe and America), made their way back across the ocean on radio waves, 78s, and LPs, and were fused with indigenous guitar, horn, and percussion styles. The colonized (and decolonizing) Africans were innovating on the styles of their (formerly enslaved) sistren and brethren on the other side of the black Atlantic. Interestingly, the success of "Ayiko" (and the record as a whole) is due, in no small part, to the surging and emotive tenor work of Yusef Lateef—revealing his versatility and sensitivity in changing musical contexts, and the rock-solid bass ("base") provided by Ahmed Abdul-Malik.

28. David Rosenthal (1992) gives and analogous breakdown, categorizing them as the "hip," the "tortured," the "lyricists," and the "experimentalists" (44–45). Again, these delineations are pragmatic and heuristic, as all of these musicians played in all of these various contexts. For example, Art Blakey, the hard bopper par excellence, was also the first jazz musician to begin seriously exploring and recording Afro-diasporic collaborations (as mentioned above). Meanwhile, the compositions of "soul" jazzmen Benny Golson and Gigi Gryce were widely performed and recorded by a variety of ensembles. Similarly, Golson appears on Ahmed Abdul-Malik's *East Meets West*, while Gryce appears on Randy Weston's *Uhuru Afrika*. The examples proliferate.

29. The album covers themselves present an interesting juxtaposition. Roach's LP cover features a black-and-white photograph of three college-aged African Americans seated at an obviously hostile lunch counter, clearly invoking the sit-in movement that had begun in North Carolina that same year. The lettering is bold and black across the top of the album cover, suggesting both a pragmatic immediacy and militancy—direct political action. Weston's cover is more subtle and subdued. The composer appears in photographic negative on the left quarter of the album cover, foregrounded by banners/

stripes of black and white. The title of the LP appears italicized in the upper right corner, almost as a thought bubble emerging from the composer's head, suggesting a more idealistic (quixotic?) and visionary approach.

30. Fred Moten's poetic meditations on the "scream" provide a useful description of one of the aspects of Yusef Lateef's tonality: "shriek turns to speech turns to song" (2003, 22).

31. Above-mentioned songs are from Lateef's output from 1956 to 1962; see discography.

32. "My music, as I've said on many occasions, is a reflection of my endeavor to express beauty, to the degree that Almighty God has permitted me to do so" (Lateef 2006, 180).

33. Kelley's research shows that both of Abdul-Malik's parents had immigrated from St. Vincent in the 1920s. Interestingly, as Kelley points out, "Virtually all of his critics and fans have come to accept this story of origins"; even Randy Weston repeats this story (Kelley 2012, 92; Weston 2010, 25, 60). Hence, this claim of Sudanese heritage is fascinating on many levels. Did the story somehow explain or authenticate his eclectic musical interests and directions? Did Sudan metaphorically reference the larger African continent in Arabic ("Sounds of Africa," "Music of Nubia")? As Kelley points out, this is no mere fabrication, but rather a reflection of the sociopolitical and cultural milieu in which Abdul-Malik moved. This self-refashioning points to the diversity of cultures, ideas, and identities circulating in Afro-diasporic communities and the strong desire to reconnect with non-Western roots and routes.

34. Calypso had long been popular in the black and Afro-diasporic communities (and the mainstream), and many musicians had been incorporating calypso rhythms and melodies into their compositions for sometime (Sonny Rollins's "St. Thomas" is perhaps the best known). In the mid-fifties calypso emerged as a national craze. Harry Belafonte's *Calypso* sold millions of records and re-revealed both the danceability and profitability for the form. See chapter 1.

35. "Afro-Blue" is often mistakenly attributed to John Coltrane, due to the latter's definitive version. On Coltrane's 1963 *Live at Birdland* he is given composer credit. On Lincoln's recording of the tune, from *Abbey Is Blue*, the song is attributed to Herbie Mann and Oscar Brown Jr.

36. The personnel consisted of Clark Terry, Benny Bailey, Richard Williams, and Freddie Hubbard (trumpets); Slide Hampton, Jimmy Cleveland, and Quentin Jackson (trombones); Julius Watkins (French horn); Ron Carter and George Duvivier (basses); Cecil Payne, Jerome Richardson, Sahib Shihab, Budd Johnson, and Gigi Gryce (saxes); Yusef Lateef and Les Spann (flutes; Spann doubles on guitar); Kenny Burrell (guitar); Max Roach, Charlie Persip, G. T. Hogan, Armando Peraza, Candido, and (the ubiquitous) Olatunji (percussion); Tuntemeke Sanga, a U.N. diplomat from Tanzania, narrates the Kiswahili portions of the work.

37. Significantly, for the purposes of our discussion, "Kucheza Blues" was originally a tune written by Randy Weston entitled "Gee Blues Gee" and dedicated to Gigi Gryce. The latter had recorded the tune under its original name earlier that same year on his LP

Reminiscin'. Importantly, in 1955 Gryce, with partner Benny Golson, founded a publishing company, Melotone, to control their music rights and royalties. As Bruce Wright put it: "[o]ne of the reasons [Gryce] was setting up Melotone and Totem with Benny was that he felt that black jazz musicians were being cheated by record companies, by producers" (in Cohen and Fitzgerald 2002, 165). This bold move for self-determination by Gryce and Golson resonated with the political atmosphere and left a lasting impression on many musicians. "This was definitely a period of organizing and increased consciousness among black musicians, and Gigi was at the vanguard of the self-determination movement" (Weston 2010, 84).

38. "Monk brought the mystery back into music, a kind of magic, a wonderful way of saying you can play music beautifully going this way" (Weston 2010, 62).

39. Crouch eloquently describes Weston's influences and dimension and is worth quoting at length: "From Monk and Ellington he has learned that harmony and rhythm can work for each other, the surprising note, chord, voicing, or sound providing accentual power through its startling effect on the ear. With peerless rhythmic control, Weston uses tunes or their motives as refrains that are constantly mutated by means of subtle or dramatic changes of key, tempo, color, and meter. There is always a summoning or expanding mind at work, rendering a rich parade of life, from the part piano in the parlor to the aloofness of a master drummer in sacred ritual" (1983, 8).

40. See discography for *Melba and Her 'Bones.*

41. "*Uhuru Afrika* was not just another jazz record. It was a manifesto, a declaration of independence for Africa and mutual interdependence between the continent and its descendants. The entire project, from the music to the program notes, celebrates the bonds between Africans and the African diaspora—past, present, and future" (Kelley 2012, 61).

42. AMSAC was formed by a group of African American intellectuals and artists who had attended the International Conference of Negro Artists and Writers in Paris in 1956. The society was to be an information service, resource center, and library, promoting tours, lectures, and offering fellowships. Unbeknownst to many of its members, it had been infiltrated and funded by the CIA as early as 1957 (Plummer 1996, 254; Kelley 2012, 65).

43. As Weston has said: "For me, the most compelling aspect of African culture is its music, magnificent in its power and diversity, with drums—African rhythms—always at the heart. The music of no other civilization can rival that of Africa in the complexity and subtlety of its rhythms. All modern music—jazz, gospel, Latin, rock, bossa nova, calypso, samba, soul, the blues, even the music of the avant-garde—is in debt to African rhythms.... When we go to Africa we realize we just left, historically, because America is such a young country. We think we left a long time ago, but it wasn't very long at all when you consider that African was the birthplace of man and civilization. We are the children of the traditional music of African that happened thousands and thousands of years ago as part of a great civilization" (Kanzler n.d., 20).

44. See Gerald Horne's (1996) excellent analysis of the roots and results of the Watts insurrection, which some have called "modern day slave rebellions."

Chapter 4

1. The title of the chapter is taken from two albums that I think uniquely represent the period under question. The first, *Cosa Nuestra*, is taken from a 1970 Willie Colón record. Colón was one of the most successful salsa performers of the period, and his music was an important articulation of the spirit and sound of the barrio youth in the late 1960s and early 1970s (see below). The second reference is to the album *Concepts in Unity* (1977) by Grupo Folklórico Y Experimental Nuevayorquino, significantly featuring an all-star lineup of Puerto Rican, Cuban, and other musicians from throughout the Caribbean. The band performs an array of Afro-Caribbean music: guajiras, plena, toques dos santos, descargas, etc. The range and virtuosity make it one of the most important albums of the period. The juxtaposition of the two provides an interesting lens on the Nuyorican musical continuum of period.

2. Boggs (1992; 127–32) and Rondón (1980) give good accounts of the life and death of the Palladium Ballroom from its heyday in the forties and fifties to the decline of the 1960s. Salazar dates the closing of the Palladium to May 1, 1966 (2002, 93).

3. By 1975 the term had come into widespread acceptance to describe the music not only of New York City but also of Puerto Rico as well.

4. Mario Bauzá expresses this viewpoint succinctly: "What they call salsa is nothing new. When Cuban music was really in demand the kids didn't go for it. Now they call it salsa and think it belongs to them. It's good as a gimmick" (in Roberts 1990, 188). Tito Puente, an ardent opponent of the term, once quipped that the only salsa he knew was "tomato sauce." Jose Mangual Jr., one of the younger generation of musicians (who played with Willie Colón, among others), took a more pragmatic approach while still denying the validity of the label: "Now, you have to go along with what people are saying, so I adapted the world salsa but it doesn't really mean anything to me" (qtd. in Blum 1978, 144).

5. See Jones (1963) and Mackey (1993).

6. Bomba, like most slave musics, was alternately tolerated and outlawed. After emancipation it was generally stigmatized and associated more with "blackness" than "Puerto Ricanness" (See Alvarez Nazario 1974; Duany 1984).

7. "Music has served as one of the most important symbols of Puerto Rican cultural identity. With the growth of nationalism in the latter 19th century, when literacy was discouraged by Spanish policy it was only natural that Creole music, rather than literature, should come to be celebrated as a quintessential expression of island culture" (Manuel 1994, 249).

8. I am borrowing this idea from Pensri Ho and her recent work on Taiwanese immigrant communities in the United States (personal communication).

9. Following Davila, we can think of this nationalism as cultural nationalism, as a way of shifting the terrain of political action to cultural politics and practices; culture becomes the idiom and domain of contestation, resistance, and collective action (1997, 3). A (trans)nationalism arises at the interstices of the nation and the diaspora, expressing collective mentalities and shared sentiments of identity and alterity through cultural

production. This transnationalism has its roots in the nineteenth and the early waves of the twentieth centuries. It is significant that the great Puerto Rican composer Rafael Hernandez wrote his classic patriotic protest "Lamento Borincano" ("El Jibarito"), depicting the hardships and difficult conditions on the island, in 1930 in New York. The Harlem riots of 1935 came two years before Albizu Campos's uprising in Ponce.

10. Machito and his Afro-Cubans, an all-black family band, were tremendously popular amongst African Americans in New York. The Apollo and the Savoy, among other clubs, began to have mambo nights to respond to audiences' and dancers' desires for Latin music.

11. The contributions of Rafael Cortijo and Ismael Rivera go beyond the brief mention made here. In the fifties and early sixties, Cortijo y Su Combo was one of the most important bands on the island. Using the standard conjunto format, Cortijo (along with Mon Rivera) re-energized the bomba tradition, long stigmatized by many Puerto Ricans as primitive. They blended bombas, plenas, and guarachas, but with a distinctly Afro-Puerto Rican flavor, addressing everyday life in the ghettos to create a sophisticated urban folklore. As a predominantly black band they broke through the color bar at an important time in the history of the island, playing exclusive nightclubs and regularly on television. Although the original band split in 1962, Cortijo and Ismael Rivera both continued to record throughout the 1960s and 1970s.

12. René Lopéz states that the music of the period performed an integrative function for the community by uniting "uptown" and "downtown" styles, due in part to postwar economics and the popularity of the Palladium: "It was that music [the 'hotter' uptown sound] breaking through downtown, when Latinos and blacks were getting a little more purchasing power and could now go down to these places and spend a bit more" (qtd. in Waxer 1994, 157).

13. Musical collaboration between African Americans and Puerto Ricans, and the considerable ties between the two communities, date to the early decades of the twentieth century, and has been well documented by Glasser (1995). In the late 1950s, the street sounds of doo-wop singers competed with the sounds of improvised street rumbas. Frankie Lymon and the Teenagers, an integrated group of Africans and Puerto Ricans from New York, were perhaps the most important group of the day. They were signed to Gee Records in 1954 by George Goldner, an important producer and music impresario who also helped found the important Latin labels Tico and, later, Cotique.

14. The musical diversity of the boogaloo period belies its simplistic industry label. There were important musical predecessors to the new music, and many of the definitive bands of the period had diverse repertoires and playbooks. As Flores points out, "the boogaloo repertoire actually ranges along a continuum from basically Latin sounds and rhythms with the trappings of African American styles on one end, to what are R&B, funk, and soul songs with a touch of Latin percussion, instrumentals, Spanish-language lyrics or inflections" (2000, 88).

There were two important antecedents to boogaloo that are worth mentioning. In 1962 Ray Barretto, a conga player who (significantly) was inspired to take up the instrument after hearing Chano Pozo's playing on the song "Manteca," released a song that became a Top 20 hit called "El Watusi." The watusi was a popular dance and a hit song by the Orlons; Barretto "latinized" the groove to create a hit party record. Barretto was one of the most important congueros of the hard bop period, essentially the house conga player for Prestige, Blue Note, and Riverside (the three most important hard bop labels; see chapter 3), and recorded countless classic hard bop sessions with musicians like Grant Green, Lou Donaldson, Eddie Davis, Gene Ammons, and Charlie Parker, to name a few. These sessions were important to his own musical development as well as in advancing the fusions of jazz and African American music with Afro-Cuban rhythms. He would also play a seminal role in the creation of "salsa" and the "típico revolution" that took over the music in the late sixties and early seventies.

The other significant prelude to boogaloo was Mongo Santamaria's 1963 hit "Watermelon Man." The song itself was a popular jazz tune written by Chicago-born pianist Herbie Hancock, a gospel-inspired sixteen-bar blues anchored by a simple piano vamp, meant to mimic the rhythm of the wheels of the cart of a watermelon vendor from his childhood on the South Side of Chicago. Santamaria took the tune, added a heavier emphasis on the backbeat with congas and timbales, and added some grunts and shouts (for the party effect) to create what was essentially the first boogaloo. Santamaria was also a pioneering conguero important in both jazz and Latin music generally. Again, boogaloo, like hard bop, was a rich period of musical experimentation and cross-fertilization that elided the narrow codifications of marketing labels.

15. The crossover worked both ways. African American multi-instrumentalist Jimmy Castor, born and raised in Spanish Harlem, was also good friends with the young men who formed the Teenagers, even substituting on vocals at times for Frankie Lymon. In 1967 he had a hit on Smash Records, "Hey Leroy, Your Mama's Callin' You" ("Tu Mama Te Llama"). The liner notes were written in both English and Spanish and the song reached the Top 40 on the *Billboard* charts. Modeled closely after "Bang Bang" (which he also covered on the album), "Hey Leroy" was a swinging boogaloo anthem, combining a funky backbeat, nonsensical lyricism, and a solid groove.

16. We must be careful not to over-romanticize the clearly close historical ties between the Puerto Rican and African American communities. While sharing long-standing linkages, culture, religion, language, racism, and generational differences clearly complicated the communities' interactions. Nuyorican poet Tato Laviera captures this complexity in a poem: "El negrito / vino a Nueva York / vio milagros/ en sus ojos / su tía le pidió / un abrazo y le dijo, / "no te juntes con / los prietos, negrito."

17. Many of the records from the period are replete with bad pop tunes and generally uninspired versions of late-sixties "now" sound material ("Grazing in the Grass," "You've Lost That Loving Feeling," "My Way," etc.). While Flores (2000) argues that boogaloo was both a "bridge and a break," it seems that it was more of a musical way-station, which despite the often crass commercialization succeeded in producing some lasting and important music.

18. The boogaloo style is generally considered typical of the period from 1965–68, and the biggest hits of the time were R&B-influenced affairs. The typical boogaloo record generally contained a variety of musical styles, the familiar Afro-Cuban son, guaracha,

and guaguanco and new combinations and blends of older styles and rhythms from Afro-Cuba and the Afro-Antilles in general (e.g., Mozambique, wobble-cha, pachanga, jala-jala). The music was an amalgam of musical and cultural influences coming together in the vibrant cauldron of Afro-diasporic creativity that was New York City in the 1960s. Boogaloo provided the platform for the rise of many young Latinos who were to go on to become salsa stars.

19. Numerous musicians and historians have attributed the demise of boogaloo to a virtual conspiracy between established musicians, booking agents, record labels, and disk jockeys to silence the music. While this may be the case, this was also a period when popular musical trends were coming and going in quick succession as the recording industry and radio were playing an unprecedented role in catering to and shaping the rapidly changing tastes of consumers.

20. Rondón and others prefer the term salsa dura to describe the music of the period. I prefer típico because it highlights the aspects of rootwork, historical memory, and stylistic change that I want to interrogate. The 1974 album *Típico* by timbalero and vibist Louie Ramirez is emblematic. Moving through a variety of rhythms and genres, the album blends original compositions ("Típico," "Feo Como El Oso"), Arsenio Rodriguez covers ("Tocoloro," "Caminante Y Labori"), and plena and guaguanco standards ("Plena de San Anton," "Sabrosso Guaguanco").

21. Not coincidentally, by the late 1960s conga drums had gone from adding an exotic tinge in African American music to being a rhythmic staple in virtually all black popular recorded music, from the spoken-word recordings of Gil Scott-Heron and the Last Poets to the jazz lofts of New York and Newark, and from street rumbas in Oakland to the studios of Motown. There was a reassertion of rhythm (and hence roots) and the conga in particular, and the conga drum became a symbol of Black Power and cultural authenticity.

22. United Artists was one of the few majors actively involved at the time; their UA Latino division produced a series of important recordings in the early 1970s, due largely to the A&R work and promotion of Bobby Marin and Chico Alvarez.

23. Beginning in 1961 the Alegre All-stars recorded four volumes of *Jam Sessions*, modeled on the earlier Panart sessions. These were eloquent experiments blending the descarga tradition with jazz and the soulful sounds of more contemporary "latinidad." The repertoire included jams improvised in the studio and Latin-jazz standards. "The music was mostly classic descarga building on fairly brief head arrangements, a great deal of soloing and . . . excellent vocals with coro sections and all [not to mention some hilarious studio chatter]. . . . they were joyous and unself-conscious, their solo style echoed small-band jump as much as bebop, and they swung like the devil . . ." (Roberts 1999, 142). The Alegre All-Stars consisted of shifting personnel, a veritable who's who of the New York Latin scene; but the core of the unit was the inimitable Bobby Rodriguez on bass, Jose "Chombo" Silva (who, incidentally, was on the first two volumes of the Panart *Cuban Jam Sessions*, and was one of the finest sax players in the music), Kako on timbales and percussion, and Charlie Palmieri on piano. The latter two members also served as A&R men for the label. The Alegre crew continued the all-star jam session

tradition that would be picked up later by other labels. Tico would release three volumes of their all-stars beginning in 1966; the Fania All-stars beginning in 1968 would record two volumes at the Red Garter, and in 1971 two more volumes at the Cheetah; the United Artists all-stars ("La Crema") would record their own version of the tradition in 1973, appropriately entitled *El Party Con La Crema*.

24. This combination of commercial opportunism and cultural nationalism was not unique (the easy conflation of Black Power and black capitalism being only the most obvious). Numerous small, independent funk and soul record labels also emerged during the period, producing recordings of local talent for specifically regional demographics ignored by major record labels. Dante Carfagna has done exhaustive work on small soul and R&B labels in the late sixties and seventies (his encyclopedia of funk and soul 45s is forthcoming).

25. The dynamic output of the Willie Colón/Hector Lavoe unit is worthy of a full-length exploration. Their music consistently challenged típico convention. Colón and Lavoe innovated, recycled, and "rican-structed" old Puerto Rican forms and freely borrowed and rootworked other Caribbean and Afro-diasporic forms—Panamanian, Venezuelan, Brazilian, etc. The song "Ghana'e" was inspired by a tune he learned from an "African" in New York. The voice of Hector Lavoe (like Ismael Rivera) was evocative of the jíbaro forms and styles. They had a unique, distinct, and distinguished sound in the midst of the típico hegemony.

26. Willie Colón's early record covers reiterated and reinforced the bad-boy image. His first, appropriately titled *El Malo* (1967), pictures him and Hector Lavoe in a back alley. His second, *The Hustler* (1968), has him and the band all in a pool hall. His third, *Guisando* (Doing a Job), shows Colón and Lavoe breaking a safe; Lavoe squats and fans out a large wad of money, while Colón points a gun at the camera. His next album, *Cosa Nuestra* (1970), takes the image further, with Colón beneath the Brooklyn Bridge, dressed in black, Mob-style, standing over a body wrapped in carpet with a rock tied to it at his feet. He holds his trombone case under one arm like a tommy gun and has hat in his hand over his heart, a salute to the recently departed. Finally, his classic *La Gran Fuga* (1971), the logical culmination to a life of musical crime and infamy, took the form of a wanted poster, and on the back pictured him and the band breaking out of prison. In an interesting intersection of art and politics, designer Izzy Sanabria describes the genesis of the cover: "I had wanted to play up the whole gangster image to subvert it. I had seen those posters of Bobby Seale and other Black Panthers who were wanted by the FBI . . . from that idea I came up with [the] album cover" (Yglesias 2005, 112–13).

27. In addition to the regular releases of their roster, Fania also organized important live shows featuring their All-stars as well as producing two movies, *Our Latin Thing* and *Salsa*, in 1971 and 1973, respectively. Through independent labels and self-generated productions, the Latino community in New York created full multi-media expressions.

28. While many of the album covers of the period were extremely innovative, like the contemporary Black and Brown Power movements much of their symbolism was over-dominantly masculinist and homosocial. It was about the streets, pool halls, alleyways, and the public and private, traditionally male spaces that get claimed and reclaimed by

the dispossessed and disenfranchised of color. The majority of the migrants, like the black folks they shared the ghetto with, were predominantly poor and working class; and in such a situation, the image of the "badman," the pimp, the hustler—that man-of-the-streets aesthetic and ideology that figured so prominently in assertions of Black Power—were often the aspired ideal. It was largely a "brothers" kind of thing: "the fellas," hanging out acting bad, and women were relegated to the sidelines and kitchens of the male imaginary. As in most commercial production, the music and imagery of the period amounted to "an extended masculinity ritual, with virtually no women involved in any aspect of the musical scene beyond that of chorus and audience, and with the sexual playfulness of the songs generally from a masculine point of view" (Flores 2000, 91). Of course, there were important exceptions: popular during this period were Celia Cruz (whose 1972 record on Vaya with Johnny Pacheco is classic típico and one of her best), La Lupe, and Graciela (Machito's sister), all of whom continued to release successful recordings during the period and simultaneously asserted and appropriated spaces for women and alternative views to the male-dominated scene.

29. "Version" here should be read here in the full and nuanced Afro-Antillean sense: not simply a cover, a "version" is part of the rich Caribbean tradition of cultural interchange that has always characterized the region. Although there were many blatant copyright violations (made the more egregious by some record labels withholding composer credits by simply printing "D.R." or "derechos reservados"—rights reserved—on the labels), many of the bands of the period used the sounds and rhythms as points of departure.

30. Arsenio was also active in New York for the beginnings of the típico period, and a number of younger musicians either played with him or saw his groups perform. García (2006) has meticulously documented Arsenio's time in New York and his importance to the development of típico (salsa dura). His style directly influenced the development of the pachanga. Arsenio put out several recordings in the early and mid-sixties that, ironically, met with little commercial success.

31. These are just a few of the bands that were clearly influenced by and worked within traditional Puerto Rican styles and genres, whose most popular expositor was the ridiculously deep conjunto of Cortijo with vocalist Ismael Rivera. There is also an interesting filiation at work here. In 1961 Cortijo's band broke up and basically split into two units: Rivera formed Los Cachimbos, and pianist Rafael Ithier formed El Gran Combo. El Gran Combo, one of the seminal salsa outfits, featured a young and talented bongocero named Roberto Roena, who was to be a very successful típico recording artist on Fania with his Apollo Sound.

32. Palmieri's playing style was greatly influenced by McCoy Tyner (longtime pianist with the quartet of John Coltrane). He incorporated Tyner's dense block chords, modal progressions, "forearm smashes," and tone clusters into his own playing style. His collaborator and lead trombonist, Barry Rogers, was influenced by jazz musicians like J. J. Johnson and the sounds of Arsenio and Chappotin (Carp 2004).

33. This rhythm section was part of Atlantic Records' studio band, and backed up many hits by artists like Aretha Franklin and Wilson Pickett.

Bibliography

Abrahams, Roger D. *Deep Down in the Jungle: Black American Folklore from the Streets of Philadelphia*. New Brunswick, NJ: Transaction, 2006.
——. *The Man-of-words in the West Indies: Performance and the Emergence of Creole Culture*. Baltimore: Johns Hopkins University Press, 1983.
Acosta, Leonardo. *Cubano Be, Cubano Bop: One Hundred Years of Jazz in Cuba*. Washington: Smithsonian Institution, 2003.
Alleyne, Mervyn C. *Roots of Jamaican Culture*. London: Pluto Press, 1988.
Amin, Samir. *Spectres of Capitalism: A Critique of Current Intellectual Fashions*. New York: Monthly Review Press, 1998.
Amira, John, and Steven Cornelius. *The Music of Santería: Traditional Rhythms of the Batá Drums*. Crown Point, IN: White Cliffs Media, 1992.
Anderson, Perry. *In the Tracks of Historical Materialism*. Chicago: University of Chicago Press, 1984.
Aparicio, Frances R. *Listening to Salsa: Gender, Latin Popular Music, and Puerto Rican Cultures*. Hanover, NH: University Press of New England, 1998.
Appadurai, Arjun. "Disjuncture and Difference in the Global Political Economy." *Theory, Culture and Society* 7 (1991): 295–310.
Armstrong, Robert Plant. *The Affecting Presence: An Essay in Humanistic Anthropology*. Urbana: University of Illinois Press, 1971.
Austerlitz, Paul. *Jazz Consciousness: Music, Race and Humanity*. Middletown, CT: Wesleyan University Press, 2005.
Baker, Houston A. *Modernism and the Harlem Renaissance*. Chicago: University of Chicago Press, 1987.
Baldwin, James. "A Negro Assays the Negro Mood." *New York Times*, March 3, 1961.
Baraka, Imamu Amiri [LeRoi Jones]. *Black Music*. London: MacGibbon & Kee, 1969.
——. *Home: Social Essays*. London: MacGibbon & Kee, 1968.
——. *Blues People: Negro Music in White America*. New York: W. Morrow, 1963.
——. *Digging: The Afro-American Soul of American Classical Music*. Berkeley: University of California Press, 2009.
Barry, Boubacar. *Senegambia and the Atlantic Slave Trade*. Cambridge, UK: Cambridge University Press, 1998.

Bascom, William Russell. *African Art in Cultural Perspective: An Introduction*. New York: Norton, 1973.

Bastide, Roger. *The African Religions of Brazil: Toward a Sociology of the Interpenetration of Civilizations*. Baltimore: Johns Hopkins University Press, 1978.

Battle, Ellen. "Randy Weston—Spirits of Our Ancestors." Antilles Records press release (1992).

Benítez Rojo, Antonio. *The Repeating Island: The Caribbean and the Postmodern Perspective*. Durham, NC: Duke University Press, 1996.

Benveniste, Emile. *Problems in General Linguistics*. Coral Gables, FL: University of Miami Press, 1971.

Bergad, Laird W. *The Cuban Slave Market, 1790-1880*. Cambridge, UK: Cambridge University Press, 1995.

Blaut, James M. *The National Question: Decolonizing the Theory of Nationalism*. London: ZED Books, 1987.

Blum, Joseph. "Problems of Salsa Research." *Ethnomusicology* 22, no. 1 (January 1978): 137-49.

Boggs, Vernon. *Salsiology: Afro-Cuban Music and the Evolution of Salsa in New York City*. New York: Greenwood Press, 1992.

Borneman, Ernest. "Creole Echoes." *Jazz Review* 2, no. 8 (September 1959): 13-15.

Bourdieu, Pierre. *Outline of a Theory of Practice*. Cambridge, UK: Cambridge University Press, 1977.

Brathwaite, Kamau. *Roots*. Ann Arbor: University of Michigan Press, 1993.

———. *The Folk Culture of the Slaves in Jamaica*. London: New Beacon Books, 1981.

———. *Contradictory Omens: Cultural Diversity and Integration in the Caribbean*. Mona, Jamaica: Savacou Publications, 1974.

———. *The Development of Creole Society in Jamaica, 1770-1820*. Oxford, UK: Clarendon Press, 1971.

Brereton, Bridget. *A History of Modern Trinidad, 1783-1962*. Kingston, Jamaica: Heinemann, 1981.

———. *Race Relations in Colonial Trinidad, 1870-1900*. Cambridge, UK: Cambridge University Press, 1979.

———. "The Trinidad Carnival 1870-1900." *Savacou* 11/12 (1975): 46-57.

Cabral, Amílcar. *Return to the Source: Selected Speeches*. New York: Monthly Review Press, 1974.

Cabrera, Lydia. *El Monte, Igbo Finda, Ewe Orisha, Vititinfinda; Notas Sobre Las Religiones, La Magia, Las Supersticiones Y El Folklore De Los Negros Criollos Y Del Pueblo De Cuba*. Habana: Ediciones C. R., 1954.

Carp, David. "Salsa Symbiosis: Barry Rogers, Eddie Palmieri's Chief Collaborator in the Making of La Perfecta." *Centro Journal* 16, no. 2 (Fall 2004): 43-61.

Carpentier, Alejo. *Music in Cuba*. Minneapolis: University of Minnesota Press, 2001.

Cedeno, Rafael A. Nunez. "The Abakua Secret Society in Cuba: Language and Culture." *Hispania* 71, no. 2 (Fall 2004): 43-611; (March 1988): 148-54.

Certeau, Michel de. *The Practice of Everyday Life*. Berkeley: University of California Press, 1988.

Chernoff, John Miller. *African Rhythm and African Sensibility: Aesthetics and Social Action In African Musical Idioms*. Chicago: University of Chicago Press, 1979.

Clarke, John Henrick. "The New Afro-American Nationalism." *Freedomways*, vol. 1, no. 4 (Fall 1961), 285–95.

Courlander, Harold. "Musical Instruments of Cuba." *Musical Quarterly* 28, no. 2 (April 1942): 227–40.

Cowley, John. *Carnival, Canboulay and Calypso: Traditions in the Making*. Cambridge, UK: Cambridge University Press, 1996.

———. "Cultural 'Fusions': Aspects of British West Indian Music in the USA and Britain 1918–51." *Popular Music* 5 (1985): 81–96.

Crahan, Margaret, and Franklin Knight (eds.). *Africa and the Caribbean: The Legacies of a Link*. Baltimore: Johns Hopkins University Press, 1979.

Crouch, Stanley. "Randy Weston's Pan-African Piano." *Village Voice*, January, 25, 1983.

Crowley, Daniel J. "Folk Etymology and Earliest Documented Usage of 'Calypso.'" *Ethnomusicology* 10, no. 1, Latin American Issue (January 1966): 81–82.

———. "Toward a Definition of Calypso (Part I)." *Ethnomusicology* 3, no. 2 (May 1959): 57–66.

———. "Toward a Definition of Calypso (Part II)." *Ethnomusicology* 3, no. 3 (September 1959): 117–24.

Daaku, K. Y. *Trade and Politics on the Gold Coast, 1600–1720: A Study of the African Reaction to European Trade*. London: Clarendon, 1970.

Davies, Carolyn Boyce. "The Africa Theme in Trinidad Calypso." *Caribbean Quarterly* 38, no. 2 (1985): 67–86.

Debord, Guy. *The Society of the Spectacle*. New York: Zone Books, 1994.

de la Fuente, Alejandro. *A Nation for All: Race, Inequality, and Politics in Twentieth-Century Cuba*. Chapel Hill: University of North Carolina Press, 2001.

DeVeaux, Scott Knowles. *The Birth of Bebop: A Social and Musical History*. Berkeley: University of California Press, 1997.

Dodge, Roger. "The Cuban Sexteto." *Jazz Review*.

Du Bois, W. E. B. *Black Reconstruction in America*. 1935. New York: Free Press, 1998.

Duany, Jorge. "Popular Music in Puerto Rico: Toward an Anthropology of 'Salsa.'" *Latin American Music Review* 5, no. 2 (Autumn–Winter 1984): 186–216.

Dudziak, Mary L. *Cold War Civil Rights: Race and the Image of American Democracy*. Princeton, NJ: Princeton University Press, 2000.

Elder, J. D. "Cannes Brulees." *TDR (1988-)* 42, no. 3, Trinidad and Tobago Carnival (Autumn 1998): 38–43.

———. "The Male/Female Conflict in Calypso." *Caribbean Quarterly* 14, no. 3 (1968): 23–41.

———. "Kalinda: Song of the Battling Troubadours of Trinidad." *Journal of the Folklore Institute* 3, no. 2 (August 1966): 192–203.

———. "Color, Music, and Conflict: A Study of Aggression in Trinidad with Reference to the Role of Traditional Music." *Ethnomusicology* 8, no. 2 (May 1964): 128–36.
Eldridge, Michael. "There Goes the Transnational Neighborhood: Calypso Buys a Bungalow." *Callaloo* 25, no. 2 (Spring 2002): 620–38.
Ellington, Duke. *Music Is My Mistress*. Garden City, NY: Doubleday, 1973.
Ellison, Ralph. *Shadow and Act*. New York: Random House, 1964.
Emery, Lynne Fauley. *Black Dance: From 1619 to Today*. Princeton, NJ: Princeton Books, 1988.
Engels, Friedrich. *Dialectics of Nature*. Moscow: Progress Publishers, 1972.
Erin, Ronald. "Cuban Elements in the Music of Aurelio de la Vega." *Latin American Music Review* 5, no. 1 (Spring-Summer 1984): 1–32.
Escobar, Wilson A. Valentin. "El Hombre Que Respira Debajo Del Agua: Trans-*Boricua* Memories, Identities, and Nationalisms Performed Through the Death of Hector Lavoe." In *Situating Salsa: Global Markets and Local Meanings in Latin Popular Music*. Lise Waxer (ed.). New York: Routledge, 2002.
Fage, J. D. *A History of West Africa: An Introductory Survey*. London: Cambridge University Press, 1969.
Feld, Steven. *Jazz Cosmopolitanism in Accra: Five Musical Years in Ghana*. Durham, NC: Duke University Press, 2012.
———. *Sound and Sentiment: Birds, Weeping, Poetics, and Song in Kaluli Expression*. Philadelphia: University of Pennsylvania Press, 1990.
Ferrer, Ada. *Insurgent Cuba: Race, Nation, and Revolution, 1868–1898*. Chapel Hill: University of North Carolina Press, 1999.
Fick, Carolyn E. *The Making of Haiti: The Saint Domingue Revolution from Below*. Knoxville: University of Tennessee Press, 1990.
Flores, Juan. *From Bomba to Hip-hop: Puerto Rican Culture and Latino Identity*. New York: Columbia University Press, 2000.
———. *Divided Borders: Essays on Puerto Rican Identity*. Houston: Arte Público Press, 1993.
Floyd, Samuel A. "Black Music in the Circum-Caribbean." *American Music* 17, no. 1 (Spring 1999): 1–38.
———. *The Power of Black Music: Interpreting Its History from Africa to the United States*. New York: Oxford University Press, 1995.
Freyre, Gilberto. *The Masters and the Slaves (Casa-grande & Senzala) a Study in The Development of Brazilian Civilization*. Berkeley: University of California Press, 1986.
Fu-Kiau, Kimbwandènde Kia Bunseki. *African Cosmology of the Bantu-Kongo: Tying the Spiritual Knot: Principles of Life & Living*. Brooklyn: Athelia Henrietta Press, 2001.
García, David F. *Arsenio Rodríguez and the Transnational Flows of Latin Popular Music*. Philadelphia: Temple University Press, 2006.
Gitler, Ira. "Randy Weston." *Down Beat* (February 1964).
Gayle, Addison (ed.). *The Black Aesthetic*. Garden City, NY: Doubleday, 1971.
Genovese, Eugene. *From Rebellion to Revolution: Afro-American Slave Revolts in the Making Of the Modern World*. Baton Rouge: Louisiana State University Press, 1979.

Gerard, Charley. *Music from Cuba: Mongo Santamaría, Chocolate Armenteros, and Cuban Musicians*. Westport, CT: Praeger, 2001.
———. *Salsa! The Rhythm of Latin Music*. Crown Point, IN: White Cliffs Media, 1989.
Gillespie, Dizzy. *To Be, or Not . . . to BOP: Memoirs*. Garden City, NY: Doubleday, 1979.
Gilroy, Paul. *The Black Atlantic: Modernity and Double Consciousness*. Cambridge, MA: Harvard University Press, 1993.
———. "There Ain't No Black in the Union Jack": *The Cultural Politics of Race and Nation*. Chicago: University of Chicago Press, 1991.
Glasser, Ruth. *My Music Is My Flag: Puerto Rican Musicians and Their New York Communities, 1917–1940*. Berkeley: University of California Press, 1995.
Glissant, Edouard. *Caribbean Discourse: Selected Essays*. Trans. by J. Michael Dash. Charlottesville, VA: University Press of Virginia, 1989.
Goldmann, Lucien. *Essays on Method in the Sociology of Literature*. St. Louis: Telos Press, 1980.
———. *Cultural Creation in Modern Society*. St. Louis: Telos Press, 1976.
———. *Towards a Sociology of the Novel*. London: Tavistock, 1975.
Gomez, Michael. *Black Crescent: The Experience and Legacy of African Muslims in the Americas*. Cambridge, UK: Cambridge University Press, 2005.
———. *Exchanging Our Country Marks: The Transformation of African Identities In the Colonial and Antebellum South*. Chapel Hill: University of North Carolina Press, 1998.
Greaves, Gail-Ann. "Call-Response in Selected Calypsoes of Political Commentary from the Republic of Trinidad and Tobago." *Journal of Black Studies* 29, no. 1 (September 1998): 34–50.
Guilbault, Jocelyn. *Governing Sound: The Cultural Politics of Trinidad's Carnival Musics*. Chicago: University of Chicago Press, 2007.
Hall, Gwendolyn Midlo. *Africans in Colonial Louisiana: The Development of Afro-Creole Culture in* the Eighteenth Century. Baton Rouge: Louisiana State University Press, 1992.
Heisenberg, Werner. *Physics and Philosophy: The Revolution in Modern Science*. New York: Harper & Row, 1962.
Hentoff, Nat. "The Continuous Growth of Randy Weston." *Musician* (November 1964).
Helg, Aline. *Our Rightful Share: The Afro-Cuban Struggle for Equality, 1886–1912*. Chapel Hill: University of North Carolina Press, 1995.
Herskovits, Melville J. *The Myth of the Negro Past*. Boston: Beacon Press, 1990.
———. *Dahomey, an Ancient West African Kingdom*. Evanston, IL: Northwestern University Press, 1967.
———. *Trinidad Village*. New York: Octagon Books, 1964.
———. *Life in a Haitian Valley*. New York: A. A. Knopf, 1937.
Higman, B. W. *Slave Populations of the British Caribbean, 1807–1834*. Baltimore: Johns Hopkins University Press, 1984.
Hill, Donald R. "West African and Haitian Influences on the Ritual and Popular Music of Carriacou, Trinidad, and Cuba." *Black Music Research Journal* 18, no. 1/2 (Spring-Autumn 1998): 183–201.

———. *Calypso Calaloo: Early Carnival Music in Trinidad*. Gainesville: University Press of Florida, 1993.
Hill, Errol. "Calypso and War." *Black American Literature Forum* 23, no. 1 (Spring 1989): 61–88.
———. *The Trinidad Carnival: Mandate for a National Theatre*. Austin: University of Texas Press, 1972.
———. "On the Origin of the Term Calypso." *Ethnomusicology* 11, no. 3 (September 1967): 359–67.
International African Institute. *African Worlds: Studies in the Cosmological Ideas and Social Values Of African Peoples*. London: Oxford University Press, 1954.
Jahn, Janheinz. *Neo-African Literature: A History of Black Writing*. New York: Grove Press, 1969.
———. *Muntu: An Outline of the New African Culture*. New York: Grove Press, 1961.
James, C. L. R. *A History of Pan-African Revolt*. Chicago: C. H. Kerr, 1995.
———. *Notes on Dialectics: Hegel, Marx, Lenin*. London: Allison & Busby, 1980.
———. *The Black Jacobins: Toussaint L'Ouverture and the San Domingo Revolution*. New York: Vintage, 1963.
Jameson, Fredric. *The Ideologies of Theory: Essays 1971–1986*. Minneapolis: University of Minnesota Press, 1988.
Johnson, Hafiz Shabazz Farel, and John M Chernoff. "Basic Conga Drum Rhythms in African-American Musical Styles." *Black Music Research Journal* 11, no. 1 (Spring 1991): 55–73.
Johnson, Sara. "*Cinquillo* Consciousness: The Formation of a Pan-Caribbean Musical Aesthetic." In *Music, Writing and Cultural Unity in the Caribbean*. Timothy Reiss (ed.). Trenton, NJ: Africa World Press, 2005.
Johnson, Walter. *Soul by Soul: Life Inside the Antebellum Slave Market*. Cambridge, MA: Harvard University Press, 1999.
Kasinitz, Philip. *Caribbean New York: Black Immigrants and the Politics of Race*. Ithaca: Cornell University Press, 1992.
Keil, Charles, and Steven Feld. *Music Grooves: Essays and Dialogues*. Chicago: University of Chicago Press, 1994.
Kelley, Robin D. G. *Africa Speaks, America Answers: Modern Jazz in Revolutionary Times*. Cambridge, MA: Harvard University Press, 2012.
———. *Thelonious Monk: The Life and Times of an American Original*. New York: Free Press, 2009.
———. "New Monastery: Monk and the Jazz Avant-Garde." *Black Music Research Journal* 19, no. 2 (Autumn 1999): 135–68.
Kodat, Catherine Gunther. "Conversing with Ourselves: Canon, Freedom, Jazz." *American Quarterly* 55, no. 1 (March 2003): 1–28.
Klein, Herbert S. *African Slavery in Latin America and the Caribbean*. New York: Oxford University Press, 1986.
Klein, Martin A. *Slavery and Colonial Rule in French West Africa*. Cambridge, UK: Cambridge University Press, 1998.

Knight, Franklin W. *The Caribbean, the Genesis of a Fragmented Nationalism*. New York: Oxford University Press, 1978.

———. *Slave Society in Cuba During the Nineteenth Century*. Madison: University of Wisconsin Press, 1970.

Kołakowski, Leszek. *Main Currents of Marxism: Its Rise, Growth, and Dissolution*. Oxford, UK: Clarendon Press, 1978.

Kofsky, Frank. *Black Nationalism and the Revolution in Music*. New York: Pathfinder Press, 1970.

Kojève, Alexandre. *Introduction to the Reading of Hegel*. Ithaca, NY: Cornell University Press, 1980.

Korsch, Karl. *Marxism and Philosophy*. London: NLB, 1970.

Kubik, Gerhard. *Africa and the Blues*. Jackson: University Press of Mississippi, 1999.

Lateef, Yusef. *The Gentle Giant: The Autobiography of Yusef Lateef*. Irvington, NJ: Morton Books, 2006.

Law, Robin. *The Oyo Empire, c. 1600–c. 1836: A West African Imperialism in the Era of the Atlantic Slave Trade*. Oxford, UK: Clarendon Press, 1977.

Lefebvre, Henri. *Dialectical Materialism*. London: Cape, 1968.

León, Argeliers. *Del canto y el tiempo*. Havana: Editorial Letras Cubana, 1984.

———. *Música Folklórica Cubana*. Havana: Ediciones del Departmento de Música de la Biblioteca Nacional José Marti, 1964.

Levine, Lawrence W. *Black Culture and Black Consciousness: Afro-American Folk Thought from Slavery to Freedom*. Oxford, UK: Oxford University Press, 1978.

Lipsitz, George. *The Possessive Investment in Whiteness: How White People Profit from Identity Politics*. Philadelphia, PA: Temple University Press, 1998.

———. *Dangerous Crossroads: Popular Music, Postmodernism, and the Poetics of Place*. London: Verso, 1994.

———. *Time Passages: Collective Memory and American Popular Culture*. Minneapolis: University of Minnesota Press, 1990.

Liverpool, Hollis. *From the Horse's Mouth: An Analysis of Certain Significant Aspects in the Development of the Calypso and Society As Gleaned from Personal Communication with Some Outstanding Calypsonians*. Diego Martin, Trinidad: Juba Publications, 2003.

———. *Rituals of Power and Rebellion: The Carnival Tradition in Trinidad and Tobago 1763–1962*. Chicago: Frontline Distribution/Research Associates School Times Publications, 2001.

———. "Researching Steelband and Calypso Music in the British Caribbean and the U.S. Virgin Islands." *Black Music Research Journal* 14, no. 2 (Autumn 1994): 179–201.

Lott, Eric. "Double V, Double-Time: Bebop's Politics of Style." *Callaloo* 36 (Summer 1988): 597–605.

Lovejoy, Paul (ed.). *Identity in the Shadow of Slavery*. London: Continuum, 2000.

———. *Transformations in Slavery: A History of Slavery in Africa*. Cambridge, UK: Cambridge University Press, 1983.

Lukács, György. *History and Class Consciousness: Studies in Marxist Dialectics.* Cambridge, MA: MIT Press, 1971.

MacGaffey, Wyatt. *Religion and Society in Central Africa: The BaKongo of Lower Zaire.* Chicago: University of Chicago Press, 1986.

Mackey, Nathaniel. *Discrepant Engagement: Dissonance, Cross-Culturality, and Experimental Writing.* Cambridge, UK: Cambridge University Press, 1993.

Mahabir, Cynthia. "Wit and Popular Music: The Calypso and the Blues." *Popular Music* 15, no. 1 (January 1996): 55–81.

Manuel, Peter. *Caribbean Currents: Caribbean Music from Rumba to Reggae.* Philadelphia: Temple University Press, 1995.

———. "Puerto Rican Music and Cultural Identity: Creative Appropriation of Cuban Sources from Danza to Salsa." *Ethnomusicology* 38, no. 2, Music and Politics (Spring–Summer 1994): 249–80.

———. *Essays on Cuban Music: North American and Cuban Perspectives.* Lanham, MD: University Press of America, 1991

Martin, Tony. *The Pan-African Connection: From Slavery to Garvey and Beyond.* Cambridge, MA: Schenkman Publishing Co., 1983.

Marx, Karl. *The German Ideology, with Selections from Parts Two and Three.* New York: International Publishers, 1970.

———. *The Eighteenth Brumaire of Louis Bonaparte.* New York: International Publishers, 1963.

———. *Capital (vol. I).* Moscow: Foreign Languages Publishing House, 1959.

Mason, John. *Orin Òrìṣà.* Brooklyn: Yoruba Theological Archministry, 1992.

Mbiti, John S. *African Religions and Philosophy.* New York: Praeger, 1969.

McCloud, Aminah Beverly. *African American Islam.* New York: Routledge, 1995.

Merod, Jim. "Jazz as a Cultural Archive." *boundary 2* 22, no. 2, Jazz as a Cultural Archive (Summer 1995): 1–18.

Meyer, Leonard B. *Emotion and Meaning in Music.* Chicago: University of Chicago Press, 1956.

Miller, Ivor. "A Secret Society Goes Public: The Relationship between Abakuá and Cuban Popular Culture." *African Studies Review* v. 43, n. 1 (April 2000): 161–88.

Miller, Joseph Calder. *Way of Death: Merchant Capitalism and the Angolan Slave Trade, 1730–1830.* Madison: University of Wisconsin Press, 1988.

Mintz, Sidney Wilfred. *The Birth of African-American Culture: An Anthropological Perspective.* Boston: Beacon Press, 1992.

———. *Caribbean Transformations.* New York: Columbia University Press, 1989.

———. *Sweetness and Power: The Place of Sugar in Modern History.* New York: Penguin, 1986.

———. *Caribbean Contours.* Baltimore: Johns Hopkins University Press, 1985.

———. *Slavery, Colonialism, and Racism: Essays.* New York: Norton, 1975.

———. *Worker in the Cane: A Puerto Rican Life History.* Westport, CT: Greenwood Press, 1974.

Monson, Ingrid T. *Freedom Sounds: Civil Rights Call out to Jazz and Africa*. New York: Oxford University Press, 2007.

———, ed. *The African Diaspora: A Musical Perspective*. New York: Garland, 2000.

———. *Saying Something: Jazz Improvisation and Interaction*. Chicago: University of Chicago Press, 1996.

———. "Doubleness and Jazz Improvisation: Irony, Parody, and Ethnomusicology." *Critical Inquiry* 20, no. 2 (Winter 1994): 283–313.

Montejo, Esteban. *The Autobiography of a Runaway Slave*. New York: Vintage, 1973.

Moten, Fred. *In the Break: The Aesthetics of the Black Radical Tradition*. Minneapolis: University of Minnesota Press, 2003.

Moore, Robin. *Nationalizing Blackness: Afrocubanismo and Artistic Revolution in Havana*. Pittsburgh: University of Pittsburgh Press, 1995.

Moreno Fraginals, Manuel (ed.). *Africa in Latin America: Essays on History, Culture, and Socialization*. New York: Holmes & Meier, 1984.

———. *El Ingenio: Complejo económico social cubano del azúcar*. La Habana: Editorial de Ciencias Sociales, 1978.

———. *The Sugarmill: The Socioeconomic Complex of Sugar in Cuba, 1760–1860*. New York: Monthly Review Press, 1976.

Murray, Albert. *Stomping the Blues*. New York: McGraw-Hill, 1976.

Nettleford, Rex M. *Caribbean Cultural Identity: The Case of Jamaica: An Essay in Cultural Dynamics*. Kingston: Institute of Jamaica, 1978.

———. *Inward Stretch Outward Reach: A Voice from the Caribbean*. Caribbean Diaspora Press, 1995.

Nketia, J. H. Kwabena. *The Music of Africa*. New York: W. W. Norton, 1974.

Nodal, Roberto. "The Social Evolution of the Afro-Cuban Drum." *Black Perspective in Music* 11, no. 2 (Autumn 1983): 157–77.

Northrup, David. *Trade Without Rulers: Pre-colonial Economic Development in Southeastern Nigeria*. Oxford, UK: Clarendon Press, 1978.

Odinga, Sobukwe. *Mediums of Conspiracy and Existential Acts of Rebellion: Slave Resistance in Spanish Colonial New Orleans, 1766–1803*. M.A. thesis, New York University, 2003.

Ortiz, Fernando. *Cuban Counterpoint: Tobacco and Sugar*. Durham, NC: Duke University Press, 1995.

———. *La Música Afrocubana*. Madrid: Ediciones Júcar, 1975.

———. *Los Bailes Y El Teatro De Los Negros En El Folklore De Cuba*. Ciudad de La Habana, Cuba: Editorial Letras Cubanas, 1981.

———. *Los Negros Esclavos*. La Habana: Editorial de Ciencias Sociales, 1975.

———. *Hampa Afro-cubana. Los Negros Brujos (apuntes Para Un Estudio De Etnología*. Miami: Ediciones Universal, 1973.

Palmer, Robert. "From Africa—Where His Roots Are." *New York Times*, January 7, 1973.

Palmié, Stephan. *Wizards and Scientists: Explorations in Afro-Cuban Modernity and Tradition*. Durham, NC: Duke University Press, 2002.

Pearse, Andrew. "Carnival in 19th Century Trinidad." *Caribbean Quarterly* 4, nos. 3 & 4 (March/June 1956): 175–93.
——— (ed.). "Mitto Sampson on Calypso Legends of the 19th Century." *Caribbean Quarterly* 4, nos. 3 & 4 (March/June 1956): 250–62.
Peñalosa, David. *The Clave Matrix: Afro-Cuban Rhythm: Its Principles and African Origin*. Redway, CA: Bembe Press, 2009.
Pérez, Louis A. *On Becoming Cuban: Identity, Nationality, and Culture*. Chapel Hill: University of North Carolina Press, 1999.
———. *Cuba: Between Reform and Revolution*. New York: Oxford University Press, 1988.
———. *Cuba under the Platt Amendment, 1902–1934*. Pittsburgh, PA: University of Pittsburgh Press, 1986.
———. *Cuba between Empires, 1878–1902*. Pittsburgh, PA: University of Pittsburgh Press, 1983.
Peretti, Burton W. *The Creation of Jazz: Music, Race, and Culture in Urban America*. Urbana: University of Illinois Press, 1992.
Plummer, Brenda Gayle. *Rising Wind: Black Americans and U.S. Foreign Affairs, 1935–1960*. Chapel Hill: University of North Carolina Press, 1996.
Porter, Eric. *What Is This Thing Called Jazz? African American Musicians As Artists*. Berkeley: University of California Press, 2002.
———. *Out of the Blue: Black Creative Musicians and the Challenge of Jazz, 1940–1995*. PhD thesis. University of Michigan, 1997.
Post, Ken. *Arise Ye Starvelings: The Jamaican Labour Rebellion of 1938 and Its*. The Hague: Nijhoff, 1978.
Price, Richard (ed.). *Maroon Societies: Rebel Slave Communities in the Americas*. Baltimore: Johns Hopkins University Press, 1979.
Quevedo, Raymond. *Atilla's Kaiso: A Short History of Trinidad Calypso*. St. Augustine, Trinidad & Tobago: University of the West Indies Press, 1983.
Quintero Rivera, Angel G. *Salsa, Sabor Y Control!: Sociología de la Música "Tropical."* Ciudad México: Siglo Veintiuno Editores, 1998.
Ramsey, Guthrie P. *Race Music: Black Cultures from Bebop to Hip-hop*. Berkeley: University of California Press, 2003.
Reddock, Rhoda. *Women, Labour & Politics in Trinidad & Tobago: A History*. London: Zed Books, 1994.
Reis, João José. *Slave Rebellion in Brazil: The Muslim Uprising of 1835 in Bahia*. Baltimore: Johns Hopkins University Press, 1993.
Robbins, James. "The Cuban 'Son' as Form, Genre, and Symbol." *Latin American Music Review* 11, no. 2 (Autumn-Winter 1990): 182–200.
Roberts, John Storm. *Latin Jazz: The First of the Fusions, 1880s to Today*. New York: Schirmer Books, 1999.
———. *The Latin Tinge: The Impact of Latin American Music on the United States*. New York: Oxford University Press, 1979.
———. *Black Music of Two Worlds*. New York: Praeger, 1972.

Robinson, Cedric J. *Black Marxism: The Making of the Black Radical Tradition.* Chapel Hill: University of North Carolina Press, 2000.

Rodney, Walter. *A History of the Guyanese Working People, 1881–1905.* Baltimore: Johns Hopkins University Press, 1981.

———. *How Europe Underdeveloped Africa.* Washington: Howard University Press, 1974.

———. *A History of the Upper Guinea Coast, 1545–1800.* Oxford, UK: Clarendon Press, 1970.

———. *The Groundings with My Brothers.* London: Bogle-L'Ouverture Publications, 1969.

Rohlehr, Gordon. "The Calypsonian as Artist: Freedom and Responsibility." *Small Axe* 5, no. 1 (March 2001): 1–26.

———. "The Culture of Williams: Context, Performance, Legacy." *Callaloo* 20, no. 4, Eric Williams and the Postcolonial Caribbean: A Special Issue (Autumn 1997): 849–88.

———. *Calypso and Society in Pre-independence Trinidad.* Port of Spain, Trinidad: G. Rohlehr, 1990.

———. *The Development of Calypso, 1900–1940.* St. Augustine, Trinidad: University of the West Indies Press, 1972.

Rondon, César Miguel. *El Libro De La Salsa: Crónica De La Música Del Caribe Urbano.* Caracas, Venezuela: s.n., 1980.

Rosenthal, David H. *Hard Bop: Jazz and Black Music, 1955–1965.* New York: Oxford University Press, 1992.

———. "Jazz in the Ghetto: 1950–70." *Popular Music* 7, no. 1 (January 1988): 51–56.

———. "Hard Bop and Its Critics." *Black Perspective in Music* 16, no. 1 (Spring 1988): 21–29.

Saakana, Amon Saba. "Africanity and Continuum in Sacred and Popular Trinidadian Musical Forms." In *Music, Writing and Cultural Unity in the Caribbean.* Timothy Reiss (ed.). Trenton, NJ: Africa World Press, 2005.

Salazar Primero, Max. *Mambo Kingdom: Latin Music in New York.* New York: Schirmer Books, 2002.

Sánchez-Korrol, Virginia. *From Colonia to Community: The History of Puerto Ricans in New York City.* Berkeley: University of California Press, 1994.

Saussure, Ferdinand de. *Course in General Linguistics.* LaSalle, IL: Open Court, 1986.

Shepherd, John. *Music As Social Text.* Cambridge, MA: Polity Press, 1991.

Shepherd, Verene, et al. (eds). *Engendering History: Caribbean Women in Historical Perspective.* New York: St. Martin's Press, 1995.

Sidbury, James. *Ploughshares into Swords: Race, Rebellion, and Identity in Gabriel's.* Cambridge, UK: Cambridge University Press, 1997.

Singer, Roberta L. "Tradition and Innovation in Contemporary Latin Popular Music in New York City." *Latin American Music Review* 4, no. 2 (Autumn–Winter 1983): 183–202.

———. *My Music Is Who I Am and What I Do: Latin Popular Music and Identity in New York.* PhD. diss., Indiana University, 1982.

Singh, Kelvin. *Race and Class Struggles in a Colonial State: Trinidad 1917–1945.* Mona, Kingston, Jamaica: University of the West Indies Press, 1994.

Small, Christopher. *Musicking: The Meanings of Performing and Listening.* Hanover, NH: University Press of New England, 1998.

———. *Music of the Common Tongue: Survival and Celebration in Afro-American Music.* London: J. Calder, 1987.

Smallwood, Lawrence. "African Cultural Dimensions in Cuba." *Journal of Black Studies* 6, no. 2 (December 1975): 191–99.

Snead, James A. "On Repetition in Black Culture." *Black American Literature Forum* 15, no. 4, Black Textual Strategies, Volume 1: Theory (Winter 1981): 146–54.

Soyinka, Wole. *Myth, Literature, and the African World.* Cambridge, UK: Cambridge University Press, 1976.

Spellman, A. B. *Four Lives in the Bebop Business.* New York: Pantheon, 1966.

Stewart, Alexander. "'Funky Drummer': New Orleans, James Brown and the Rhythmic Transformation of American Popular Music." *Popular Music* 19, no. 3 (October 2000): 293–318.

Stuckey, Sterling. *Slave Culture: Nationalist Theory and the Foundations of Black America.* New York: Oxford University Press, 1987.

Sublette, Ned. *Cuba and Its Music: From the First Drums to the Mambo.* Chicago: Chicago Review Press, 2004.

Taylor, Art. *Notes and Tones: Musician-to-musician Interviews.* New York: Da Capo, 1993.

Thompson, E. P. *The Poverty of Theory and Other Essays.* New York: Monthly Review Press, 1978.

———. *The Making of the English Working Class.* New York: Vintage, 1966.

Thompson, Robert Farris. *Face of the Gods: Art and Altars of Africa and the African Americas.* New York: Museum for African Art, 1993.

———. *Flash of the Spirit: African and Afro-American Art and Philosophy.* New York: Random House, 1983.

———. *African Art in Motion: Icon and Act in the Collection of Katherine Coryton White.* Los Angeles: University of California Press, 1974.

Thornton, John. *Africa and Africans in the Making of the Atlantic World, 1400–1680.* Cambridge, UK: Cambridge University Press, 1992.

Trouillot, Michel-Rolph. *Silencing the Past: Power and the Production of History.* Boston: Beacon Press, 1995.

Turner, Richard Brent. *Islam in the African-American Experience.* Bloomington: Indiana University Press, 1997.

Turner, Victor Witter. *The Forest of Symbols: Aspects of Ndembu Ritual.* Ithaca, NY: Cornell University Press, 1967.

———. *The Ritual Process: Structure and Anti-structure.* Ithaca, NY: Cornell University Press, 1977.

Van Norman, William C. *Shade-grown Slavery: The Lives of Slaves on Coffee Plantations in Cuba.* PhD thesis. University of North Carolina at Chapel Hill, 2005.

Vansina, Jan. *Kingdoms of the Savanna.* Madison: University of Wisconsin Press, 1966.

Vogt, John. *Portuguese Rule on the Gold Coast, 1469–1682.* Athens: University of Georgia Press, 1979.

Voloshinov, V. N. *Marxism and the Philosophy of Language.* Cambridge, MA: Harvard University Press, 1986.

Von Eschen, Penny M. *Satchmo Blows Up the World: Jazz Ambassadors Play the Cold War.* Cambridge, MA: Harvard University Press, 2004.

———. *Race Against Empire: Black Americans and Anticolonialism, 1937-1957.* Ithaca, NY: Cornell University Press, 1997.

Wagner, Roy. *An Anthropology of the Subject: Holographic Worldview in New Guinea and Its Meaning and Significance for the World of Anthropology.* Berkeley: University of California Press, 2001.

———. *Symbols That Stand for Themselves.* Chicago: University of Chicago Press, 1986.

Warner, Keith Q. *Kaiso! The Trinidad Calypso: A Study of the Calypso As Oral Literature.* Washington: Three Continents Press, 1982.

Warner-Lewis, Maureen. *Central Africa in the Caribbean: Transcending Time, Transforming Cultures.* Kingston, Jamaica: University of the West Indies Press, 2003.

———. *Trinidad Yoruba: From Mother Tongue to Memory.* Tuscaloosa: University of Alabama Press, 1996.

———. *Guinea's Other Suns: The African Dynamic in Trinidad Culture.* Dover, MA: Majority Press, 1991.

Washburne, Christopher. "The Clave of Jazz: A Caribbean Contribution to the Rhythmic Foundation of an African-American Music." *Black Music Research Journal* 17, no. 1 (Spring 1997): 59–80.

———. "Play It 'Con Filin!': The Swing and Expression of Salsa." *Latin American Music Review* 19, no. 2 (Autumn–Winter 1998): 160–85.

Waterman, Richard. "African Influence on the Music of the Americas." In *Acculturation in the Americas.* Sol Tax (ed.). Chicago: University of Chicago Press, 1952.

Watkins-Owens, Irma. *Blood Relations: Caribbean Immigrants and the Harlem Community, 1900–1930.* Bloomington: Indiana University Press, 1996.

Waxer, Lise. "Of Mambo Kings and Songs of Love: Dance Music in Havana and New York from the 1930s to the 1950s." *Latin American Music Review* 15, no. 2 (Autumn–Winter 1994): 139–76.

Weinstein, Norman. *A Night in Tunisia: Imaginings of Africa in Jazz.* Metuchen, NJ: Scarecrow Press, 1992.

Weston, Randy. *African Rhythms: The Autobiography of Randy Weston.* Durham, NC: Duke University Press, 2010.

White, Bob. "Congolese Rumba and Other Cosmpolitanisms." *Cahiers d'Études Africaines* 42, no. 168 (2002): 663–86.

White, Hayden V. *Metahistory: The Historical Imagination in Nineteenth-century Europe.* Baltimore: Johns Hopkins University Press, 1973.

———. *Tropics of Discourse: Essays in Cultural Criticism.* Baltimore: Johns Hopkins University Press, 1978.

Whorf, Benjamin Lee. *Language, Thought, and Reality: Selected Writings.* Cambridge, MA: Technology Press of Massachusetts Institute of Technology, 1956.

Williams, Eric Eustace. *Capitalism and Slavery*. Chapel Hill: University of North Carolina Press, 1994.

———. *From Columbus to Castro: The History of the Caribbean, 1492–1969*. New York: Vintage, 1984.

———. *The Negro in the Caribbean*. New York: Haskell House, 1971.

———. *History of the People of Trinidad & Tobago*. New York: Praeger, 1964.

Williams, Raymond. *Marxism and Literature*. Oxford, UK: Oxford University Press, 1977.

Wilmer, Valerie. *As Serious As Your Life: The Story of the New Jazz*. London: Quartet Books, 1977.

Wilson, Peter J. *Crab Antics: The Social Anthropology of English-speaking Negro Societies of the Caribbean*. New Haven: Yale University Press, 1973.

Wolf, Eric R. *Peasant Wars of the Twentieth Century*. New York: Harper & Row, 1969.

———. *Europe and the People without History*. Berkeley, CA: University of California Press, 1997.

Wood, Donald, and Institute of Race Relations. *Trinidad in Transition: The Years After Slavery*. Oxford, UK: Oxford University Press, 1986.

Yglesias, Pablo Ellicott. *Cocinando!: Fifty Years of Latin Album Cover Art*. New York: Princeton Architectural Press, 2005.

Zuckerkandl, Victor. *Sound and Symbol*. Princeton, NJ: Princeton University Press, 1969.

Select Discography

Chapter 1

Growling Tiger. *Knockdown Calypsos*. Rounder R-5006 (1977).
Lord Invader. *Calypso Travels*. Folkways FW-8735 (1959).
Various Artists. *The Real Calypso 1927-1946*. Folkways RBF-13 (1966).
———. *Native Calypso Songs*. Halo-50244 (n.d.).
———. *Le Jazz Primitif from Trinidad*. Cook 1082 (n.d./ca. 1957).
———. *Dance Calypso*. Cook 1180 (n.d./ca. 1957).
———. *Calypso Pioneers 1912-1937*. Rounder CD 1039 (1989).
———. *Calypso Breakaway*. Rounder CD 1054 (1990).
———. *Calypsos from Trinidad*. Arhoolie CD 7004 (1991).
———. *Calypso Carnival 1936-1941*. Rounder CD 1077 (1993).
———. *The Fall of Man: Calypsos on the Human Condition*. Rounder CD 1141 (1999).
———. *Roosevelt in Trinidad*. Rounder CD 1142 (1999).
———. *Calypso Awakening*. Smithsonian Folkways CD 40453 (2000).

Chapter 2

Cachao y Su Ritmo Caliente. *Cuban Jam Sessions in Miniature*. Panart LP-2092 (1957).
———. *Jam Session with Feeling*. Maype US 122 (1962).
Chappottin Y Su Conjunto. *Sabor Tropical*. Puchito SP-107 (ca. 1957).
———. *Alto Songo*. Panart LP 2072 (1957).
———. *Musicalidad en Sepia*. Maype US-110 (1962).
Mendez, Silvestre. *Oriza*. Seeco CELP 4062 (ca. 1959).
Patato y Totico (Carlos Valdes and Eugenio Arango). *Patato y Totico*. Verve V6-5037 (1967).
Rodriguez, Arsenio. *Palo Congo*. Blue Note BLP-1561 (1957).
———. *Cumbanchando con Arsenio (Fiesta en Harlem)*. SMC-ProArte SMC-1074 (1960).
———. *Y Su Conjunto vols. 1 & 2*. Ansonia ALP-1337 and 1418 (1964–65).

———. *Quindembo: Afro Magic*. Columbia CLT-7049 (1964).
———. *Primitivo*. Roost RST-2261 (1965).
Zayas, Alberto. *Guaguanco Afro-Cubano*. Panart 2055 (ca. 1960).
———. *Afro-Frenetic*. Panart 3053 (ca. 1960).

Chapter 3

Abdul-Malik, Ahmed. *East Meets West*. RCA Victor LPM-2015 (1959).
———. *The Music of Ahmed Abdul-Malik*. New Jazz NJLP-8266 (1961).
———. *Sounds of Africa*. New Jazz NJLP-8282 (1962).
———. *Eastern Moods*. New Jazz NJLP-8298 (1963).
Blakey, Art. *Art Blakey and the Jazz Messengers*. Blue Note BLP-4003 (1958).
———. *The African Beat*. Blue Note BLP-4097 (1961).
Coltrane, John. *Coltrane Live at Birdland*. Impulse A-50 (1963).
Davis, Miles. *Miles Davis Sextet*. Prestige PRLP-182 (1954).
Gillespie, Dizzy. *Afro*. Norgran MGN-1003 (1954).
Gryce, Gigi. *Reminiscin'*. Mercury MG-202628 (1961).
Lateef, Yusef. *The Sounds of Yusef Lateef*. Prestige PRLP-7122 (1957).
———. *Jazz Mood*. Savoy MG-12103 (1957).
———. *Jazz for the Thinker*. Savoy MG-12109 (1957).
———. *Prayer to the East*. Savoy MG-12117 (1957).
———. *Before Dawn*. Verve MGV-8217 (1958).
———. *Into Something*. New Jazz NJLP 8272 (1961).
Lincoln, Abbey. *Abbey Is Blue*. Riverside RLP 1153 (1959).
Roach, Max. *Deeds, Not Words*. Riverside RLP 1122 (1958).
———. *We Insist!—Freedom Now Suite*. Candid CD 8002 (1960).
Weston, Randy. *Jazz A La Bohemia*. Riverside RLP 12-232 (1957).
———. *Little Niles*. United Artists UAL-4011 (1959).
———. *Uhuru Afrika*. Roulette R-65001 (1961).

Chapter 4

Barretto, Ray. *Acid*. Fania LP-346 (1967).
———. *Hard Hands*. Fania LP-362 (1968).
———. *Power*. Fania LP-391 (1970).
———. *Que Viva La Musica*. Fania LP-427 (1972).
Colón, Willie. *El Malo*. Fania LP-337 (1967).
———. *Guisando ("Doing a Job")*. Fania LP-370 (1968).
———. *Cosa Nuestra*. Fania LP-384 (1969).
———. *La Gran Fuga*. Fania LP-394 (1970).
Gomez, Kent. *My Ghetto*. Mio MS-1002 (ca. 1969?).

Cortijo Y Kako. *Ritmos y Cantos Callejeros*. Ansonia ALP-1477 (ca. 1965?).
Harlow, Larry. *Tribute to Arsenio*. Fania LP-404 (1972).
Ocho. *Ocho*. United Artists Latino. L-3110 (1972).
Pacheco, Johnny. *Live at the World's Fair*. Fania LP-326 (1965).
———. *Sabor Tipico*. Fania LP-339 (1967).
Palmieri, Eddie. *Justicia*. Tico LP-1188 (1969).
———. *Superimposition*. Tico LP-1190 (1970).
———. *Harlem River Drive*. Roulette SR-3004 (1970).
La Protesta. *La Protesta*. Rico LP-706 (1970).
Pucho and the Latin Soul Brothers. *Yaina*. Right On Records RR0-5000 (1972).
Ramirez, Louie. *Tipico*. United Artists LT-LA 208 (1974).
Various Artists. *Caliente=Hot: Puerto Rican and Cuban Musical Expression in New York*. New World Records NW 244 (1977).

Conclusion

Villafranca, Elio. *Caribbean Tinge*. Motema MTM-147 (2014).

Index

Abakuá, 58, 64, 68, 147n7
Abdul-Malik, Ahmed, 90–91, 93–95, 100–101, 105, 155nn27–28, 156n33
Abdurahman, Bilal, 94–95
Abrams, Ray, 100
Acid (Barretto), 128
Africa, 4, 75, 92–93, 97, 104–6, 123, 137, 157n43
African Academy of Arts and Research (AAAR), 85–86, 153n20
African Americans: Afro-Caribbeans and, 120–21, 124, 132, 159n13; Puerto Ricans and, 159n13, 160n16. *See also* civil rights movement; jazz
African Beat, The (Art Blakey's Afro-Drum Ensemble), 93, 155n27
"African Bossa Nova" (Abdul-Malik), 95
Afro (Gillespie), 87
Afro-Asian conference, 75–76
"Afro-Blue," 156n35
Afro-Caribbean music, 128
Afro-Caribbeans, African Americans and, 120–21, 124, 132, 159n13
Afro-Cuban culture, 11–12, 55–60, 61, 68–69, 135
Afro-Cubanismo, 13, 41, 58, 63, 67, 69, 147n7
Afro-Cuban music, 51, 85–87, 149n17, 149n19, 149n21, 149n22, 150nn23–27, 160–61n18; Afro-Cuban funk, 126; Afro-Cuban jazz, 120; appropriation of, 109–10; influence of, 110; jazz and, 118–19; salsa and, 109, 118, 124, 127–31
Afro-Cubans: black nationalism and, 60–72; exclusion of, 60–61; North American racism and, 60
Afro-diaspora, 3, 7–10, 12, 49–50, 69, 94, 97–98, 106, 134, 136, 140n16; consciousness, 5, 12–14, 49, 85–86, 95, 132, 137, 147n7, 148n9, 151n3, 155n27, 157n41, 157n43, 162n25
Afro-French creole, 19–20
"Afro-modernism," 80, 152n12
Afro-Puerto Ricans, 14, 115–16, 135, 159n11
agregados, 115
aguinaldo, 115, 118
Akow, 15–16
Alegre All-Stars, *Jam Sessions*, 161–62n23
Alegre Records, 109, 125, 130, 161–62n23
Alfredo Zayas and his Grupo Afro-Cubano, 147n7
Allada, 58
"All Africa" (Roach), 97
"Alto Songo" (Chappotín), 61
Alvarez, Chico, 124, 161n22
American Society of African Culture, 103
Amira, John, and Steven Cornelius, 147n2
Angelou, Maya, 74
Angola, 59
Ansonia label, 125
anticolonialism, 13, 41, 76, 79–80, 89, 106, 135, 150n1, 150–51n2

181

anti-communism, 106
Antilles, 53
Aparicio, Frances R., 110
apesi drums, 97
apprentices, 23
"Aquí Como Allá" (Rodriguez), 49
Arabic music, 94–95
Arango, Eugenio, and Carlos Valdez, *Potato Y Totico*, 147n7
Arará, 58–59, 148n8
Archie Bell and the Drells, 125
Armenteros, Alfredo "Chocolate," 144n22
Armstrong, Robert Plant, 138–39n5
Asante, 143–44n19
Aslan, Djamal, 94
Atilla the Hun, 22, 27, 33–38, 41–43, 45, 141n1, 142n7, 144n20
At the World's Fair (Johnny Pacheco), 127
Austerlitz, Paul, 118
"Ayiko Ayiko" (Blakey), 155n27
Ayti. *See* Haiti

Baker, Houston, 76–77
Baldwin, James, 74
Bandung, Indonesia, 12, 75
Bandung Conference, 12
Bandung period, 14, 80, 84–85, 90–91, 97, 106, 153n18
"Bang Bang" (Joe Cuba Sextet), 121
Bantu, 60, 148n11
Baraka, Amiri, 5, 91, 105. *See also* Jones, LeRoi
Barbados, 24, 115
barrack yards, 27–28, 32, 46
barracónes, 58
Barretto, Ray, 128, 150n26, 159–60n14
Barrio, El, 108, 117, 124
Basie, Count, 82
Bataan, Joe, 128
bata drums, 59, 149n17
Bauzá, Mario, 85, 118, 120, 158n4
bebop, 13, 80–83, 86–88, 101, 118, 153n14, 153n16. *See also* hard bop

Beginner, 43, 45
Begorrat, "Lawa" ("King"), 21
Belafonte, Harry, 156n34
Bel-Air (bele), 21
Belgium, 73
Belmont, Trinidad, 25
Benin, 58
Benson, Bobby, 104
Benton, Walter, 96
Biafran war, 106
big bands, 81–82, 85, 91, 93, 95
"Bilongo" (Rodriguez), 131
Birdland, 119
black activism, 73–74, 87, 90, 155–56n29. *See also specific movements*
black aesthetic, 4, 6–7, 10, 12, 123, 135–36
Black Arts movement, 123
black consciousness, 89. *See also* Afro-diaspora: consciousness
black nationalism, 76–77, 87, 151n3
blackness, 10, 50, 60–72, 79, 89, 135–36, 139n8, 158n6
Black Panther Party, 123
Black Power, 12–13, 79–80, 106, 108, 122–23, 132–33, 150n26, 161n21, 162n24, 162–63n28
black pride, 68, 70
Blakey, Art, 90–91, 93–95, 150n27, 154n23, 155nn27–28
Bluebird label, 43, 88
Blue Note Records, 72, 95, 150n27, 159–60n14
blues, 13, 84, 77–87, 90–106, 126, 145n24, 152n13
Blues People (Jones/Baraka), 140n15
Boggs, Vernon, 158n2
bois bataille, 27. *See also* stickfighting
bolero, 68
bomba, 21, 115, 118–19, 130, 158n6, 159n11
bongo, 67, 69
Boobull Tiger, 30
boogaloo, 108, 119–22, 124–28, 132, 159–60n14, 160n17, 160–61n18, 161n19

boogie-woogie, 84
bop. *See* bebop; hard bop
Borinquen. *See* Puerto Rico
bossa nova, 95
botija, 67
bourgeoisies, 8
bozales, 55, 57, 70
brass bands, 95
Bravo, Sonny, "Tighten Up," 125
Brazil, 35, 137
Brereton, Bridget, 19
Briggs-Hall, Austin, 86
Bríkamo, 58
Brilliant Corners, 84
British Empire, 18–19, 20, 23–24, 30, 53
British Guiana, 22, 45
Brooklyn, New York, 100–102, 104, 108, 116–17
Broun Fellinis, "Chocolate Surrealism," 138n1
Brown, James, 124, 132
Brown, Oscar, Jr., 96–97, 156n35
Brown, Ray, 153n16
Brown Power, 108, 133, 150n26, 162–63n28
Brown v. Board of Education, 12, 74–76
"Bruca Maniguá" (Rodriguez), 70–71, 150n26
Brunswick, 43, 66
bugalú, 119. *See also* boogaloo
Burrell, Kenny, 91
Butler, Uriah "Buzz," 41–42
Byas, Don, 94
Byrd, Donald, 91

cabildos, 57, 61
Cabrera, Lydia, 63, 64
Cachao, "La Luz," 109
cachimbo, 149n17
Cachimbos, Los, 163n31
caja, 149n17
cajones, 64
calinda. *See* kalinda

call-and-response (antiphony), 111, 115, 149n19
Calloway, Cab, 82
Calo, 95
calypso, 50, 71, 93, 102, 104, 137, 141n1, 143–44n19, 144n22, 155n27, 156n34; Anglicization of, 40; boom in the thirties and forties, 144–45n23; class and, 39, 46; fusion, 95; gender and, 46–47; "golden age" of, 45, 145n24; growing popularity of, 44; history of, 16; incorporation of elements from other genres, 45; lyrics, 46–47; market for, 42–44, 45; "new school," 45; "Old Brigade," 45; politicization of, 41–42; popularity of, 146n26; rootwork and, 44–45; sales of recordings, 15–16; salsa and, 110, 115; swing, 85; technology and, 44; in the US, 42, 146n27, 146n29; in West Africa, 146n29
calypsonians, 35–37, 39, 41, 144n20, 144n22, 145n24, 145–46n25, 146n28; as chroniclers and critics of racial and class tensions, 41; patronage and, 39–40; professionalization of, 40, 43–44
Cameron, Candido, 87, 102, 144n22, 155n27
Cameroon, 58
campana (cowbell), 69–70, 125
Campos, Albizu, 158–59n9
canboulay, 26, 31, 142n10, 143n17
Canboulay Riots of 1881, 31, 32
Cannes Brulees, 26
capitalism, 10, 11, 15, 27–28, 50, 110, 113, 115, 135, 162n24
Carabalí, 58, 59
Carfagna, Dante, 162n24
Caribbean region: capitalism and, 10; development and, 10; historiography of, 9–10; as locus, 7; plural societies in, 11; social history of, 7; unrest in, 144n21. *See also specific countries and islands*
carieto, 22

carisos, 22, 30–31, 34, 143n16
Carmichael, Stokely, 75
carnival, 13, 17–20, 22, 25–26, 28, 30–32, 34, 43, 47, 141n3, 143n17; songs, 34; class and, 32–33, 39; middle-class cooptation of, 37–38; yard rehearsals for, 32, 36
Carnival Improvement Association, 39
Carpentier, Alejo, 63
Casino de la Playa, 71
caste, 24. *See also* class
Castor, Jimmy, 160n15
cedula, 17
Cedula of Population of 1783, 17–18
censorship, 40–41, 44, 145n24
centrales, 56–58
Central Intelligence Agency (CIA), 73, 106
cha-cha, 51, 119
Chambers, Paul, 91
"Changing Same," 77–78, 140n15
changüí, 68
chants, 34
chantwells, 21, 28–29, 36, 142n6
Chappotín, Felíx, "Alto Songo," 61
charangas, 108, 119, 127
Charles, Ray, 153n16
Cheetah (nightclub), 161–62n23
Chief Bey, 95
"Chinee Patrick," 36
"Chocolate Surrealism" (Broun Fellinis), 138n1
cinquillo, 148n8
civil rights movement, 12–13, 74–78, 87–90, 95–97, 105, 108, 120, 122–23, 132, 135, 151nn4–5, 155–56n29
Clark, Gerald, 42, 144n22
Clarke, John Henrik, 74, 150n1
Clarke, Kenny, 81, 91
class, 8, 11, 134, 139n10; calypso and, 16–17, 24–25, 30–32, 37–39, 42, 48; carnival and, 32–33, 39; in Cuba, 62; kaiso and, 37–38, 42, 48; language and, 32–33; in Puerto Rico, 116; salsa and, 110, 126; in Trinidad, 16–17, 24–25, 30–32, 37–39, 40–42, 46–48, 143n12
clave, 65, 67, 129, 146n2, 155n27; consciousness, 50, 51–52, 65, 69, 86, 126; as root of salsa, 111–12
COINTELPRO, 150n26
Cold War, 75–76, 103, 105, 109
Coleman, Ornette, 90
Collins, Rud, 95
Colón, Willie, 110, 127–28, 162nn25–26
colonialism, 10–11, 17, 63, 66, 75, 115, 134, 136, 150n1, 150–51n2
colonias, 116
Colpix Records, 104
Coltrane, John, 153n18, 156n35
Columbia Records, 66–67, 149n21
columbia rumba, 64–65
Columbus, Christopher, 52
combos, small, 81
"Communication" (Abdul-Malik), 95
communism, 74–75
"Con Alma" (Gillespie), 87
Concepts in Unity (Grupo Folklórico y Experimental Nuevayorquino), 158n1
conga drums, 161n21
Congo, 59, 73, 104, 142n5, 148n10
congueros, 128, 159–60n14
conjunto, 69–71, 108, 126–30, 159n11, 163n31
Connor, Edric, 141n1
Conquistadora, La, 130
consciousness, 5–6, 12, 14. *See also* black consciousness; clave: consciousness; national consciousness
Conspiracion, La, 130
Continental label, 43
"cool jazz," 89
Copeland, Ray, 100, 104
Cortijo, Rafael, 159n11, 163n31
Cortijo y Su Combo, 119, 159n11
Cosa Nuestra (Colón), 158n1, 162n26
cosmogony, 8
cosmology, 8–9

cosmopolitanism, 49–50, 55, 62–63, 68, 80, 152n12
Cotique label, 122, 125, 159n13
counterculture, 12, 122
counterpoint, 12, 51, 89
creolization, 12, 16–24, 26, 28, 32–33, 59–60, 84
cross-fertilization, 84, 119, 120
Cross River delta (Old Calabar), 58
crown colony system, 18, 23–24, 40
Crusader, 41
cua, 115
cuatro, 115
Cuba, 11–13, 35, 49–72, 109–10, 114, 134–35, 137; Afro-diasporic cultures in, 147nn7–8; blackness in, 50; British occupation of, 53; class in, 62; defeat of Spain, 60; development in, 52–54; *guerra de razas* in, 61, 148n13; Haitian refugees in, 58, 65; labor unrest in, 62; national consciousness in, 62; nationalizing blackness in, 60–72; recording ban of 1961, 50, 122; as satellite of the US, 62, 107; slavery in, 55, 57, 147n5; slave trade to, 59–60; sugar industry in, 55–56, 61–62; tourism in, 68; US and, 50, 60–62, 67–68; "white" immigration from Spain, 60
Cubanidad, 50, 55, 63, 68, 147n7
Cuban music: Cosmopolitanism, 49–50; in West and West Central Africa, 146n1. *See also* Afro-Cuban music
Cuban Revolution, 13, 50, 76, 108, 122
CuBop, 118, 120
Cyrille, Andrew, 94

Dafora (Horton), Asadata, 86, 145–46n25, 153–54n21
Dahomey, 58
dance, 12, 20–21; central role in black cultural life, 8–9; Latin crazes, 119, 125
dance clubs, 107–8, 118–19, 158n2, 159n12
Davila, Arlene, 158–59n9

Davis, Miles, 87, 100
Dawud, Talib, 91
Decca Records, 15–16, 42–43, 66, 125, 144n22
decimas, 115
decolonization, 12, 75–78, 95–98, 103, 105–6, 150n26
Deeds Not Words (Roach), 96
de la Fuente, Alejandro, 63
Dessalines, Jean-Jacques, 18
Dirlik, Arif, 106
doo-wop, 108, 119, 159n13
Douglas, Railway "Chieftain," 38–39, 43, 45
Duboney, La, *Salsa Na' Ma'*, 109
Dunham, Katherine, 86
DuVall, Tomas, 96–97

East Indians, 24–26, 32, 36, 40
East Meets West (Abdul-Malik), 94
"Échale Salsita" (Septeto Nacional), 109, 149n22
el Bakkar, Mohammed, 94
Elder, J. D., 20, 30
El Din, Hamza, 95
Eldridge, Michael, 144–45n23
Eldridge, Roy, 82, 91
Ellington, Duke, 82, 85, 101, 153n19, 157n39
Ellison, Ralph, 3, 6
emancipation, 12, 23, 34, 97, 115, 142n9
Engels, Friedrich, 6–7
Ervin, Booker, 103–4
ethnicity, 8, 10, 14, 17, 19, 50–51, 56, 71, 110
Evans, Bill, 91. *See also* Lateef, Yusef

Faílde, Miguel, 147n7
Fania Records, 108, 126–29, 161–62n23, 162n27, 163n31
Febles, "Juanillo," 147n7
Feld, Steven, 111, 139–40n11, 152n12
Feliciano, Cheo, 109
Felix, Gregory, 144n22
Fields, Ernie, 91
"Fire Down Below" (Weston), 102

Index

Fitzgerald, Ella, 146n29
Flamboyan, La, 130
Flanagan, Tommy, 91
Flores, Juan, 115, 120, 159–60n14, 160n17
Flowers, Brock, 98
Floyd, Samuel A., 152n13
folk songs, 25, 45
Fon-Ewe, 58
Fraser, L. M., 141n2
freedom movement, 76, 81, 135, 151n5
freed people, 10–11, 16, 18, 25–28, 34, 60, 71, 115, 143n12
French Caribbean, 17–20, 33, 53, 141n4
Fuller, Curtis, 91, 94
funk, 89, 126, 132, 159–60n14, 162n24

Galliard, Slim, 85
García, David, 150n25, 163n30
Garvey, Marcus, 40
Garveyism, 13, 40, 43, 62, 100
gayap, 22, 36, 142n8
Gee Records, 159n13
Gema label, 125
gender, 8, 16–17, 31, 110, 126; calypso and, 46–47; jazz and, 151–52n9; masculinity, 27–31; politics and, 151–52n9; stick-fighting and, 30; in Trinidad, 31–32, 46–47
Gerald Clark and his Caribbean Serenaders, 42
Getz, Stan, 154n22
Ghana, 76, 95, 106
Gillespie, Dizzy, 81, 85–87, 91–93, 100, 103, 118, 120, 137, 147n7, 159–60n14
Gilroy, Paul, 5
Glasser, 115, 159n13
Glissant, Eduoard, 33
Gold Coast, 95
Goldner, George, 159n13
Golson, Benny, 94, 155n28, 156–57n37
Golson-Farmer-Fuller Jazztet(s), 90
gospel, 84, 87, 89–90, 104
Gramophone Company, 146n1
gramophones, 44
Gran Combo, El, 163n31
Great Migration, 79, 81, 152n10
Grenada, 23–24
Griffin, Johnny, 87, 94
griottage, 22
Growling Tiger, 36, 43, 45–47, 144n22
Grupo Folklórico y Experimental Nuevayorquino, *Concepts in Unity*, 158n1
Gryce, Gigi, 91, 155n28, 156–57n37
Gryce-Byrd Jazz Lab, 90
guaguancó rumba, 64–65, 70, 131, 160–61n18, 161n20
guajeos, 67, 69, 131
guajira, 68
guaracha, 124, 129, 159n11, 160–61n18
Guilbault, Jocelyne, 16
Guillén, Nicolas, 63
guiro, 115
guitar, 67, 115, 128
guraracha, 51, 68
"gustatory imperative," 110
Guy, Rosa, 74
Guzman, Pablo, 124

habanera rhythm, 85
Habitual Idlers Ordinance, 40
Hadi, Shafi, 91
Haiti, 13, 18–19, 53, 58, 65, 115, 137, 148n8
Haitian Revolution, 53, 58, 115, 148n8
Hall, Stuart, 150n23
Hancock, Herbie, 159–60n14
Handy, W. C., 85
hard bop, 12, 72, 77–90, 105–6, 154nn22–23, 155n28, 159–60n14. *See also* bebop
Harewood, Al, 94, 100
Harlem, New York, 42–43, 108, 123; riots of 1935, 158–59n9
Harlem Renaissance, 13, 41, 63, 118
Harlem River Drive (Eddie Palmieri), 131
Harlow, Larry, 128
Harris, Barry, 91
Havana, Cuba, 49, 52–53, 55, 58, 66

Hawkins, Coleman, 94, 96, 101
Hayes, Louis, 91
Henry, Ernie, 100
Hernandez, Raul, 110; "Lamento Borincano," 158–59n9
Herskovits, Melville, 86
Heywood, Eddie, 100
highlife, 50, 95, 104, 155n27
Higman, B. W., 19
Hill, Andrew, 87
Hill, Donald, 27
Hill, Erroll, 36, 141n1, 143–44n19
"hillbilly" music, 15
hip-hop, 142–43n11
history, 6–7, 9–10, 50, 138n2, 140n14; materialism, 10–11; regional, 14
Holder, Geoffrey, 102–3
Hosein festivals, 32, 143n18
Hughes, Langston, 98–99, 102–3
hybridity, 4, 51, 94, 116, 125

Iglesias, Yeyo, 109
Illori, Solomon, 95, 150n27
imperialism, 13, 76, 106, 135, 146n27. *See also specific empires*
indentured servants, 16, 23–24, 26, 36, 40
independent labels, 162n24
ingleses, los, 115
Islam, 76, 91
Ithier, Rafael, 163n31

Jamaica, 115, 142–43n11, 142n10
Jamal, Ahmad, 91
"jambassadors," 76
James, C. L. R., 145–46n25
jamette, 27–30, 32, 34–35, 37–38, 42, 45–46, 143n17
Jamette Carnival, 30
jazz, 12–14, 45, 76–77, 92, 104, 152n13, 159–60n14; Afro-Cuban music and, 50, 66, 71, 118–19; Afro-diasporic traditions and, 84; as cerebral art form of contemplation, 153n16; civil rights movement and, 78–79, 151n4; commercial success of, 89; gender and, 151–52n9; hard bop and, 87–88, 89; history of, 78, 105, 151–52n9, 154n24; psychedelic, 126; record sales, 88–89; rhythms of, 84; salsa and, 110, 124, 126, 128, 131–32; as symbol of American democracy and freedom, 76, 103
"jazz cosmopolitanism," 152n12
Jazz Messengers, 90, 154n23
jazz radicalism, 91–92
Jemmott, Jerry, 131
Jhouba (juba), 21
jibaros, 114–15, 118, 127, 162n25
Joe Cuba Sextet, 109, 120–21
John Canoe, 142n10
Jones, Elvin, 91
Jones, Hank, 91
Jones, LeRoi (Amiri Baraka), 74, 77, 153n14; *Blues People*, 140n15
Jones, Quincy, 103
Jones, Thad, 91
Jordan, Clifford, 89
Jordan, Duke, 100
Jordan, Louis, 85, 146n29
juju, 50
jukeboxes, 88–89
Justicia (Eddie Palmieri), 130–31

kaiso, 13, 35, 41–44, 47–48, 141n1, 144n22, 144–45n23, 145n24, 145–46n25, 146n29; class and, 37–38, 42, 48; as commodity and export, 43; creole society and, 24; English language, 33; "kaiso epistemology," 26–29, 47–48; kalinda and, 15–22, 27–30, 34; new-style, 34, 39–40; social role of, 42. *See also* calypso
Kako, 161–62n23
kalinda, 15, 20–22, 26–27, 28–31, 34–35, 39, 142n5, 143n15
Karacand, Naim, 94
Keepnews, Orrin, 96
Kelley, Robin D. G., 93, 153n17, 156n33

Kennedy, John F., 73
Keskidee Trio, 146n28
King, Martin Luther, Jr., 75
King Radio, 36-37, 42
Klain, Gaylan, 123-24
Klein's Show Bar, 91
Knight, Franklin W., 147n5
Kodat, 83
Kofsky, Frank, 80
Kongo, 19, 58-60, 147n7, 148nn10-11
Korean War, 75
"Kucheza Blues" (Weston), 98-99, 156-57n37
Kuti, Fela, 104

Labat, Pierre, 21
labor, 9, 17, 22, 24, 30-32, 40-41, 62, 144n21
Labor Party, 40-41
Lam, Wilfredo, 63
languages: African, 57; Afro-Cuban Creole Spanish, 59; Afro-French creole, 19-20; class and, 32-33; English, 32-33; linguistic literature, 10; patois, 25, 40; slavery and, 32-33; in Trinidad, 19-20, 25; West African, 33
Lateef, Yusef, 90, 91-93, 95, 105, 126, 154n23, 155n27, 156n30
Latin dance crazes, 119, 125
Latin identity, 119, 123, 161-62n23
Latino/a blues, 126-28
Latinos, 122, 126
Latin soul, 12, 108
"Latin sound," 107
"Latin tinge," 118
Laviera, Tato, 160n16
Lavoe, Hector, 127-28, 162n25, 162n26
lavways, 31
"leopard" societies, 58
liberation, 12-13, 76-77, 96, 105, 151-52n9. *See also* emancipation
Lincoln, Abbey, 74, 96-97, 156n35
"lining out," 34
Liston, Melba, 98-99, 103-4

Little, Booker, 96
Liverpool, Hollis, 22, 141n3
Lopez, Orestes "Cachao," 150n24
López, René, 159n12
Lord Beginner, 36, 43-47
Lord Caresser, 36, 45
Lord Destroyer, 36, 45
Lord Executor, 36, 45
Lord Iere, 36
Lord Invader, 36, 45
Los Angeles, California, 142-43n11
L'Ouverture, Toussaint, 18
Luciano, Felipe, 107, 123-24
Lukumí (Lucumí), 58-60, 147n7, 149n17
Lumumba, Patrice, 73-74
Lymon, Frankie, and the Teenagers, 159n13, 160n15

Macbeth, 102
Machado, Gerardo, 66-68
Machito (Frank Grillo), 107, 118, 120, 150n24, 159n10
Malcolm X, 73, 75, 123
mambo, 51, 69, 107-8, 119, 124, 150n24, 159n10
Mañana label, 125
Mandika, 19
Mangual, Jose, Jr., 158n4
Mann, Herbie, 156n35
Manning, Sam, 145-46n25
"man-of-words," 31
"Manteca" (Gillespie), 87, 120, 147n7, 159-60n14
mantecerización, 127
Mantillo, Ray, 96-97
Manuel, Peter, 122
maracas, 67, 115
Marcano, Neville, 46. *See also* Growling Tiger
marímbula, 67
Marin, Bobby, 161n22
Martí, Jose, 60
Martin, Tony, 62

Martinez, "Chihuahua," 155n27
Martinez, Luis "Sabu," 91, 155n27; *Palo Congo*, 71–72
Marx, Karl, 3, 6–7; and black Marxism, 6–9
Mary Lou label, 125
mas, 38–39
masculinity, 27–31
masquerade, 25–26, 141n3
mass media, 62–63
mass popular culture, 87, 119
Masucci, Jerry, 126
Mbadiwe, Kingsley Ozoumba, 86, 153–54n21
Mendez, Silvestre, "Oriza," 132
Mendoza, Chico (Ira Roberts), 131
Mericana label, 125
meringue, 110
Merod, Jim, 79
Meyer, Leonard, 139n6
Middle Passage, 4, 7–9
migration, 17, 50; Great Migration, 79, 81, 152n10; to New York City, 44; to Puerto Rico, 115; from Puerto Rico, 116–18; to Trinidad, 17–20, 23–25, 142n9; West Indian emigration, 43
Miller, Joseph Calder, 147n7
Millinder, Lucky, 91
Mingus, Charles, 90
Minns, Al, 103
Minton's Playhouse, 81
MIO label, 125
modernism, 80, 152n12
modernity, 6–7, 10, 62, 68
Monk, Thelonious, 81, 83–84, 86, 90, 94, 101–2, 153nn17–19, 157n39
Monroe's Uptown, 81
Monson, Ingrid, 151n4, 152n12, 155n27
Montego Joe, 95
montuno aesthetics, 12, 49–72, 121, 131, 149n19
Moore, Robin, 63–64
Moré, Beny, 59

Moreno Fraginals, Manuel, 54
Morgon, Lee, 94
Morton, Jelly Roll, 85
Moten, Fred, 139n8
music: central role in black cultural life, 8–9; discourses, 89–90; forms, 3; history and, 5–6, 138n2, 140n14; phenomenology of, 6; politics and, 89, 138n4, 141n4, 151n4, 151–52n9; studied from different vantage points, 5–6
musical communities, 89–90. *See also specific communities*
Music Inn, 102

NAACP, 76
ñáñigos, 58, 147n7
Nanton, "Tricky Sam," 85
"nation," 13
national consciousness, 11–13, 41, 49–50, 62–63, 68, 110, 116, 135
nationalism, 11–13, 49, 63, 76–77, 135, 144n21, 158–59n9, 162n24
Negritude, 13, 41, 63
Negro World, 41
Nelson, David, 123–24
neocolonialism, 12–13, 103–4, 106
Nettleford, Rex, 19–20
New Jazz/Prestige label, 94
new nationalism, 12–13
"new Negro," 40
New Orleans, Louisiana, 84–85, 95
New York, New York, 12, 42–44, 67–68, 100–102, 104, 107–8, 112–25, 142–43n11, 159n10
"New York Sound," 108, 110
Nieto, Ubaldo, 87
Nigeria, 58, 93, 104, 106
non-aligned movement, 12, 75
Nuyoricans, 13, 106, 108, 112–13, 116–22, 124, 126–30, 135, 160n16

obeahmen, 21
Ocho, 131–32

Odetta, 94
OKeh (record label), 43
Olatunji, Babatunde, 96–97, 102; *Zungo*, 93
Oratorical calypso, 34–35, 37, 40, 45
Oriente, Cuba, 61, 65–66, 148n8, 149nn19–20
Original Last Poets, 123–24, 161n21
Ortiz, Fernando, 50, 56–57, 63, 148n14
Oyó, 58–59

Pacheco, Johnny, 109, 126–27
Pacheco, Victor, 144n22
Padmore, George, 145–46n25
Page, Hot Lips, 91
pa'lante, 126
Palladium Ballroom, 107–8, 118–19, 158n2, 159n12
Palmié, Stephan, 66
Palmieri, Charlie, 109, 161–62n23
Palmieri, Eddie, 130–31, 163n32
Palo Congo (Martinez), 71–72
Palo Mayombe (Palo Monte), 59, 61
"Pam's Waltz" (Weston), 102
pan-Africanism, 40–41, 44, 89–90, 102, 106, 155n27
Panart label, 125
panderetas, 116
pan-Latino culture, 118, 124, 132
Parker, Charlie, 81, 85, 87, 153n20, 154n23
Partido Independiente de Color (PIC), 60–61
Party con la Crema, El (United Artists), 161–62n23
patois, 25, 40
Payne, Cecil, 100
Pearse, Andrew, 26
peasants, 7, 8. *See also* working class
Peña, Enrique, 147n7
percussion, 90, 92, 94, 96, 115–26. *See also* drums
Pérez, Louis A., 147n5, 148n13
Perfecta, La, 130
Peters, Brock, 98

picong, 31, 34–35
pierrots, 28–29
Piñero, Ignacio, 68, 109, 149n21
plantations, 11, 13, 18–19, 25, 53–56
planters, 20, 24, 115, 141n4, 148n8
Platt Amendment, 60
plena, 115–16, 118–19, 130, 159n11, 161n20
plural societies, 8, 11
political economy, 7, 10
politics, 12–13, 89, 151n4, 151–52n9
Pollard, Terry, 91
polyrhythm, 4–5, 9–11, 14, 68, 78, 89, 95, 97–98, 106, 134–37; Afro-Cuban music and, 50–52; bebop and, 82–83; salsa and, 110–15, 125
Ponce, Puerto Rico, 115, 158–59n9
Porter, Cole, 102
Porter, Eric, 80, 88, 91
Port of Spain, Trinidad, 17, 19, 23, 24–28, 32, 36, 42, 143n12
postcolonialism, 96, 105–6, 150–51n2
Powell, Bud, 81
Pozo, Chano, 83, 85–86, 91, 118, 120, 147n7, 159–60n14
Prado, Perez, 150n24
Prestige label, 88, 94, 159–60n14
Priester, Julian, 96
Primus, Pearl, 86
Protesta, La, 130
Puente, Tito, 107, 119, 158n4
Puerto Ricans, 13–14, 112–13, 116, 119, 122, 159n13, 160n16; identity, 117–18, 129, 133, 158n7; music, 124, 158n7, 159n11, 162n25, 163n31. *See also* Afro-Puerto Ricans
Puerto Rico, 13, 107, 109–10, 112–13; coerced labor in, 115; demography of, 114; ecology of, 114; economy of, 114–17; Haitian immigration to, 115; independence movement in, 122; investment in, 115; migration from, 116–18; migration to, 115; national identity in, 116; slavery in, 115–16; struggle for independence from Spain, 116; as

territory of the US, 115; US invasion and occupation of, 114, 116
Purdie, Bernard, 131

Quevedo, Raymond, 142n7. *See also* Atilla the Hun
Quintana, Ismael, 130
quinto, 65

rabat, 92
race, 11, 16, 24–25, 50–51, 56, 71, 110, 126, 135, 144n21; consciousness, 83; in Puerto Rico, 116; segregation in Cuba, 60; in Trinidad, 18–19; in the US, 74–76; violence, 74–75. *See also* ethnicity
"race" records, 15, 67, 145n24
racism, 10, 60, 76. *See also* segregation
Radas, 25
radio, 44, 66, 88–89, 125, 155n27
Railroad Millionaires, 38–39
Ramirez, Louie, *Típico*, 161n20
Ramsey, Guthrie, 77, 80, 88
Randolph, A. Phillip, 79
Ray, Richie, 121
RCA Victor, 43, 125; Bluebird label, 15–16
rebellion, 10, 12, 20, 134, 141n4
recording industry, 43–44, 50, 66–67, 88–89, 109, 145n24, 155n27, 160n17, 161n19, 162n24; growth and development of, 15–16; independent labels, 125–26; newer labels, 125–26; small labels, 125; World War II and, 81
Redd, Vi, 103
Red Garter (nightclub), 161–62n23
reggae, 142–43n11
requinto, 115
Revolutionary Worker, 41
revolutions, 18–19, 23
rhythm, 3, 11–12, 89, 137, 161n21. *See also* polyrhythm
rhythm & blues (R&B), 87–89, 92, 108, 119, 121, 125, 128, 153n16, 159–60n14, 160–61n18

Rico label, 125
Rigaud, Andre, 18
ritual, 4, 13–14, 20–21, 34, 59, 61, 148n9
Rivera, Ismael, 119, 159n11, 163n31
Riverside Records, 84, 88, 102, 159–60n14
Roach, Max, 74, 81, 85, 91, 100–101, 105, 153n20, 155n29
Roaring Lion, 15, 36, 42–43, 45, 47
Roberto Roena y Su Apollo Sound, 130
Roberts, Ira, 131
Robinson, Cedric J., 140n16, 143n17
rock 'n' roll, 119, 125, 128
Rodriguez, Arsenio, 49, 59, 68–70, 118, 128–30, 150nn24–25, 161n20, 163n30; Afro-Cuban tradition and, 70–71; "Aquí Como Allá," 49; black pride and, 69, 70–71; "Bruca Maniguá," 70–71, 150n26; instrumentation of, 69–70; lyrics of, 70–71; move to New York, 71–72; "No Ha Viste Caridad," 132; "Pa Huele," 131; rootworking by, 70–71; sound ideal, 132; style of, 69–70
Rodriguez, Bobby, 161–62n23
Rodriguez, Tito, 107, 119
Roena, Roberto, 130, 163n31
Rogers, Barry, 163n32
Rohlehr, Gordon, 27, 29, 45
Roman, Manny, 132
Rondón, César Miguel, 127, 129, 158n2, 161n20
Roosevelt, Franklin Delano, 146n27
rootwork, 4–5, 9–14, 78, 134, 137, 162n25; Afro-Cuban music and, 50; bebop and, 84, 87; calypso and, 44–45; salsa and, 110, 112, 123, 129
Rosenthal, David, 84, 88, 155n28
Roulette Records, 99
rumba, 13–14, 50–51, 59, 61–64, 67–68, 124, 137, 149n15, 155n27, 159n13, 161n21; genres of, 64–65; instrumentation of, 64–65, 149n17. *See also* son/rumba complex
Russell, George, 100
Russia, 62. *See also* Soviet Union

Sabater, Jimmy, 120–21
Sa Gomes, Edward, 15–16, 43
Saint Domingue, 17–18
salidor, 65
Salim, A. K., 91
salsa, 12, 14, 108, 122–33, 135, 137, 149n22, 158n4; as appropriation of Afro-Cuban music, 109–10; history of, 112–13; instrumentation of, 126; literal definition of, 110–11; as pan-Latino, 124; situating, 109–10; as symbol of cultural nationalist identification, 124
Salsa, 162n27
salsa dura, 106, 124, 161n20. *See also* salsa típico
salsa "folklórico y experimental," 12, 107–33
Salsa label, 125
salsa típico, 106, 122–33, 161n20, 163n30
samba, 137
Sampson, Mitto, 21–22
Sanabria, Izzy, 162n26; and WE-2 graphics, 128–29
Sancti Spíritus, Cuba, 55
San Fernando, Trinidad, 23, 32, 36
Sankana, Amon Saaba, 143–44n19
Sans Humanité calypso, 34–35, 37, 40, 45, 143–44n19
Santamaria, Ramon "Mongo," 87; "Watermelon Man," 159–60n14
Santeria, 59, 61
Santiago, Al, 109
Santo Domingo (Spanish), 113
Savoy, 159n10
Schenck, James, 96
Scott, Calo, 94
Scott-Heron, Gil, 161n21
Second Reconstruction, 12
Seditious Publications Ordinance, 40–41
Seeco label, 109, 125
segregation, 60, 74–76
seguidora, 115
seis, 115, 118

Septeto Nacional, 68, 149n21; "Échale Salsita," 109, 149n22
septetos, 67, 69
Sexteto Habanero, 67, 147n7
Sexteto Nacional, 67
Sexteto Oriente, 149n21
sextetos, 67
Shango religion, 25, 34
Sharpeville Massacre, 90, 97
Shepherd, John, 6
Shihab, Sahib, 91
Silva, Jose "Chombo," 161–62n23
Silver, Horace, 90
Simone, Nina, 103
Singer, Roberta, 111
sit-in movement, 90, 155–56n29
sixteen-bar blues, 95, 159–60n14
slave culture, 12, 20, 32–33, 148n9
slavery, 7, 9, 11, 13, 17–18, 51, 53–54, 135–36; British abolition of, 22–24; in Cuba, 55, 57, 147n5; language and, 32–33; legacy of, 49; main areas of catchment and embarkation, 9; massive demographic displacement of, 8; in Puerto Rico, 115–16; religious ritual and, 148n9; resistance to, 20; in Trinidad, 19–20, 22–23
slave trade, 10, 22–23, 59–60
Small Island Pride, 36–37
Smash Records, 160n15
Smith, Mauricio, 144n22
Smith, Willie "the Lion," 102
Snead, James, 8, 136
social sciences, concepts inherited from, 5
society: control, 20, 32; formations, 3, 5–8, 10–11, 17, 20, 56, 138n4; unions, 32, 36
son, 13, 65–67, 69, 149n20, 160–61n18; commercial popularization of, 67–68; "golden age" of, 67–68; instrumentation of, 67; "rumbanization" of, 69. *See also* son montuno; son oriental; son/rumba complex
soneros, 67–68

songs, 9, 21, 59; carnival, 34; dance and, 20–21; folk, 25, 45; indigenous, 22; praise-singing traditions, 22; slave, 20; thirty-two bar pop, 82–83; work, 22
sonic imagination, 12
son montuno, 51, 69, 128, 129–30. *See also* montuno aesthetics
Sonora Poncena, 130
son oriental, 65–66, 126
Sonoro Mantecera, 127
son/rumba complex, 11–13, 50–52, 62, 66–69, 71, 109, 124, 129, 137, 146n1. *See also* rumba; son
soul, 89–90, 124, 126, 154n25, 159–60n14, 162n24
South Africa, 90, 97
South Bronx, New York, 108, 117
Soviet Union, 62, 73, 76
Spanish Empire, 13, 17, 20, 52, 53, 60, 116
Spanish Harlem, New York, 123
"Spanish tinge," 85
Staton, Dakota, 91
Stearns, Marshall, 102
Stevenson, Adlai E., Jr., 73
stickfighting, 17, 21, 26–30, 36–37, 142n5; gender and, 30; outlawing of, 31–32
Sublette, Ned, 53, 66
"Suffering" (Abdul-Malik), 95
sugar industry, 23, 26–27, 53–56, 58, 64, 135; in Cuba, 55–56, 61–62; the Depression and, 116; in Puerto Rico, 115–16; in Trinidad, 18–19, 23–24, 35–36
Sulieman, Idrees, 91
Sun Ra, 90
swing, 45, 82–83, 85, 102, 111
syncopation, 11, 45, 70, 90
syncretism, 77
syndicates, 36, 38

tamboo bamboo, 34–35
Tampa, Florida, 49
Taylor, Cecil, 154n22
Tentacion, La, 130

Third World, 92, 106, 150–51n2; aural making and unmaking, 73–106; consciousness, 13; identification with, 123; movements, 76–80, 86, 89, 95–97, 103–6, 129, 133, 150n1; musics, 95, 106; as political and ideological entity, 77; unity, 12. *See also specific countries and regions*
"third world creative music," 12
Thompson, E. P., 139n10
Thornton, Clifford, 151–52n9
Tico Records, 125, 130, 159n13, 161–62n23
Till, Emmett, 75
timbales, 129
Tin Pan Alley, 45
Tizol, Juan, 85
Tjader, Cal, 109
transculturation, 8, 10–12, 16, 20, 23, 44, 59–60, 63, 66, 68, 71, 84–85, 110
transnationalism, 119, 158–59n9
tres, 67, 69–70, 115
Trinidad, 11, 13, 134, 142n10; African diaspora in, 19; Afro-French character of, 141n2; Anglicization of, 30, 32–33; British takeover of, 18–19, 30; censorship in, 145n24; class in, 27, 32, 37–39, 40–42, 46–47, 143n12; creolization of, 17, 20–21, 23–24, 26, 28, 33; cultural complexity of, 25; demography of, 23; Depression-era, 41; education and literacy in, 32–33; 1881 depression in, 31; gender in, 31–32, 46–47; history of, 16; imperial powers and, 16; labor in, 27, 40–41; linguistic history of, 19–20, 25; migration to, 17–20, 23–25; new Africans in, 24–25; "open door" policy in, 18; plantations in, 18–19; political economy of, 23–24; post-Emancipation period, 17, 23–26, 142n9; race in, 18–19; record bans in, 145n24; slavery in, 17–20, 22–23; sugar industry in, 18–19, 23–24; Victorian ideals and, 31–32; women in, 31–32

Trinidad Workingmen's Association (TWA), 40
Trio and Solo (Weston), 102
"Triptych: Prayer, Peace, Protest" (Brown and Roach), 96–97
Trouillot, Michel-Rolph, 140n14
tumbadora, 65, 69–70
tumba francesa, 148n8
tumbao, 65, 70, 126, 129, 132
Tyner, McCoy, 91, 163n32

Uhuru Afrika (Weston), 90, 93, 97–100, 103, 157n41
"Uhuru Kwanza" (Weston), 98
Uñica, La, 130
United Nations, 73–76, 97
United Negro Improvement Association (UNIA), 40–41, 62
United States, 90, 106; annexation of Puerto Rico, 114, 116; black migration within, 79, 81, 152n10; calypso market in, 42, 44; Cuba and, 50, 60–62, 67–68; entertainment industry in, 67; government, 76; imperialism of, 11, 13, 43, 146n27; Puerto Rican migrants to, 116–18 (*see also* Nuyoricans); "race" records, 15, 67, 145n24; segregation in, 49, 74–76; State Department, 76, 103; Supreme Court, 74–75; West Indian emigration to, 42–44. *See also* civil rights movement; jazz; New York, New York; record industry; *specific cities and regions*

vacunao, 64
Valdez, Carlos "Patato," 147n7
Vallee, Rudy, 146n29
vaudeville, 45
Velez, Walter, and WE-2 graphics, 128–29
Venezuela, 45
Vera, María Teresa, 149n21
Verve Records, 109
Victor Records, 66–67, 149n21

Vietnam, 106, 108, 122
Von Eschen, Penny, 75, 151n4

Warner, Keith Q., 141n1
Warner-Lewis, Maureen, 25, 33–34, 141n1, 148n11
War of 1812, 142n9
Washburne, Christopher, 111
Water Riots of 1903, 38
Watkins, Doug, 91
Watts, Daniel, 74
Watts Rebellion, 106
Weeks, Daphne, 144n22
West Africa, 9, 56, 104, 141n3; calypso in, 146n29; Cuban music in, 146n1
West African languages, 33
West Central Africa, 9, 56, 59–60, 69, 141n3, 146n1
West Indian Regiment, 142n9, 145–46n25
West Indies, 17, 43, 85, 137
Weston, Randy, 90, 94–99, 100–104, 105, 153nn18–19, 155n28, 155–56n29, 156–57n37, 157n39, 157n41, 157n43; "Run Joe," 102
WestSide label, 125
White, Bob, 63
White, Hayden, 140n14
wildcat strikes, 41
Williams, Eric, 38, 54, 111, 144n21
Williams, Fess, 94
Wilson, Peter, 16
women, 31–32. *See also* gender
World War II, 81
Wright, Bruce, 156–57n37

yambú rumba, 64–65
Yetman, Ahmed, 94
Yoruba, 19, 25, 34, 58–59, 148n9
Young Lords Party, 123
yuka, 149n17

zafra, 64
Zayas, Alfredo, 147n7
Zungo (Olatunji), 93

www.ingramcontent.com/pod-product-compliance
Lightning Source LLC
Chambersburg PA
CBHW030344240426
43661CB00052B/1734